SHACKLES

To Marion

Love & Light

[signature]

SHACKLES
OVERCOMING DOMESTIC ABUSE
A MODERN DAY TABOO

Malaika Cohen with **Carole Yeoman**

CanaanPress

CanaanPress

Copyright © 2008 – Malaika Cohen and Carole Yeoman

First printed in Great Britain in 2008 by
Canaan Press
5 Willowhayne Close
Angmering on Sea
West Sussex
BN16 1PF
office@canaanpress.co.uk
www.canaanpress.co.uk

The book imprint of
Matt's Canaan Trust
www.mattscanaantrust.com

British Library Cataloguing in Publication Data
A record of this is book is available from the British Library

ISBN: 978-0-9551816-1-0

Designed by Andy Ashdown
www.andyashdowndesign.co.uk

Cover photographs © iStockphoto.com

Manufactured in Malta by Gutenberg Press Limited

For my wonderful children,
Taylor, Grace and Summer
my eternal Love to you
– and for every child suffering in silence –
that we may end the violence

Soli Deo Gloria

Acknowledgments

I would like to thank the many people who have made it possible for me to write this book and those who faithfully supported me, near and far, whilst awaiting its publication.

Taylor, I thank you for loving me, enough to sacrifice your own happiness, and for standing by me throughout. No ocean and no scheme of man could separate us and the love we share so deeply. You are such a blessing in my life. I love you.

Grace, thank you for your wisdom and tenderness. You are my biggest encouragement. Without you this book would not have been written. Thank you my beautiful child. I love you very much.

Summer my little sweetheart, thank you for always turning my tears to laughter. I hope we can now dance together in freedom. You are a priceless treasure, I love you my little princess.

Carole, thank you for believing in me and giving freely of your talents. For all the hours you spent writing, editing and loving this book into being. But most of all, thank you for your friendship. Mark, thank you for being such a wonderful friend not just to me but to my precious children, to you and Carole, always remember my children are yours also. Thank you for being part of our lives. Matthew, I cannot wait to meet you!

Selma, thank you for being the truest friend and most wonderful example of a loving family. Thank you for all your love and practical help, no matter where or when, day and night, you were always there for me. An angel sent to minister to me.

Pastor David and his wife Heather for believing in me. Also, thank you for letting me use the computer in the office to carry on writing, you have allowed my faith to grow.

Miss S for giving me her electronic typewriter to restart the whole script after it had been destroyed. Thank you so much, without it I wouldn't have had the courage to go on.

Kyla for being such a wonderful counsellor, faithful to God, and for infecting me with your passion for Jesus.

All the friends I have made both near and far, here in UK, USA, Portugal, Spain, France, Italy, Greece, Germany, Belgium and Netherlands, Switzerland Bulgaria, Sweden and Norway, and last but not least South Africa. From the East to the West and the North to the South. Thank you for your prayers and encouraging words, you have urged me to carry on despite the setbacks.

Andy, thank you for your sensitive designs and all the work you have produced. I love it all!

But most of all I thank God for giving me the amazing opportunity and life experience to write this book, for taking me on this journey. You are my God in all situations. All Glory be to you. I thank for the incredible blessing of motherhood – for showing me who I am, and that you love me – enough to die for me.

Foreword

Violence is a crime we are becoming all too familiar with every year and in the UK a quarter of all reported violent crimes are domestic. But domestic abuse is not just about physical violence, though that is often the most visible and life-threatening manifestation. Domestic abuse covers a wide range of perpetrations from the physical to the emotional. The effects are as far reaching as myriad ripples on the water when a stone breaks the surface. Domestic abuse is most certainly about power: power over other people's lives and it is seldom one isolated incident. Domestic abuse causes such total breakdown of self-esteem that the victim will almost always believe they are at fault and will undoubtedly believe they cannot escape from their situation. The shame and disgrace they feel often prevents them from crying out for help.

One important fact is not only women are victims of domestic abuse; men and children are too. I believe it is time we drag this inhumane practice out of the cupboard, shatter the secrecy, tackle all the taboos associated with the subject and raise awareness about this frightening crime. I believe it is time we help victims understand how they can break the shackles and actually walk in freedom and new life. No one should live their life in fear of another person. That is why I have written this book – so that others may read my story, understand the mental state of someone suffering from domestic abuse, and hopefully be motivated to break the insidious cycle of fear this crime has over too many lives.

Names and places have been changed to protect identities.

VICTIMS...
Winter 2003

The aged smell of the carpet and dust and damp of the house invade my nostrils as I try to sleep on the floor in an empty shell of a house I cannot call home. Forced into an unfamiliar place with no possessions; distraught and in disbelief that my life has come to this.

The night storage radiators offer no friendship against the bitterly cold night. I am frightened – feeling unwanted – chucked away like garbage. Feeling let down by everyone, including the law. Is it because I am a foreigner here? Or is it because I have been made to feel I have no rights, no defender of my cause? I am a woman but I'm not a feminist. I'm a human being who believes we are all equal when it comes to how we should be treated. A human being, not an animal.

"I am broken inside – we have nothing left and nowhere to go."

I watch my two daughters sleeping on the blanket beside me; they are exhausted too. So many troubles, so much pain in their short lives. I can barely hold back the tears. What have I done to my girls? Made another big mess in their lives – and mine. I am broken inside – we have nothing left and nowhere to go.

The fragile fairy tale life was smashed before it began. My dream of happiness only a fantasy I kept resurrecting, hoping against hope that one day my rags of sorrow and hurt would be changed for a beautiful garment of simple joy.

Is it too much to ask? Is the outcome of my life my fault? Am I being punished; am I really worthless? To seek the answers I dig deep into my past – in the hope that I may find out who I really am. My given name is Malaika – it means messenger and I hope my message will help someone else make a choice that will change their life for the better. I hope by speaking out, I can encourage someone to cut the shackles that hold them captive.

Chapter 1
BRUISES FADE BUT THE PAIN REMAINS...

I was born in East Germany in 1968 and grew up in a nation that had been living under the cloud of communism for two decades. A dictatorship and the Stasi – the secret police – kept me and my fellow countrymen and women behind a concrete curtain called the Berlin Wall. An iconic symbol of the Cold War, its menacing presence was all I knew. For me it was hard, oppressive; I knew little of freedom of choice and movement. But for those who knew of a different life before, but dare not speak against the regime for fear of imprisonment or worse, theirs was a consuming depression that led many to try and blot out reality by whatever means they could.

That was the other cloud I lived under – alcoholism and domestic violence. Conditions were hard for my parents, for everyone at that time, except the privileged few. My Dad worked as a builder in the city, and my Mother's parents worked on the same site too. I remember seeing my Grandmother sorting through bricks taken from the old houses and cleaning them before they were used on the new buildings replacing those destroyed in the Second World War.

My Mother worked in a factory yards from our home. Dad would catch the coach from our village, leaving very early in the morning and we would not see him before we went to bed at night. Many men were weekend fathers, if at all. Mum would take us to the state-run nursery or kindergarten as early as six o'clock when they opened. In the former East Germany, women were praised for managing a full-time job and a family at the same time. Later, when my older sister and I attended infant school, our Mother would leave for work before us, entrusting us to walk to school with a few neighbourhood friends.

As my sister and I lay sleeping in bed at night, Mum would come into the room and wake us, saying she was going out to look for Dad as it was late and he was not home. She always said there was no need to worry, but I did. I didn't want her to go out looking for Dad. I was scared being left alone in the house with my sister who was only two years older than me. Terrified in the silence, I would lie awake waiting to hear the door downstairs open and hear her voice. She usually found him – sleeping in the pub or lying on some roadside in the village.

"The arguing, and shouting sounds drifted through the door into our room. Mum begging Dad to stop hitting her and not to waken us."

Sometimes he came home by himself, but they were often the worst nights. The arguing, and shouting sounds drifted through the door into our room. Mum begging Dad to stop hitting her and not to waken us. But it was too late, I was already awake and frozen in fear, in case he should come into our room. My Father was incredibly strong, and all too quick to use his hands to discipline us with a forceful slap behind the head or in the face. There were also nights when men would bring my Father home, supporting him as he couldn't stand up by himself. If we were still up my Mother would tell us to go upstairs to our bedroom and stay there. I was too young to understand why Dad was like he was, but I remember feeling sorry for him as he often had cuts and bruises on his face. Occasionally, these same men would knock on our door to say that Dad had fallen asleep on the bus and missed his stop, or stumbled off too early. Mum would then go off on her bike and search for him, leaving us alone again. I hated those times. I was angry that the other men would not help Dad get home. But more than that I was angry because I missed having a Dad I could spend time with. He never seemed to be there for me or my sister.

The daily routine of Dad not coming home and Mum leaving the house to search for him was normality for me and my sister. We presumed it was how all families lived. In fact I learned later, many did. I remember episodes when Dad would not come home for long periods of time. My Mother would stay home from work and lie inertly on the couch until finally, forced into action by our incessant pleas, she would take us into the town, knocking on door after door, enquiring as to the whereabouts of my Father. We generally located him but the glazed expression of his eyes confirmed he seldom knew where he was or what he was doing there.

Although my parents were home from work at weekends, they were always stressful times. Mum was always busy cleaning and washing, though she did manage to make delicious cakes every Sunday for tea. That small event was the highlight of our week, looking forward to those cakes, helping her bake them and squabbling over eating the leftover mixture in the bowl. That and playing outside with our neighbourhood friends I remember were the few times I felt happy. Hiding in the cornfields around our home, watching the combine harvesters in front of our house and jumping in and out of the bales of straw in our friends' barns. Sometimes we were allowed to stay over for dinner with friends' families; that was the best. The other parents appeared to have time to listen to a child's incessant chatter. They seemed to enjoy having us in their homes.

Not so at our house. We were never allowed to have friends come and play. My Father was repeatedly harsh with us and other children. His spare time was spent watching local football matches or sitting watching football on the television and, of course, drinking. Invariably my Mother would tell us to be quiet, not make a noise, we were not to disturb Dad under any circumstances. Desperate for some attention I would pretend I wanted to watch the football with him, just to be able to sit with him and feel his nearness. But he never acknowledged my presence. He never gave me the hugs I craved.

My sister and I did not get on well together. Whether it was the strained atmosphere created by my parents' constant quarreling and violence that influenced our acrimonious relationship, I don't know, but it was always a relief that our Mother would frequently take us out to see an aunt who lived nearby. We would also visit old Mrs Becher in the same block of flats. She gave us lovely food and often sat in her chair with her eyes closed, giving the impression she was asleep. She spoke with kindness and wisdom whenever I bombarded her with questions. I was especially intrigued with a picture on her wall depicting a man hanging, in obvious agony, on a wooden cross. Being raised in an East Germany that forbade religious freedom, I was fascinated to be told there was a God who loved me and knew everything about me. I learned later Mrs Becher spent many hours praying for me. The walk home from infant school took us past the old lady's flat and I grew used to the friendly waves from her vantage point at the window. I felt inexplicably saddened to learn of her death, but no one took the time to explain to a young and vulnerable child that death was as much a part of life as living.

Learning at school was not something that came easily to me, I was always anxious about my home life and could not concentrate on anything for long. I struggled with an inner sense of failure that was reinforced by a total lack of encouragement from my parents, who were constantly dealing with their own shortcomings. I felt sure their arguing was due to some fault of mine, and I was terrified of disappointing them, of failing, of causing them additional stress. My sleep was filled with fearful dreams, fed by my insecurities. I battled nightly with monsters trying to imprison me against my will, never finding the safe haven of parental love and attention.

When I was ten, my parents took on the job of caretakers for the new local school which included accommodation. Their marriage was inadequately held together by bandages of pretence and lies as the arguments and violence increased and though they looked upon this change as an upward career move, it only served to pile more guilt and anxiety on my already overburdened young mind. My obsessive worrying led me to daydream in class, getting reprimanded by teachers and chastised by my parents, who were now conveniently on-hand all the time. In search of acceptance and craving love so much from my Dad, I sought friendships with my peers, inevitably finding myself in the company of boys to compensate. I nurtured a dream of happiness that spelled a perfect family – a fairy tale marriage, beautiful children – and all away from the smallness of the village where I lived. Where people gossiped and hid behind lives of quiet desperation, blotted out by alcohol and apathy.

By the time I was twelve, music had become an important part of my life. I could not speak English, but instinctively understood many of the lyrics to the popular songs of the time. They often seemed to mirror my life with all its disappointments and struggles. My Mum and Dad never told me they loved me and my heart cried out for something more than our insignificant village with its many drunken men and unemotional, secretive women; for some reciprocal love that would fill the huge aching gap inside of me. Sometimes I recalled the God of whom old Mrs Becher spoke – who apparently knew me, my every thought and need – and I cried out to this God if he was there, to give me some happiness and beautiful children of my own I could love in the way they were meant to be loved. I also clearly remember asking this God not to give me a man!

I was angry with both my parents – but especially my Mother for never talking to me about human relationships, about love, anger, frustrations, hopes, dreams, the expectations and downfalls of life. My sister and I started to smoke and although we thought we were pretty smart at hiding our habit, Dad found out and imposed impractical restrictions, grounding us for weeks at a time. Protracted periods of confinement to the house motivated me to even more acts of rebellion. Taking advantage of my Father's drinking bouts I continued to smoke; friends would visit me at my ground floor bedroom window and I would even escape from that same window and disobey my parents by sneaking off to local discos.

"As the frequency and intensity of the violence increased I used music to drown out the all-too familiar sounds, because if I heard them, they would terrify and haunt me."

As the frequency and intensity of the violence increased I used music to drown out the all too-familiar sounds, because if I heard them, they would terrify and haunt me. One night in particular when my sister was away at a friend's house, I heard my Father return home and the customary drone of raised voices. But suddenly what was usually background noise made the hairs on my body stand up. Turning down the music I heard my Mother crying on the other side of the door and shouting at my Father, telling him to "do it – get it over with – finish it"! Caustiously opening the door a little, I peered into the living room. My Mother was sitting, forced into a chair with Dad standing over her, holding a knife to her throat.

I screamed and Dad turned around; I saw straight into his eyes. The look there made me cower back into my room and seek cover on my bed. My heart was racing, banging against my chest and I could feel the blood pounding in my ears as Dad walked straight past my room and out of the flat. Mum came in very distressed and in tears but trying to calm me, saying everything was okay. We sat together on the bed and for the first time I could ever recall she put words to the terrifying situation, excusing Dad explaining he was drunk and would never do anything like that again. She tried to use her familiar reasoning that things were only half as bad as they seemed, and everything would be fine in the morning. My fears could not be so easily allayed: I was fighting the many demons I saw in my dreams. I wanted to leave the apartment, get away and never see my Dad again. I begged my Mother to leave with me immediately and go somewhere far away and safe. Eventually, she consented and I spent a terrified and sleepless night with her in a friends' bedroom overlooking the street, listening to my Dad searching for us. Providence miraculously prevented him from knocking on the house where were in hiding.

With the morning the shroud of pretence crept back over my Mother's face and we returned home. Although it was a Sunday, Dad was working all that day and so when my sister came home from her sleep-over, the three of us talked again about the reality of our situation, and Mum shared something of the details she had lived with for many years. My Father's drinking and violence caused most of the problems, but there had been her affair with my maths teacher too. Shockingly, we were told that my Father never liked my sister, and had no interest in her from birth, preferring me. I felt betrayed by everyone. I felt sick, and I felt angry on behalf of my Mum and sister. I decided never to speak to my Father again and begged my Mum to divorce him, frightened that he would try to stab her again – or even us.

"Living in a country dominated by a suppressive regime and the cold war meant that many East Germans were emotionally stunted. We were not encouraged to love one another…"

Living in a country dominated by a suppressive regime and the cold war meant that many East Germans were emotionally stunted. We were not encouraged to love one another, rather to be suspicious of everything, spy on one another and trust no one. I'm sure now that is partly why my Mother chose to accept her situation as unchangeable and hopeless, but I also know that there are too many people living in liberated societies who remain with these shackles on their lives, too afraid to claim the freedom that is their right. When my Mother began divorce proceedings, I was encouraged at the prospect of a better life, without alcohol or fear of beatings, only to have those dreams shattered when she dropped the petition. I began to hate what I saw as my Mother's weakness and our lives returned to how they had always been, dominated by drunkenness, arguments and violent outbursts.

Chapter 2
TAINTED LOVE...

Alongside our physical needs, inside all of us are basic emotional needs that cry out to be met. If we grow up with these needs unmet, our human nature will strive to find another way to satisfy those requirements. I was no exception. Starved of love and attention at home and growing up in an environment that allowed bullying and cruelty to reign, I looked for every opportunity to fulfill my deepest desire: to have a loving, supportive partner and create a stable, safe and happy home where children could grow up without fear. I decided at a fairly young age that in order to achieve my dreams I needed two main essentials: a husband and to live far, far away from my home village. With its small-minded attitudes and excessive dislike and mistrust of outsiders, this also meant that the husband I desired needed to be from far away too.

My teenage years at home continued in much the same vein as my earlier childhood: betrayals, alcohol abuse, physical violence, fights and cold, cold hearts. Without realising it I was erecting protective walls around my own heart that would not be dismantled for a long time. Whenever I could, and if I was not being punished for one misdemeanor or another, I would escape to life outside our home and frequent the discos and places popular with my friends at that time. It was not long before I met a boy. At only fourteen it was hardly the relationship to change the world, though truly in my heart I was looking for my Romeo. Someone who loved me so much they would do anything for me – to the point of death I guess. Inside I was empty, I knew I was missing something in my life that I wanted badly; that and to escape to the far away. This boy came from the city which seemed far away to me in my small fourteen year old world and he was older than me – another advantage in my eyes: someone who could defend me.

But I was not reckoning on the controlling obsession of my parents who had spent all their lives in our village with its narrow thinking and prejudices against outsiders. In my efforts to pursue a one-way ticket out of town I had to engage in elaborate escapades to continue my illicit friendship with this boy. One evening, letting my parents think I was in bed asleep, I climbed out of my bedroom window before changing my clothes and disappearing for an evening at the local disco with my knight in armour. The boy even asked me to go back to the city with him on the last bus out of the village that night but torn between my desperate need to escape and a sudden overwhelming fear of the unknown I chose to stay. I stood in the road watching the bus disappear out of sight.

"Through the initial searing pain of the blows, I looked up at my Mother, pleading with her silently to stop my Father, but she did nothing."

Had I known what awaited me at home I might have jumped on the bus without a backward glance. But too often we stay in familiar situations because we are scared to leave, and we hope against hope that things will get better. Instead I spent that night at a friends' house, innocently returning home the next morning, as if I had been on an early outing, instead of an all-night one! But Dad already knew about my evening out and before I realised what was happening, he pushed me into my room following close on my heels, taking his belt from his trousers as he did so. He threw me on the bed violently, hitting me uncontrollably with the belt. I was aware my Mother and sister were standing in the room, watching, but doing nothing to intervene. Through the initial searing pain of the blows, I looked up at my Mother, pleading with her silently to stop my Father, but she did nothing. My whole body was numb from the initial shock and pain of the beating. I remember thinking it was shutting itself down because it could not deal with the ferocity of the blows raining down on me.

As blood ran down my face, my sister taunted me, saying I deserved my punishment. My Mother said absolutely nothing and only tried to comfort me after Dad left the room. I escaped into the bathroom shouting to everyone to leave me alone. The mirror revealed how badly I had been beaten: I couldn't see properly as my eyes were swollen and rapidly discolouring. My lips were puffed up and bleeding. My back, chest and bottom felt very sore and I had so many bruises over my body I couldn't sit or lie down properly.

Later, my sister said she discovered my escape and told my Mother who immediately relayed the story to my Dad, thinking I had run away from home for good. How could I tell them this place where I lived never felt like a home to me – only a place of unhappiness and punishment. Feeling nothing but hatred for my whole family, I vowed never to speak to my Father again. Even though I had disobeyed his rules, I did not think the punishment suited the crime; it was uncontrolled and unreasonable. As for my Mother, I hated her for not speaking out in my defense, and her own decision to remain in a living hell rather than take a risk and leave. Forced to go to school the next day, I sat in the classroom covered in bruises for all to see, wishing my Dad would get run over by a lorry freeing us from his bullying regime. But I never voiced my opinions and deep hurts; what was the point – no one ever listened, I had no voice, I was only a child. Even if there were those who disagreed with the way I had been treated, no one said anything against my Father; apparently he had a reputation outside the home as an aggressive bully, quick to use his fists.

I struggled with schoolwork, but it was assumed I was a slow learner and no one bothered to look behind the façade to see what was really going on. I didn't realise our nightmare life had a name called 'domestic violence'. It was all I knew, and my daily reality. There was no one I could talk to. My Mother never seemed to have time for me or my sister. I have no memories of her playing with us when we were little, only running around after my Father, pandering to his volatile moods. She, too, was terrified if she did not keep our boat on an even keel incase another huge storm brewed without warning, and we'd all be shipwrecked or worse – drowned. More than anything, I craved a happy family of my own. Children of my own, whom I could love and care for and make up for all the times my broken, empty heart cried out against the loneliness. I found myself praying more and more to a God I desperately hoped was there and listening, taking care not to let the family know, sure they would have me declared insane.

Neither God nor religion was discussed in East Germany at that time and we certainly didn't learn anything on the subject in school. Incongruously there were two churches in our village and I always felt peaceful when the bells rang. I would open my bedroom window and breathe in the air as their soothing sound seemed to envelope my whole being. Freedom of religion was forbidden behind the wall of Communism though some church leaders continued in their faith and helped others do the same, even to the point of losing their lives for their beliefs.

When it was time to choose school subjects for my future, I had no idea what I wanted to do. When I asked my Mother for guidance and motivation, she said she had always been there to do everything for me; the time had come for me to stand on my own two feet and make my own decisions. I wanted to scream at her that she had never been there for me. I had always felt alone.

I had few friends, thanks to the strangeness of our home and ones I did make, my parents never approved of. So much of our lives was ordered by the East German dictatorship, it went against our natures to be decisive in choosing a future for ourselves. Kept in ignorance of what really went on in the outside world, we were told the Berlin Wall was there to protect us from the enemy's evil plans, not realising it kept us as prisoners and no threat to the regime.

Eventually I decided to work towards becoming a retail saleswoman. The teachers in school worked hard with me in my last year and I finished with satisfactory grades. My sister was working towards a secretarial post and so was away from home during the week for some time. My parents made another change in their lives then and bought some land available through the dictatorship and set about building their own house. Many families were doing so at that time. I still refused to speak to my Father, and relationships at home continued in their strained pattern, but my Mother's continual pleading to forget the past and be reconciled to him finally wore me down. I found it impossible to overlook his excessive drinking and abusive behavior towards us, but I finally agreed to her requests just for some peace. The house they were building looked promising – but I personally couldn't wait for the two years to pass until I was eighteen when I hoped to move away from their influence and control.

'Things are only half as bad as they seem' was my Mother's stock answer for every disaster in life. But to my adolescent mind, things seemed twice as bad – with no hope of getting better unless I could escape from my situation. The following two years, studying for my future career, gave me more opportunities to be away from home and it helped me to cope with each day. My parents accused me of using their house like a hotel, which I suppose was true, but I didn't feel I had a family deserving of my time and loyalties. I silently withheld from them the respect they demanded, taking care to avoid further beatings by simply remaining silent instead of challenging them.

"I dreamed of a perfect love that people could share."

I dreamed of a perfect love that people could share. Something capable of enduring the harshest trials and yet breathtakingly beautiful and fragile. The hurt child in me continued to rebel in as many ways as I could without invoking physical recriminations. I continued to smoke, hang out with friends instead of attending college, and even experimented with alcohol. Even though I detested what I knew it could do to lives I was led by a greater pressure than fear – that of being accepted by my peers.

After my eighteenth birthday I met another guy from the city. The main attraction for me was that he was not a local boy. We met mainly on weekends and corresponded during the week. Inevitably I ended up sleeping with him, although I had always intended to save that until I was married. Sex was one thing I believed would bond someone to me more strongly but I hadn't planned on becoming pregnant within four short months. With no knowledge of things of the world taught me by my parents and not wishing to look foolish, I had lied about using contraceptives. My periods ceased, and I could feel a swelling developing under my clothes. If there were such things as pregnancy tests in East Germany, I did not know about them. That knowledge along with so much else had been denied me. Finally concluding I must be pregnant, but shocked and frightened of telling either my parents or my boyfriend, I confided in my work colleagues who were supportive and understanding. On their advice I wrote to my boyfriend explaining the situation and invited him to come with me to see my parents. I did not receive any reply from him.

With time passing all too quickly and my condition threatening to announce itself, I finally plucked up courage to tell my Mother one evening. As I opened my mouth to utter the dreaded words, my sister and her boyfriend arrived home in a tense state and insisted on speaking to our Mother. She left me in the lounge and went outside where my sister told her she was pregnant. I could hear Mum's initial shocked answer – that my sister must have an abortion. My sister explained that as she was already sixteen weeks pregnant, that was not an option. I too felt shocked, as much for my own situation as for my sister's. How could I now also tell my Mother I was pregnant and that my boyfriend had deserted me? My Father echoed Mum's feelings when he was told later that evening. My sister was too young, this was too soon, it was a disaster for us all.

A favorite song of mine at the time was *Papa Don't Preach* by Madonna. Although I didn't understand every word, I could sense the overall meaning of the words from the video. I likened my own situation to the girl in the song. I was terrified to tell my parents about the baby I was carrying in case they forced me to have an abortion or have it adopted. I wanted more than anything to keep the baby – but feared the shame they would insist I brought upon the family. As well as the characteristic explosion of hormone activity associated with pregnancy, I was faced with the added strain of dealing with it in secret. While my officially pregnant sister complained continually about feeling unwell, I had to suffer in silence. Fortunately, my work colleagues continued to show great kindness and support to me. How tragic that strangers can offer so much kindness and help yet the one place we should be able to expect that treatment, in the home, is often the last place we find it.

I was constantly tired and suffering from pregnancy sickness, so mealtimes were a particular trial for me. I would escape to my room or the bathroom as often as I could without rousing suspicion. It was difficult learning to deal with something so profound as pregnancy at a young age, feeling alone and unloved. I told my closest friends, many of them boys, whom I had known since childhood. They were all excited for me but offered little in the way of a solution to my problems. Although travel was possible to countries such as Hungary, Poland and the Czech Republic, lifestyles there were all too similar to that of our own. It was almost impossible to travel or emigrate to countries with different cultures and freer lifestyles so it was quite common for people to start a family at a very early age. It was a way to become eligible for a flat of your own.

Despite valiant efforts by my boss to encourage me to tell my Mother of my predicament at a convenient time, it wasn't until he forced my hand by inviting her to the office one lunchtime that I tried to blurt out my news. If people do not want to receive the news you have to share, there is never a convenient moment. Fear gripped me and I kept gabbling that I had done nothing wrong, until finally my Mother got up and left the office, still unaware of the life-changing news I needed to tell her. My boss was horrified and sent me after her, telling me not to return until I had achieved my goal.

"So I told my Mother those three precious words – 'I am pregnant'…"

So I told my Mother those three precious words – "I am pregnant", on the street around the corner from where I worked. I desperately wanted it to be good news, news of life and happiness and new beginnings, but her immediate facial reaction caused the blood to freeze in my veins. Her words only compounded her disappointment and disapproval of me. What was I intending to do with the baby? I couldn't possibly keep it. I must get rid of it. What would people in the village say? And what about my Father? Fear seized me. He would get mad for sure. There was no telling what it would cause him to do. The words cut deep into my heart, my very soul. Frankly I didn't care what anyone thought or said about my conduct. All I knew was that this life I carried within me was precious and meant the world to me. Forced to admit that the father of my child had chosen to disassociate himself from me, I realise I gave my Mother more ammunition with which to beat me into submission – submission to her will anyway. Her parting words to me, before rushing off to catch her bus were, that I must get rid of it, immediately.

Back at work, my boss was happy that I had done as he asked

and commented that things were never as bad as they seemed at first. Now where had I heard that before? He was sure my parents would get used to the idea of being grandparents twice in one year and kept saying what wonderful news it was. Why couldn't he be my Father I wondered? I spent the remainder of the day anxiously contemplating what would happen at home that evening. My Father for once did not lash out in violence and beat me when he was told the news. In fact he did the only other thing characteristic of him, he stopped talking to everyone and busied himself away from us all in the cellar.

Mum kept asking me over and over what I was thinking about, what I was planning to do. It was a pointless exercise asking me my opinion because I knew in the end I would be forced to do as she wished. The choice was never mine. Though I passionately wanted to give birth to the baby I carried, and bring it up as my own, by the way she spoke of it, almost as a piece of meat, an inconvenient and shameful thing, I knew that would never happen. I kept telling my Mother there was no shame in being a single mum, there were other girls in that situation and it no longer carried the stigma it once did. But she took no notice of my wishes, torturing me by saying my sister could go ahead with her pregnancy because she was older with a boyfriend who stood by her. I, on the other hand, would be the centre of gossip, with no money and no prospects. My life would be ruined by having the child. My Dad's total inability to face the situation and talk only made matters more painful for me. But Mum was quick to defend him as always and tell me how hard the situation was for him.

Whatever he may or may not have felt, it cannot be compared to the pain and rejection I felt as my Mother hastily arranged for me to see a doctor at the hospital within a matter of days. She accompanied me, not in the caring role of a mother, but simply to ensure I went ahead with the planned abortion. Inside I screamed no, but outside I remained silent. I thought of my baby like a helpless lamb to the slaughter. Throughout the examination, I could not look the doctor in the eyes, as my soul cried out, desperate to be heard. I think she realised I was distraught because she asked my Mother to leave the room for a few minutes. She reluctantly left, but not without giving me a look that spoke volumes – it was a look she and my Father used that said you will obey or else.

"Once again it didn't matter what I wanted, it was all about pleasing others."

When the doctor and I were finally alone, she asked me if this termination was truly what I wanted, explaining I did not have to do what was against my will just because my parents put pressure on me. But she did not know what I knew. She had not grown up in a home overshadowed by a violent and drunken father, and a controlling mother who would go to any lengths to pander to his volatile temperament. Even though the doctor intimated there were ways to help me keep my baby, my insecurities screamed at me that I couldn't go through this alone. I could not bear to live with my parents but realised I couldn't live without them either. I could not wait to be housed in a residence for pregnant teenage girls. I did not have the strength to battle against my Mother until I could be moved somewhere else alone. I feared anything and everything my parents would throw at me. Exhausted before it all began, I functioned like a robot and left the room agreeing to my baby's death warrant – I would go ahead with the termination of my pregnancy. Once again it didn't matter what I wanted, it was all about pleasing others.

A possibility of reprieve presented itself when the doctor revealed the pregnancy may be more advanced than at first thought and I was given an appointment to check this in one week's time. I had one more week to enjoy my unborn child. Everyone outside my immediate family was shocked that I was to have an abortion. One friend even offered to move somewhere with me to help me raise the child. I couldn't believe anyone could be so caring, so sensitive; it was the kindest thing I had ever been told. For most of that week I sat in my room when I wasn't working, or with friends who genuinely cared about me. I spent hours crying silently, stroking my tiny bump, telling the baby how very sorry I was that I could not let it be born. I had no real knowledge of God or heaven, but I believed my baby would go straight into God's care, which I instinctively knew was a better place, where hurt and pain did not exist. I declared my love to that child, explaining I had no choice, and I hoped one day he or she would understand. I promised I would never, ever forget this, my first child.

"…so I went to the hospital with a heart shattered into a million pieces, and a darkness hanging over my life."

The week passed all too quickly and it was time to go to the hospital for the scan. No last minute stay of execution, no miraculous change of heart from my parents, no contact from my boyfriend. My Mother offered to come with me but I could not bear the thought of her being there – after all it was she who insisted I go through with the termination. My Father still refused to talk to me. How could a father treat his daughter in that way? I was unable to stop the flow of tears as I packed my few things the night before. I hardly slept before morning came crashing into my life. I wanted to stop time, to reverse all the decisions but it was not possible, and so I went to the hospital with a heart shattered into a million pieces, and a darkness hanging over my life.

Because there was doubt as to the exact length of the pregnancy, the doctors performed a scan to establish how many weeks the baby was. For this I needed to drink a lot of fluid. I was not prepared for the scan itself. I had not been warned that I would see the image of my unborn baby and I broke down in tears. The whole atmosphere in that place seemed impersonal and detached. Nurses merely took you where you needed to be, with little sympathetic bedside manner. I already felt like the lowest form of life for agreeing to this termination, now I also felt judged by everyone else. It was established the foetus was at the end of twelve weeks of life and the doctors expressed concern over whether they should go ahead.

The operation was scheduled for the following morning and if everything was successful, I would return home within a week. I did not want to be responsible for taking the life of my baby, but the fear I felt of my parents caused me to feel paralyzed with indecision. I felt numb – nothing seemed real anymore. Not surprisingly I broke down after a few hours at the hospital and the staff sent for my parents, as I was crying uncontrollably. I was standing, immobile, in the hall of the ward when I saw my parents' blue metallic East German Trabant car arrive in the car park. My Father remained outside smoking a cigarette – he would not venture in. My Mother came up to the ward, telling me again how things are only half as bad as they seem and to pull myself together. She only stayed a couple of minutes before rushing back to my Father. Her words echoed around my head for a long time after she left. "Father gets mad; pull yourself together."

I do not remember much of the following morning and its sinister schedule. I only remember being taken from and back to the ward I shared with several other women – there for many different reasons. I slept for most of that day and the next morning. By then the anesthetic had worn off and I hoped the feelings of guilt and shame would do likewise. The doctor arrived for his morning round and I was the last patient he attended. He told all the other patients their operations had gone well then approached my bed. I was expecting a similar report, but what he told me shattered my world all over again. He expressed his sorrow but said the operation didn't go as they hoped. Apparently I was between fourteen and fifteen weeks pregnant and they had only been able to remove part of the foetus and would have to operate again to remove the rest.

I thought my head would explode from the overload of emotions. How could it be? How could they get it so wrong? One minute I had been pregnant, then I wasn't. First, everything was okay then it wasn't. The only sign of my inner torment were the tears that streamed down my face, my whole being was in complete shock. When I found my voice I finally lost control, pulling the covers over my head, refusing to listen to the nurses trying to calm me, shouting that I would not have another operation. I would remain half pregnant for the rest of my life! How could I expect anyone in the hospital to understand what was going on – inside my head or inside my family. Of course I couldn't tell anyone, because my Father would get mad.

Once again my parents were summoned. But I remained absolute in my refusal to do the bidding of everyone else. I would not go through another operation. The doctors decided to give me some strong antibiotics to expel what remained of the foetus, from my body. Then I was discharged to go home to face my biggest fear: my Mother and Father. For the next two weeks I did not leave my bedroom but remained in bed, crying most of the time. My Mother kept telling me unsympathetically that life must go on. But what did she know of the brief life within me that had been snuffed out; what did she know of the excruciating pain and guilt I felt deep within?

"I was a prisoner in a war-zone called home!"

Perhaps if things had been different I may have been able to grieve properly for the loss of my child during those two weeks at home, but every-time I cried out my Mother would come into my room warning me not to let my Father see or hear how I felt or he would get mad. My sister's continuing pregnancy only made it harder to deal with what I had done. There was nothing worthwhile in my life and I lost all interest in seeing any of my friends. One evening while my Father was out somewhere getting drunk, my Mother came and told me I should be out with my friends, getting on with life. I escaped to the bathroom engulfed in my loneliness, sick of my life and my controlling parents. I was a prisoner in a war-zone called home!

Following close on my heels my Mother appeared at the bathroom door and asked me not to get mad at her. At first I didn't understand what she meant. I wasn't the one who got mad, that was my Father's speciality, but something in her tone made me pay attention. Then she dropped her bombshell: my boyfriend had contacted me by letter. When I asked why she hadn't given it to me and where it was, she said she had destroyed it, thinking it best I had nothing more to do with him. With one sweep of her controlling hand, she had destroyed any chance I had of escape. How could she do that to her daughter; what right did she have to make all my decisions for me? All the time I had thought he did not care and yet he had taken the trouble to write. Even then she had to have the last word, assuring me he was in favour of the abortion. I yelled at her to leave me alone. Now, I would never know how things might have turned out.

"…we lived like captives, deprived of free travel and free choice, ruled over by the secret police. The depression and frustration of the nation mirrored my own hopelessness."

To avoid the relentless badgering, I started to go out with my friends again, but because I had not dealt with my loss, all I could do was talk about my abortion to anyone who tried to get close, until they too abandoned me. As the date drew closer for my sister to give birth I was forced to repress all my emotions far below the surface, building up walls around my heart without being aware of it. I believe it is a common survival technique that humans adopt; whenever we are hurting but have no permission to deal with our emotions we hide them underneath layers of tight covers, like the skin of an onion. It takes much time, love and patience to peel them away. Although we had seasons like the rest of Europe, East Germany never seemed beautiful to me at that time in my life. A constant cloud hung over our nation, as we lived like captives, deprived of free travel and free choice, ruled over by the secret police. The depression and frustration of the nation mirrored my own hopelessness.

The birth of my sister's beautiful baby boy captivated my heart but with him occupying the room next to mine, there was little space for my grief – or sleep for that matter. Whilst with friends one evening I saw my ex-boyfriend unexpectedly, but his indifference to what had happened showed me he was not, and never had been, my knight in shining armour. That was the last time I ever saw him and life continued much as it always had, with a drunken Father causing arguments and fights at home, and a controlling Mother. I often had suicidal thoughts planning to take an overdose of painkillers and alcohol and had begun to self-harm by cutting my wrists. The only thing stopping me from taking my life was the fear my parents might discover me too early and I would not be able to withstand their anger. I knew they would misinterpret any cry for help as attention-seeking. I dare not risk their wrath.

Despite my continuing melancholy, I constantly socialised to escape the pervading atmosphere at home. With my sights firmly set on escaping to the far away, it was with some surprise that I found myself dating a guy I met at our youth club who did not tick any of my boxes required to realise my dream. But he did pay me a lot of attention in those early days and I was flattered, it being something I was not used to. My parents, of course, did not approve of the friendship. Along with the rest of the family and people in the village it was assumed that, as the black sheep, my life would inevitably cause them trouble and pain. This only served to keep me in my new relationship. When I finally plucked up courage to tell my boyfriend about the abortion, he was understanding. His sister was expecting her first child then and he invited me up north to visit her. Although I had not met his parents I was thrilled he included me in his life in this way. We started to have sex together and he secretly stayed overnight as I would smuggle him in and out of my parents' house considering this a small victory against their strict discipline and obsessive control of my life.

My sister with her boyfriend and baby moved into the flat that used to belong to Mrs Becher and although we still didn't get on well, I adored my little nephew and spent as much time with him as I could, looking after him. I envied my sister's independence and lifestyle, but in reality she was not coping well with young motherhood. She planned to marry and it was expected, as her sister, and the maid of honour, I should do my part in the proceedings but uncharacteristically I chose this time to make a stand for my own independence. In East Germany, it was traditional for a party to be held in the bride or groom's house before the actual wedding. Called Polterbend, old crockery is customarily smashed outside the house to alert the couple that the guests have arrived who are then greeted with cake and a drink. This celebration is usually extended and there is often a lot of heavy drinking involved. Much to my disapproval, my Father insisted on taking that opportunity of speaking to my boyfriend. To avoid a repetition at the reception itself, we escaped to go swimming as it was a hot day in May. As far as I was concerned, my family could do what they liked, I no longer felt it necessary to be part of it.

Immediately after the wedding, relationships deteriorated even more at home. For some unknown reason my Mother began to rebel against my Father's suppressive regime and his continued drinking bouts. She started going out enjoying herself socially. I did not like my Mother's new image; I could see she was drinking and felt sure it would lead to trouble. One evening, at a local dancing event a man from the village took a shine to my Mother and gave her a kiss. I was outraged at their behavior especially since I knew he too was an alcoholic. But more than that I was scared of what my Father would do when he found out, which was unavoidable in such a small community.

As it transpired, the story was told to him first hand the next day by the very man who had kissed my Mother. He was showing off in front of Dad. My Mother was at home resting on the sofa, nursing a hangover, and my boyfriend and I were there too watching television. Suddenly my Father stormed into the house and straight away demanded to know if the story was true. He did not appear to have seen us sitting in the lounge, his attention was firmly fixed on my Mother. Without warning, he pinned her down whilst attempting to strangle her. It was obvious my Mother could not defend herself and I shouted to my boyfriend to do something, but he remained frozen in shock, on the settee. I could see my Mother was clearly distressed and in a desperate attempt to stop the violence, I momentarily forgot my fear of my Father's rage and punched him hard on his back with my fist. He turned and looked at me before running out of the house. My Mother was clearly shaken, and bruises and marks promptly appeared on her neck from the attack. Although I begged my boyfriend to stay overnight, he left, with the excuse he had work very early the next morning. Thankfully my Father did not return, leaving my Mum and I alone together, but fear kept me awake all night. Although my Mother again filed for divorce soon after the incident, I gave her no support or attention, convinced she would not go ahead with it.

"I was desperate to escape from my home environment…"

My relationship with my boyfriend continued though his imminent conscription meant we would be apart for eighteen months. Compulsory service for all males in the East German Nationale Volksarmee meant few opportunities for leave and was usually served a long way from home. Urged on by this approaching deadline we discussed future plans, like getting engaged, married and having children – the kind of things that can suddenly mean so much when threatened by separation. Although I had not met his parents and did not really know him that well, my longings for a family of my own were incredibly strong. Accompanied by a passion to escape my home situation they influenced the commitments I made to my boyfriend at that time. Corresponding with each other almost every day became the norm but I was overwhelmed and confused when he declared his undying love for me and took me to meet his family during Christmas leave. I was desperate to escape from my home environment, though unsure this relationship was the 'real thing'. He was not the person I imagined myself married to for the rest of my life and was definitely not from the 'far away'. I was comforted rather than worried by the thought of our separation. It would give me valuable space to sort out my real feelings for him.

Meanwhile, his Mother invited me to meet her on my own before Christmas, and over coffee at her house she appeared a kind lady and a good mother, very different from my own. She warmly welcomed me, excusing her husband's absence explaining he was a long distance lorry driver and was sleeping. When he joined us later I could not help feeling there was something familiar about his manner and thought it odd he kept falling asleep in front of us. It wasn't until I was walking home later that afternoon the thought struck me: I was absolutely sure my boyfriend's Father was an alcoholic. Initially I felt extremely angry that my boyfriend had omitted to mention this rather important fact, especially since he knew of my own family's situation. But on reflection I presumed he too was ashamed of his Dad. I hoped that shame would deter him from following in his Father's footsteps as many young men from our village were apt to do.

By the time my boyfriend came home for Christmas, I was quite excited at the prospect of seeing him and decorated my bedroom in his honour. To have the perfect family life and wonderful children was still high on my agenda but with a year of my boyfriend's conscription to serve I chose to put off any sense of reality concerning our future. Foolishly during his leave we slept together without taking any precautions. When I discovered I was pregnant, I delayed telling my parents for as long as I could, worried that if they found out too soon they would force me to have another termination. I suddenly wanted this baby more than anything and would fight to keep it. News of any kind travels fast in a close-knit community like our village and one day my Mother came into the local grocery store where I was working at the time and asked me outright if I was pregnant. When I told her I was, her first reaction was that I must get rid of it. Despite my protestations that I intended to go ahead and have this baby, she began to ridicule my boyfriend and our relationship, intimating that neither of us would be able to deal with our remaining separation and would probably meet someone else.

Her constant stream of negativity almost drove me insane making me even more determined to escape from her control as soon as I could – even if that meant marrying someone I wasn't totally sure about. Strangely, when my Father was told of the pregnancy, and that I intended to keep the baby, he was very supportive and didn't show any outward signs of getting mad as my Mother threatened. For a while at least, a kind of peace descended on our household as my Dad spent lots of time taking care of me. Once or twice a month I would visit my boyfriend in Berlin where his unit was serving. Occasionally I was accompanied by his Mother, which I didn't mind as we got on well and I always enjoyed being away from our village with its claustrophobic atmosphere. I was slightly bothered by his Mother's habit of packing up drinks for her son as well as the food we usually took. She regarded the little bottles of alcohol she included as a treat for her son during his enforced service, whilst I saw it as unnecessary and, frankly, dangerous.

My pregnancy progressed uneventfully, with my Father surprisingly looking forward to being a grandfather again. Between the two of us we looked after my nephew as my sister found it difficult to cope. I enjoyed the opportunity to practice motherhood and my continuing strong relationship with my nephew made me hope for a boy, though it really did not matter, just as long as I was allowed to keep the baby and it was healthy. I was regularly seeing my boyfriend who was allowed home some weekends and because we seemed to enjoy each other's company I even imagined myself in love with him.

I promised to let him know by telegram as soon as the contractions began. House-phones then were something only the elite of East Germany enjoyed; it was a way of controlling the citizens of our nation from spreading too much information about real life behind the wall. It was common knowledge that phones were bugged – another efficient way to discover the nature of people's communications. When my contractions were firmly underway, I was taken to hospital alone in an ambulance, my parents standing outside their house waving me off. I was anxious but could think of little except that in a few hours I would be a Mum, holding a baby of my own that no one was ever going to take away from me. That baby turned out to be the most beautiful girl. I named her Taylor.

Although my boyfriend was granted leave after the birth, he was rather overwhelmed with fatherhood whilst I was very preoccupied with our daughter, sparing little time for him. Unlike me, he lacked confidence in anything to do with the care of Taylor, but with seven months still to serve in the military, I became accustomed to his absence, in-fact I preferred it, and settled into motherhood with a natural ease. My Father doted on his new granddaughter and supported me in every way he could whilst I drew even further away from my Mother, feeling little need for her or her constant negativity. When she announced she had to go into hospital following one of her frequent visits to the gynecologist, I was not worried as it was customary for her to believe she was ill with something. It came as a shock when, instead of saying things were only half as bad as they seemed, she looked extremely upset and said the doctors had discovered something abnormal. Dad took her to hospital and she was scheduled for an exploratory operation the very next day. He came home bearing the frightening news: my Mother had cancer and was given eight weeks to live.

We were all terribly shocked, but especially Dad, who when he wasn't with Mum, showed an incredible sensitivity I had never seen before. Receiving the call that she was out of theatre, he rushed to be with her, fearing the worst. I was unable to go as I had the baby and so remained at home anxiously awaiting news. Although our relationship was strained, she was still my Mother and I could not bear the thought of losing her. I prayed once again to the God I wasn't sure was there, to spare my Mother's life. I told Him I needed her and I wanted her to see her granddaughter growing up. My Father was soon back home, reporting that Mum looked pretty bad from the anesthetic but the doctors predicted they would know within the next few hours what her chances were. To the utter surprise of us all, my Mother did survive though my desperate prayer and the amazing answer it brought was soon forgotten.

Eventually my boyfriend returned home, his compulsory service completed. He moved in with me to my parents' house. It was strange having him around all the time and we found ourselves arguing frequently. He felt neglected and blamed our poor relationship on Taylor. I was totally besotted with my daughter and happily spent all my waking hours caring for her, giving her all the love overflowing from my full heart. From time to time my feelings of guilt motivated me to spend time alone with him but for the most part we were not exceptionally close. However, one year later we decided to get married, and there was a part of me eager to do that as it would further fulfil my desire to have a real family life of my own.

Chapter 3
CONVENIENT ESCAPE...

"...November 9th 1989 – a date never to be forgotten, not just for us but for the whole nation of East Germany..."

The date was set: November 9th 1989 – a date never to be forgotten, not just for us but for the whole nation of East Germany and indeed the world. During the preparations for the ceremony, I went through the whole gamut of emotions: I was excited at the prospect of finally changing my name from that of my parents, but there were moments when I questioned whether my boyfriend was indeed the prince of my dreams. The fact that he was only from around the corner did not satisfy my obsession to move far away either. My Father had miraculously stopped drinking from the day my Mother became ill and their relationship seemed calmer. They were both opposed to the marriage though, and I still didn't feel very loved or appreciated by them. The closer my wedding day loomed on the horizon, the more panic attacks I suffered. Even though over twenty one and escaping their home, inexplicably I still felt trapped. I continually doubted whether this man was the right choice for me. But what could I do to get out of the situation, and what was the alternative?

The pendulum would inevitably end up swinging the other way and I would feel encouraged about changing my name and not having to do as my parents insisted. The future promised better prospects if I was independent of my Mum and Dad, and at least I had the beginnings of a real family of my own. I had my daughter Taylor to care for and be the best mum I could be. Almost in contradiction to my decision, I had a big bust up with my boyfriend with only a week to go to the wedding. It was over a trifling matter about whether we should go out or not but it developed into a huge conflict and we both dug our heels in refusing to compromise. It was the closest I came to calling the wedding off and it was only my parents' smugness that turned the tide in favour of the marriage at the last minute. They were not best pleased.

The ceremony was a simple registry office affair. Thinking it diminished their control over me I refused all offers of financial help from my family and so was dressed modestly in a white skirt and blazer. My husband wore a suit bought for him by his Father: it was certainly not what my dreams were made of. Regrettably, we did not even have our daughter present, she was back home with my sister during the brief formalities. I vividly remember being shocked to smell a strong presence of alcohol on my new husband's breath. Although I realised some people partook of a shot of alcohol to steady their nerves, I also knew my Father had been so drunk when he married my Mother that he could barely repeat his vows. Alarm bells repeatedly rang in my head during our courtship as I observed the frequency that he consumed alcohol. The worrying habit his Mother had of supplying him with it, considering it as a treat he had earned, like giving puddings or sweets to a child was also cause for concern.

Instead of concentrating on what was being said by the registrar I was only conscious of my stomach churning and feeling light-headed. Was it too late for me to run out of the building? But how could I do that? I would have to face my parents afterwards and the thought of that made me feel even more sick. So I went ahead saying "I do", in all the right places and consoled myself at the reception later by reminding myself I was now completely independent of my parents, able to apply for a separate flat and be in charge of my life at last. My brief contentment was marred by witnessing my husband getting totally drunk before the end of the evening.

As the celebrations drew to a close, we were standing outside the hall waiting for transport to take my new in-laws back home. The driver appeared very excitable as he reported news that was spreading through East Germany like an infectious virus. The East German regime had finally capitulated after endless peaceful demonstrations (Montagsdemos) for more relaxed regulations on travel out of East Germany. From midnight that night, the citizens of East Germany would be allowed to travel freely to the west for the first time since the erection of the Berlin Wall in 1961.

"A new, different way of life had suddenly become open to our people and it was too late for me! "Why, JUST WHY?" I screamed in silent agony."

I felt my whole body go into shock as I absorbed the news and what it meant to me personally. A new, different way of life had suddenly become open to our people and it was too late for me! "Why, JUST WHY?" I screamed in silent agony. Why did this happen now, why not the night before? It was to be a terrible crushing secret I would carry with me for many long years because I knew in my broken heart that if it had happened just twenty four hours before I would never have gone ahead with the marriage. Acceptance was the only route for me, the one thing I could hope to do was build a strong family environment for my daughter. At all costs I realised I must make this marriage work. And so, for the time being at least, we returned back home with my parents to wait for our circumstances to change for the better.

That wait was not to be as long as I had feared. My Mother decided we should leave their home immediately and get a place of our own. Now I was married, felt she had performed her duty to me as a mother and it was time for me to be responsible for my own life. Her words came as a surprise, especially considering her incessant need to control every part of my life. But she was adamant. After her brush with cancer the previous year she considered it appropriate for her and my Father to spend time together, not always sacrificing their lives for their children. I wanted to ask her exactly what she thought she had done for me, except force me to do exactly as she dictated, but once again I remained silent, pushing all my feelings of rejection deep inside, feeling worthless and unloved. My Mother hadn't even taken the time to teach me how to be a wife or mother, all she had ever taught me was fear – of my Father's drinking and violence, and her control. Given no time and seemingly no choice, my husband and I took the first flat we were offered in a town some distance away, needing to have somewhere to put our belongings which my Mother briskly packed up and put out on the road.

Chapter 4
CAN LOVE CONQUER ALL?...

"...feeling trapped inside a marriage to someone I wasn't even sure I loved made it all the more unbearable."

I found the whole process of moving into the flat very stressful. I had to give up my job in the village as it was too far to travel with Taylor so early in the morning for Kindergarten, not returning home until late at night. Adjusting to city life was hard: I missed the familiarity of my home environment and I would spend many nights crying constantly as my husband's job also involved night shifts. It certainly wasn't the most favourable start to married life and would have been challenging enough, but feeling trapped inside a marriage to someone I wasn't even sure I loved made it all the more unbearable. I felt like a little girl and not the young woman I should have been.

I soon found a Kindergarten for Taylor close to home, which meant she was happy but my depression worsened as my life continued its destructive course. Constant arguments or desperate loneliness was the daily choice I faced. There was also the matter of my husband's alcohol consumption. Arriving home from work every night without exception, he would have to drink beer immediately and the evening would often end with him going out drinking to excess with his friends. When I told him I couldn't live like that anymore, he suggested I apply for a job as receptionist at the local Red Cross where he worked. I got the position and indeed liked it very much, so much so that I also began working night as well as day shifts and we passed like ships on the ocean, pausing only to hand over the care of Taylor to each other.

Looking at my marriage through the rose-tinted glasses of a job I enjoyed, I believed maybe it wasn't as bad as I had at first assumed and I settled into a life of pretence. Make-believe became my reality and although there were some good days, many were bad, but I chose not to dwell too much on those, being distracted with my busy job. Time passed quickly; I had adjusted to life in the town, made a few friends and we were both pleased when I became pregnant again, until I realised I would have to tell my parents. I had not talked much about my childhood to my husband and so apart from that one incident of violence he had personally witnessed, he did not know the history of control and abuse that had been my everyday life.

We chose an opportunity to share our news when my husband drove my Mother to the hospital to have a check up regarding her cancer. As they arrived outside my work place, I walked out to the car and told her the news. By the expression on her face I realised her attitude would be the same as before. She accused me of being crazy wanting to bring another child into this changing world. Although that was true to an extent and the reunification of Germany had brought many changes, we both had well paid jobs, and I intended to return to work after a year to provide a good home and life for my family. Her passing comment was she would have to tell my Father and he would not want to speak to me once he knew.

Despite wanting another child, damaging seeds of doubt had already been sown by my Mother's comments. I felt upset, guilty being pregnant again – just like the first time. No matter how much my husband tried to reassure me everything would be fine, I was devastated once again to realise I did not have my parents' blessing. During the days that followed, my Mother bombarded me with phone calls, relentlessly questioning whether I should go ahead and have the baby or have it terminated. Her constant nagging included predictions of job loss, poverty and more unhappiness. Once more I became the little child, being chastised, always in the wrong and making a mess of my life. I felt very insecure, scared her repeated suggestions of abortion would wear me down and I would be forced to make a decision against my wishes just to please my parents. In the end the verbal bullying took it's toll. I succumbed to the pressure and terminated my pregnancy.

Once more life didn't seem worth living; even though I was a married adult and mother, I could not even defend my own choices. I had yet again been forcibly pressured into doing something to please my Mum and Dad, even against the preferences of my husband. My weakness made me ashamed and I felt no peace. Then miraculously, four months later, I discovered I was pregnant again after visiting the doctor because I felt unwell. This time I resolutely decided not to tell my Mother until it was much too late to abort the pregnancy. Thus when I had passed the sixteenth week, I relaid the news to her as she was leaving our apartment. I hastily closed the door on her visit, not allowing her time to make one of her poisonous comments.

Deep inside I still felt ashamed. Only four months after a termination, here I was pregnant again. I felt I had cheapened life. I feared the reactions of people who knew me. I was again drowning in insecurities. What would friends say? Did I deserve another baby. Although it had always been my most heart-felt desire to have a family, I didn't feel like a good or successful mother to Taylor. I did not know how to behave with children. I desperately wanted to love them but didn't think I had shown that passionate love to my daughter. I had never been guided in how to do that. All I knew was criticism and negativity. Although I read bedtime stories to Taylor, I had no memories of my Mother playing with me or spending time with me, and I lacked the knowledge and confidence to share those treasured times properly with my own child.

Finally, Grace was born in 1992 – a beautiful, healthy baby girl. My husband was extremely supportive after the birth and as well as going to work full time, insisted on doing all the chores around the house, not allowing me to do any cleaning, cooking, shopping, washing or ironing. I began to think I had miraculously ended up with the world's most attentive and helpful husband and everyone commented on how lucky I was to be married to such a man. We applied for a larger flat, as it was obvious we had outgrown our small one-bedroomed home. We were able to exchange with a lady who had a three-bedroomed apartment nearby. Eventually I returned to work doing part-time night shifts, so being at home for Taylor and Grace when they needed me. My extra salary became more and more necessary. East Germany had fast become a consumer society shunning its very own Trabant as people desired new cars like the rest of the world. We had a little secondhand sports car and a loan we could just about afford but my husband soon made it known that he too coveted his very own new car. He went ahead and bought one, taking us further into debt.

"I also began to notice he had a distinctive look and always smelled overpoweringly of after-shave and chewing gum."

I noticed when my husband drove me to work for my night shifts, the girls would always sit crying in the back of the car. In the mornings he would return with them ready for me to drop off at nursery and Kindergarten and although there didn't seem to be any reason for their tears, I was a little concerned. I also began to notice he had a distinctive look and always smelled overpoweringly of after-shave and chewing gum. People would often laugh and make a comment about heavy nights, as he would arrive late, red-faced and looking like he'd just leapt out of bed. Whenever he came home from work early he would always tidy and clean especially in the girls' bedroom and with no explanation would discourage the girls from playing in their bedroom at all. His odd behaviour incited arguments but whenever I questioned him, he would loose his temper very quickly and more and more slap me around the head. I found these incidents worrying, especially since these physical outbursts reminded me all too much of my Father.

"With alarming regularity, I discovered small, empty spirit bottles concealed around our flat…"

With alarming regularity, I discovered small, empty spirit bottles concealed around our flat, especially in the girls' bedroom in their wardrobe and toy chest. I recalled his Mother saying he had done similar things at home too. At first I smiled, wondering why anyone would do that but when I confronted him he would nervously change the subject, insisting I should leave the housework for him to do when he came home. Slowly it dawned on me and I was cross with myself for not recognising the signs before. It was obvious he was drinking – not only the beers he demanded as soon as he came home from work – or the bouts of heavy drinking with his friends, he was also drinking secretly at home. Some mornings I would wake up to discover he had not been to bed at all. On those occasions, I would find him unconscious in front of the television, surrounded by empty beer and spirit bottles. The arguments became more frequent and it was obvious to me his drinking was out of control though he was in denial insisting his actions were perfectly normal. At night I lay awake staring at the ceiling, screaming at my Mother silently inside, asking why she never warned me about this side of life. Realisation hit me: this was not normal and it was not the life I wanted but I was trapped.

The fights continued to gather momentum. I had begun to hit back at him in anger and after one particularly violent episode, I ended up with concussion. Terrified to leave the girls in his care in that state, I refused to go to the hospital but ended up calling the doctor out as my head hurt so much. She examined me then sent my husband out of the room while she explained that I had suffered a severe concussion and could confide in her if I wished. I was embarrassed to tell her what had happened, after all I too had hit my husband. She left very strong medicine to take whenever I was sick, which was occurring every ten minutes. If my condition hadn't improved by morning hospitalisation would be unavoidable. My husband apologised and begged me not to tell anyone. I called my Mother to look after the girls the next day, as the drugs had a strong sedative effect. I tried to cover up the truth, blaming my headaches on a previous accident when I had been knocked down in the road at thirteen but the look on her face told me she knew; it also communicated that she had been right all along: we should never have married.

"What took me a long time to work out was, when new situations became frightening, I was drawn back to my past even with all its disturbing memories as it was all I knew."

I didn't need to recover from the concussion to think straight about my husband's behaviour. Instinctively I knew my marriage would not provide a stable life for me or my daughters. I needed to get out but could not envisage an obvious escape. I resigned from my job as receptionist and went back to being a shop assistant. One of the many changes in East Germany since reunification was lots of private firms reclaimed or bought land to develop as much needed housing, industrial estates and shopping centres. The centre I now worked in was close by my parents' house and I enjoyed being back on old familiar territory. That in itself seemed a contradiction as it was my very need to escape that had enticed me to marry and move away. What took me a long time to work out was, when new situations became frightening, I was drawn back to my past even with all its disturbing memories as it was all I knew. It was never a loving, stable environment but in my insecure state, it seemed more bearable than the unknown.

I decided to remain with my husband; there were few options in East Germany then for single mothers. Some of my colleagues lived in nice new privately commissioned apartments opposite my parents and when one became available I went to see it, having worked out we could just about afford to live there. It didn't take too much persuading for my husband to agree to the move; our nation had become very materialistic and everyone wanted to better themselves. The paradox for me was, having spent most of my life trying to escape from my small-minded home village overrun with men who were alcoholics and women who lived lives of pretence, I now desired to move back there. I cannot say for sure that my actions were premeditated but still a nagging voice in the back of my mind warned me my husband's volatile behaviour was dangerous.

Moving into the new flat was exciting on its own merit. For so long we East Germans had lived in very old, ill-maintained housing as the former regime sacrificed the nation's living standards and social services to maintain the high cost of the military – aimed at preventing people from escaping to the west. The old buildings seldom had central heating, all the windows were in desperate need of replacing and often the only means of heating whole apartments was by way of a huge oven in the lounge or kitchen and possibly a coal stove. Our new flat was what most people dreamed of. Of course, my family expressed their concerns as to how we would be able to afford it, but as my husband had taken charge of the finances from the day we were married and gave no signs of distress, I trusted all was well. I had no idea of the true level of his drinking, or that it was getting us into serious debt.

I changed jobs and went to work in the city. Although it felt strange finally working somewhere I considered far away I immediately fell in love with the city environment and enjoyed my job. The hours and pay were not really enough and I suspected we would be struggling to meet the outgoings I knew of. I befriended a female colleague originally from West Germany and I learned from her that materialism, with which so many in the East had become obsessed, was unimportant. The best things in life were still free or was it that the free things were the best? I tried to convince my husband that we didn't really need a new, expensive car, but his drinking had escalated further and most conversations ended in violent arguments. He was under the influence of alcohol most of the time and blind drunk for the remainder. It concerned me to leave the girls in his care, but not wishing to invoke the criticism and wrath of my parents, I did not share my hidden life with them. I knew my Mother would blame my situation on what she considered my poor choices and I now realised she could not fulfill her role as a Mother because she had no role model: her own Mother had died when she was a teenager and for most of her formative years she had no example to follow. Living in denial of my Father's true condition for so long convinced me that she would certainly not be sympathetic to what was happening in our home. Her constant comment was still 'things are only half as bad as they seem'!

If there was to be any chance of our marriage surviving, I believed I had to help my husband face up to and deal with his drink problem. Sadly it was easier said than done. His dependancy on alcohol increased and now he was drinking throughout the day as well as craving beers and spirits as soon as he came home from work, even if that were seven in the morning after a night shift. If we were going straight out to do the shopping, he would always insist on a couple of drinks beforehand. I cannot imagine how he managed to carry out his job at all without being reprimanded by his bosses, except for many in East Germany it was considered normal to drink excessively so perhaps no one noticed anything out of the ordinary. My pleas for abstinence or moderation went unanswered and in desperation I confided in my work colleague one day while we sat doing arts and crafts with our children. Explaining my husband's problem I was relieved when she agreed with me that in our village at least, excessive drinking was definitely a big issue. For so long I had felt like an outsider – the only one not sanctioning uncontrolled drinking habits – now at last someone was not just listening to me but agreeing with my views.

My friend offered me advice which made me more optimistic about the future. Apparently there was a clinic in the area, of which I had no knowledge and she volunteered to go there with me to seek help. We arrived at the clinic and were attended to by trained staff. It was a shocking experience as there were people there going through various stages of detoxification, some locked up in their rooms and experiencing severe withdrawal symptoms. It scared me and I remember thinking my husband was not like any of these patients. But the realisation hit me that I had little understanding of alcohol abuse, not even aware it was a serious illness. Thankfully my friend saw how anxious I was and sat in with me when I saw the therapist and nurses.

"The therapist explained that if someone needed more than two drinks each night, they probably did have a problem with alcohol."

Explaining I was there because I was concerned about my husband, the experts questioned me extensively about times and amounts he consumed. I told them he needed at least one drink whatever time he arrived home from work. He usually consumed five or six beers and a half bottle of spirits each evening whilst watching the television and he would often drive after that amount of alcohol the four kilometers to the nearest petrol station in order to purchase more. The therapist explained that if someone needed more than two drinks each night, they probably did have a problem with alcohol. It was both a shock to hear expert confirmation, but it didn't offer any hope to me because my husband refused to consider he even had a problem. There was nothing they could do; they were authorised to offer help only when asked by the individual themselves. They told me I was eligible for counselling as someone living with an alcoholic but I refused for the moment, my main priority being to get help for my husband. It seemed from their experience that people seldom asked for help until they reached their personal rock bottom. And even then there was no guarantee. They were concerned as the amount of alcohol my husband permitted me to witness him consuming was already far too much and assured me he would also be secretly drinking a great deal more.

I contemplated how often I had come across empty bottles hidden all over our apartment: in every hiding place imaginable, including in the children's room and wardrobe, secreted under toys and clothing. It was a relief to be told that I wasn't imagining it: my husband did have a drink problem. Conversely, all I could picture was my parents' terrible home life; how my Father's addiction had ruined their lives and relationship and mine too. I had suffered because of his illness all my life. I had been made to feel abnormal for disliking drink and what it made people do. My situation was not so much the exception in our village as the norm. People, predominantly male, were consuming excesses of alcohol all the time, both at work and home and women everywhere were covering up their secrets with masks of pretence. Even my Mother-in-law both encouraged and hid the extent to which her son was drinking when I first met him. When I did muster up courage to confront my husband, he shouted at me for even going to the clinic calling my accusations insane.

Armed with this alarming knowledge, I racked my brains trying to think of a way to get my husband to admit his condition and seek help. With the aid of my friend, whose house overlooked ours, we regularly spied on my him, gathering undeniable proof of the extent of his illness. It became clear all the apparently helpful things he undertook around the house were merely to hide his drinking. Even to the point of sneaking a drink when putting out the rubbish or hanging washing on the line. As I distanced myself from him, spending more time with my girl friend, he accused us of being lesbians but I realised it was intended to distract us from his increasing propensity to drink. I asked him to at least cut down, not to drink during the day and especially when he was at home with the children, supposedly looking after them. He promised to try if I stopped nagging him about it, but if he succeeded in cutting down at all, it was always short-lived and hardly apparent by his abusive language and behaviour.

Meanwhile I read everything I could find on the subject, desperate to help him so that we could provide a safe, loving home for our children. I learned about the different factors influencing the addiction. I found out that alcoholism can be genetic: there is evidence of children becoming alcoholics in later life if their childhood was overshadowed by a parent's addiction. But it sometimes had the opposite effect and if alcohol abuse ran in the family the children were also just as likely never to touch it. I was sure that was where I stood, since I abhorred everything associated with drinking.

I genuinely wanted to help my husband overcome his illness, but for all the promises he made, little change occurred. For the few times he would have the girls in bed, with a meal waiting on the table when I returned from work, there were countless other times when I arrived home to chaos. As often as not I was confronted by his overly red nose, sweating face and instantly smell the unmistakable combination of drink, after-shave and chewing gum. Always there was the characteristic glazed look in his eyes. I felt so let down by the continual broken promises and of course I didn't understand, he was still in denial, not believing he had a problem and humouring me to stop me nagging him incessantly. What I also did not appreciate was this kind of illness requires help from experts who know what they are doing and are not intimately involved with the sufferer. I also felt humiliated because he believed he was deceiving me. Visits to the playground with our daughters would inevitably result in him disappearing to the shops nearby on the pretext of buying bread or milk, but always it was to buy liquor. Another woman I newly befriended confirmed she observed my husband going into a store near her apartment and drinking his purchase immediately outside before discarding the empty bottle in the nearby field, with seemingly no desire to cover up his behaviour.

A surprise visit to my work place turned into a worrying incident when my husband came into the store looking distressed. I couldn't make out what had happened until, finishing work, I joined him in the car outside. Taylor and Grace were in the back, also looking very upset. Then my husband told me they had been involved in an accident. He said a bus had driven into our car. My first reaction was to turn and see if the girls were unhurt. I asked Taylor what had happened; my husband kept interrupting but she managed to tell me that her Daddy tried to overtake the bus, didn't make it in time and rammed into the bus in order to avoid an oncoming car. He denied it was his fault, accusing Taylor of lying, but I could see the truth in his face – he had obviously been drinking. Our car was totally smashed in on the driver's side. I was in shock as I realised he was prepared to put his daughters' lives in danger to satisfy his craving for alcohol. It dawned on me I could not help him and I told him his drinking was totally out of control and his conduct unacceptable: either he sought professional help or we were finished.

The weeks passed and he made more superficial efforts to convince me he was over his addiction, all the time assuring me he would seek help soon. In desperation, I moved out of our bedroom and slept with the girls in their room. This roused his anger against me and he accused me of being the one with the problem by always inciting arguments. He quickly resorted to violence when I refused to react to his claims. I began to lock the door to my daughters' bedroom when we were in there, no longer feeling safe. His attempts to make up as soon as he was sober would frequently include buying presents for us. One afternoon, after a shopping expedition, Grace came home clutching two huge cuddly toys from the new Disney movie, Lion King, one for her and one for Taylor. Knowing how tight our finances were I expressed surprise that we had money for these toys when Grace, who was three at the time, told me Daddy had walked out of the store without paying for them. I was outraged: not only was my husband guilty of shoplifting but had committed the crime while his daughter was with him. He failed to see he had either done anything wrong, or was giving wrong messages to our children.

All this time he remained in charge of our finances and always accompanied me on trips to buy groceries. Although the account was in joint names and our salaries were paid into it, I never saw bank statements. Occasionally he would ask for my signature on forms, usually at times when I was distracted with the children or about to leave for work and foolishly I would consent and sign without asking questions. I trusted he had our best interests at heart. In my naivety I failed to see it was all a ploy to prevent me from finding out the extent of our debt. On one occasion, I put all the items we needed into the trolley and my husband paid at the checkout as usual. We were about to leave when an in-store detective stopped us and asked to see the contents of our pockets. I was in shock, not fully understanding what was happening. The detective again addressed my husband, asking him to cooperate or he would have to call the police. I anxiously asked my husband what he had done – what he had stolen. Initially he denied doing anything wrong but agreed to go with the detective into a separate room. When they eventually emerged, the detective explained my husband had tried to steal a perfume. He of course tried to excuse his behaviour, saying he had done it for me. What little respect I had left for him was rapidly disappearing.

Taylor was due to start infant school and it was customary to have a big celebration for this special event. For a few days I was busy organising the party helped by friends. My husband did little except creep around taking every opportunity to drink when I couldn't see him. Although he promised to help the day before, it was obvious when he came home from work he had been drinking heavily although he tried to hide the fact from me. Taking the car on the pretext of getting something from the shops, he crashed it into a fence outside our apartment. I removed the key from the ignition and he went back into the flat to sleep and sober up. He slept all that afternoon, evening and night. By the next day, I had made up my mind enough was enough and I told him I no longer wanted him living with us. I requested he find other accommodation, explaining I would be filing for divorce.

He remained in shock most of that day, possibly because I had never before mentioned such drastic action. I had issued ultimatums to seek help for his drinking habit but never indicated I wanted a divorce. After considering my decision he dug his heels in and refused to leave and, almost as if he was mocking me, drank more and more in front of me and the children. I did not know what to do. I could not go on living like this any more. He needed help but more than that, so did I. In desperation I told my Mother about the situation but I was so nervous of her reaction all my words came out slow and wrong. She just sat there, very much in control, actually enjoying the feeling of power she held. Her words were like a slap in the face: I'd had things my way and now wished I'd listened to her. I couldn't believe the spitefulness in her voice, but having nowhere else to turn, I begged her for her support and asked if I could move back home with the girls. She said she would have to ask my Father first and let me know.

"Forced to look honestly at my life, I realised there was no way I could help my husband beat this addiction because he did not believe he had a problem."

Trying to think ahead, I made some preparations to divorce my husband and I opened a bank account in my sole name. When I went to see the bank manager where we had a joint account, I was horrified to discover the extent of our debt. We were up to the absolute limit on our seven thousand Deutsche Mark overdraft!

When I asked to see evidence of this shocking situation, the manager showed me all the transactions as well as all the papers I had jointly signed with my husband applying for higher and higher overdraft facilities. All the times I had signed paperwork and trusted him, my husband was deceiving me and feeding his habit. Now I was equally liable for this debt, as it appeared everything had been done with my full approval. I could not believe it had all come to this. Forced to look honestly at my life, I realised there was no way I could help my husband beat this addiction because he did not believe he had a problem. All the threats on earth would not force him to give up drinking, I had to carry out the only action I knew would get through to him.

Refusing to leave, he cleverly played the victim and made contact with all our friends and his family, telling them I was divorcing him. His partly respectable act during much of our relationship meant most people were shocked when they found out what I planned to do. We seemed a close couple to outsiders, a happy family. Even the girls had no real comprehension of what had been going on for such a long time as I had taken pains to protect them from the awful truth about their Dad. Of course they had witnessed the arguments and fights, but I think, with a childlike innocence, they hoped things would get better. My husband played a convincing part seeking their attention and trying to make me look like a bad person. Surreptitiously, our conflict was moving from a physical plane to an emotional one and I had no idea of the mind games he would play to frighten me.

Having no reply from my Mother about moving into my parents' house temporarily, I remained in the marital home, continuing to sleep in the girls' bedroom. More bad news arrived in the form of a letter from the property agents informing us we were three months behind with our rent. I secretly disposed of our credit cards to prevent my husband running up any further debt and arranged for my salary to be paid into my new sole account. As expected, it wasn't long before he missed his credit card, asking me where it was. I told him I had destroyed them all and he could no longer get money we did not have. He obviously needed a drink badly as his body was shaking all over. I was sitting on the sofa with the two girls when he suddenly jumped on top of me, punching and hitting me uncontrollably, demanding the return of his credit card. All three of us were terrified, he seemed like some mad animal. The girls tried to fight him off but he suddenly turned on them. Grace's little body was flung over the sofa like a rag doll, stopping when she hit the lamp in the corner causing Taylor to scream but still he would not stop raining down blows on me. I put my arms up over my head and face to protect myself. Finally, he seemed to have a notion of what he was doing and left the lounge, but not before warning me not to mess with him.

The three of us fled to the bathroom, driven by sheer terror, locking ourselves in. I glanced in the mirror and was surprised to see I was not bleeding anywhere visibly. Deciding we needed outside help and convinced he would come back if he could not feed his habit, I asked Taylor if she felt brave enough to jump out of the bathroom window and run to her grandparents' house, two minutes around the corner to tell them what had happened. She was only seven years old and had just witnessed a frightening scene but she went willingly. I was so proud of her, my eyes filled with tears. After she left, I waited anxiously with Grace. Within a few minutes, the doorbell rang and I was relieved to hear my father's strong voice through the speaker phone demanding we open the door. As I did, he stormed into the flat, searching every room looking for my husband. Satisfying himself he had left, he escorted us to their house where Mum and Taylor were waiting anxiously outside. Relief overwhelmed me.

It wasn't until we were all safely inside that I realised how much my body hurt from the beating. There was a great deal of pain in my hip area where my husband had been kneeling on me, the severe bruising was already turning black. My Mother took pictures of my injuries – she said for evidence. My mind was in such turmoil I could barely think of the future but I knew I did not want to see a doctor, I knew most of them from my job working for the ambulance service – I felt too ashamed of our situation for everyone to know. As soon as we were safe inside the house my Father went back to our apartment to confront my husband. Part of me wanted him to get a taste of his own medicine. I knew only too well my Father was physically strong enough to deal with him and angry enough, so I was surprised when Dad came back pale and in shock. Apparently my husband had tried to run him over in the car, so compelled was he by his addiction. Fortunately, Dad jumped aside in time and when my husband drove into a nearby fence, pulled him out of the car by his ear warning him to stay away. If only he had. Whatever we had experienced so far was nothing compared to what we would have to endure for the next two years!

Chapter 5
FROZEN
IN FEAR...

My Mother prepared a bedroom for me, Taylor and Grace and we settled in as best we could in cramped conditions. That first night none of us had much sleep. We were all clearly traumatised by what had happened, and were kept awake by the sound of our car screeching up and down the streets outside. Our apartment was only two minutes away and we all recognised the distinctive sound of the car immediately. The girls were both upset that their father had beaten me, not knowing what to make of his behaviour but seriously intimidated, thinking he might try to break in to reach us. My mother insisted I saw their doctor in order to have an official report of the injuries I had sustained. She was very kind and so I didn't feel embarrassed telling her all that had happened. I had further swellings on my shoulder and nose and looked a bruised mess for some time.

As soon as I was well enough, I returned to work but travelling back and forth became a nightmare as I feared for my safety. In attempts to speak to me my husband visited the store where I worked, invariably under the influence of drink. He would suddenly appear from nowhere, causing me acute anxiety and distress. I wasn't sure how much of his harassment I could endure. Fortunately my boss was very sympathetic and always asked him to leave before he caused serious problems. The feeling I was being watched everywhere I went grew so strong, I imagined I could hear his breathing over my shoulder. Each evening when I got off the bus, my father would be waiting there to walk me the few minutes home but even that didn't discourage my husband lingering or hiding near the bus stop, making attempts to reach me, speak to me. I was terrified and had no wish to speak to him, and certainly did not want to be confronted by him when I was alone.

As time passed, he became more stealthy in his attempts to speak to me or simply watch me. One night, my Mother went to the kitchen to get a drink and saw his face looking at her through the window. She screamed and ran into the lounge, obviously very startled, as my Father ran outside to try to catch him. I was amazed how my Mother still insisted things were only half as bad as they seemed; I couldn't imagine them being worse. Then my husband began using the telephone in his assault. It would sometimes ring constantly in the day or night. Stopping only while he would redial or possibly fall asleep drunk, then the sound would start again, jarring every nerve in my body.

I continued to work full-time, aware that I needed to earn as much money as I could if I was to have any chance of surviving alone with my daughters. I would see them for breakfast each morning, leaving my Mother to take them to school and Kindergarten, while I travelled the route to work each day, always in fear of being apprehended by my husband. By the time I arrived back home in the evenings, Taylor and Grace would already be in bed. It was painful to live that way, I missed them so much but I kept telling myself it was only for a short time and soon we would be able to move to an apartment of our own and live a normal life. To begin with, both girls seemed calmer at my parents' house and so I was happy to make sacrifices. I kept reminding myself there would be time enough for me to be the best mum I could be.

One day, as I made my way to work, I suddenly sensed someone walking very close behind me. I looked round instinctively putting my hand out to defend myself. I saw my husband and my heart leapt. He didn't appear to be drunk nor was he chewing gum or smelling overly of after-shave; it was usually apparent in his eyes first, this time it was difficult to tell. His job with the ambulance service gave him knowledge of many medications and I later found out he was taking drugs illegally to conceal the effects of his drinking which was by then a serious threat to his job. He asked if we could talk, suggesting coffee. I had time before I started work and the city was a crowded place so I agreed. I remember thinking that if I did not show the incredible fear I was feeling, it may reduce the control he felt he had over me. He told me he missed me and the girls and was sure they must be missing their Father too. I did not tell him they were too frightened of him to be missing him and were happier than they had been for a long time without him. He asked me to come back home, promising he would seek help for his drinking problem.

"Being in close proximity to him again made me feel uneasy, breathing seemed difficult and the hair on the back of my neck stood up."

Being in close proximity to him again made me feel uneasy, breathing seemed difficult and the hair on the back of my neck stood up. All I could think about, sitting there with my coffee, was how I could escape without him lashing out at me physically or verbally. Something didn't add up in the recesses of my frightened mind: the phone calls, far from lessening or stopping were still continuing. If this was a man who was in control of his actions and wanted to make things better between us, why would he continue to behave so irrationally? I made the excuse that I had to leave or I would be late for work and I rushed off, feeling physically sick, terrified he might follow me again. Arriving at work I slammed the security door shut and leaned against it, my heart thumping inside my chest.

As the day progressed, I became calmer and my shoulders relaxed. In that safe environment I wondered if I was exaggerating the seriousness of my situation. But the beating and violence was very real and the extent of my husband's drinking was serious. There is nothing quite like your own instincts and gut feelings to tell you whether something is right or not and it didn't feel right. Later that day, circumstances would prove my instincts reliable. After an eight hour shift, I was about to board the bus home when my husband appeared again standing close to me, very drunk and by the look on his face, extremely angry. I later learned that instead of going back home he had waited all that time for me to finish work, spying on me in the store. I felt sick.

He aggressively demanded I talk to him, expecting me to get off the bus but I didn't. He boarded directly behind me, standing in the doorway, trying to force my hand by making a scene. When the bus driver asked him to either get on or off, he just remained there, staring, trying to intimidate me with a look that demanded my obedience to disembark, or else. Trembling, I stood my ground, not acknowledging him until the driver once again asked him to pay or leave. I looked away, my heart was racing, I prayed he would leave. Finally, he got off and disappeared into the crowd. When we arrived at a shopping mall near my parents' home, I jumped off the bus and rushed into a phone booth. I called them and told them where I was, what had happened and explained I was too scared to either walk or get the next bus to my stop. I waited, pretending to shop until my Father arrived and took me home. From then on the menacing conduct increased. Every time I went out, my husband would invariably turn up. I discovered later he had stopped working altogether by then and was free to follow me continually.

Arriving late at his own place of work, my Father put his job in jeopardy in order to take me to work each morning and I would wait until he had finished work in the evenings to collect me before heading home under his protection. But even my Dad's stalwart presence could not shield me from each new act of harassment conjured up by my husband. He phoned me at work incessantly throughout the day. All the staff had a personal number announced over a loudspeaker if they received a call. One morning, my number was announced fifty times in thirty minutes. I was a physical wreck. Fortunately, without exception, my colleagues were understanding and supportive and along with my boss did everything they could to ease the tension of the phone calls: changing numbers around and even barring calls. Various people took it in turns to give me lifts home in the evenings.

"My husband induced only fear in me now, not love and respect."

I contacted a mutual family friend in the hope he may have some influence with my husband: to talk to him about his drinking, persuade him to return to work before he lost his job and even talk some sense into him about his absurd stalking. My husband insisted he would only return to work when I moved back into the family home, or gave him a definite date to do so. My dilemma was huge. On the one hand was my desire to have a good family life with love and stability but on the other hand was the experience of my husband's unreasonable conduct almost right back to the beginning of our marriage. Whatever he said could not undo or condone what he had actually done. He continued with his drinking addiction, not making any attempt to seek real help and for the most part refusing to acknowledge he had a problem. I had seen an unwelcome side of my husband's character in the violence and stalking, now one side of the scales hugely outweighed the other. My husband induced only fear in me now, not love and respect. I declined to go back home. Having learned from the professionals at the clinic that I was not able to give him the help he so desperately needed in order to get well, I knew it was the right decision.

His boss and friend finally managed to persuade him to stop

drinking day and night. It had only been three weeks since I left but if he continued like that for much longer he risked killing himself. Rumours had spread like wild-fire that we had separated and other friends tried to help him see what his behaviour was doing to us. I think people were shocked to learn about the degree of his alcohol abuse and our subsequent marital problems. He had cleverly hidden it from everyone else as well as me and I shunned confiding in anyone, too ashamed that people would know the truth. Several of my former colleagues blamed me for the break-up, some even accused me of having an affair. Sadly it was considered normal to have extra-martial affairs where I came from and they presumed my behaviour followed the accepted pattern. It didn't. Even though I had grown up in a dysfunctional family, without love, I had an inherent sense of loyalty and commitment. I realised that it was not ideal for my daughters to live apart from their Father but I truly believed their equilibrium would be better maintained away from his continual presence, although he never failed to use them to try and browbeat me and make me feel I was a failure as a Mother. Throughout the see-saw emotions and changing moods, the drunken outbursts and the stage-managed sober moments I kept focusing on the fact that my husband's condition was actually an illness that I was not able nor qualified to cure. Until he sought professional help, our marriage could not survive.

The phone calls and personal harassment continued relentlessly as the weeks went by. Somehow, the three of us managed to survive in a perpetual state of tension, waiting for the next big onslaught yet cocooned in a close family unit. Day or night it appeared he had endless strategies to wear us down. The sound of his car screeching past my parents house would always make us look at each other fearfully. We could never go out alone for fear of being confronted, even to the shops. Against my Father's advice I answered the phone in desperation one day knowing that it was my husband, hoping that by doing so I could persuade him to stop his manic behaviour. It was immediately obvious my husband had been drinking heavily, his speech was slurred and he rambled. He had called to say goodbye – he wouldn't be around anymore – and hung up the phone. I presumed he was moving back to his parent's house, but then realisation dawned – he was threatening to kill himself. I told my parents but they simply laughed it off, intimating I would be better off without him. I couldn't relax and called a friend who lived near our old apartment, but she too didn't think there was any real threat of my husband committing suicide.

Unconvinced, I arranged to meet my friend and walk the short distance to the flat. I still had my key and so let myself in the front door. The pervading smell of alcohol was overpowering. Inside it was eerily silent. I found my husband lying on the bottom bunk of our daughters' bed. I called his name but he made no move or reply. I shook him lightly; still no movement. I could not tell if he was breathing or not as I shook him slightly harder, still calling out his name. Suddenly, he opened his eyes, staring at me from a drunken stupor asking why I was there. I realised then that it had only been a threat after all – a trick to gain my attention and sympathy. I was trying to communicate with someone who didn't understand their actions were ruining four lives. I left him there lying on the bed and walked back to my parents' house. My Father vehemently opposed any attempt at reconciliation, perhaps because he recognised from his own past the Jekyll and Hyde characteristics my husband displayed. I think both he and my Mother knew what my husband's obsessive behaviour would lead to, having lived it themselves for so long. I deeply regret they never talked about their own problems or sought help themselves, it may have made a huge difference in my life and that of my children.

Until I had enough money to be financially independent and stable, we remained with my parents. To their credit, they made us as comfortable as possible and whenever we could gain access to my flat without my husband being there we would move more of our belongings out. The children needed their clothes and toys and that was all we took along with some bedding. I did not for one minute think there would be huge reprisals for such a simple act. One day however, my husband called to say he was ready to sign the divorce papers and those to terminate the tenancy on the flat. Dad warned me not to go to see him as he suspected a trap, but as my husband had sounded calm and approachable on the phone, I ignored his advice and went. If a divorce was inevitable I desperately wanted it to be as amicable as possible for life to assume a degree of peacefulness.

"When my husband answered the door and let me in I knew it was a big mistake to be there."

When my husband answered the door and let me in I knew it was a big mistake to be there. The tell-tale smell of drink was all around him and he did not look happy. Ignoring the screaming alarms in my head, I handed him the papers I'd had prepared but he just laughed in my face saying he wouldn't sign a thing after what I and my parents had done to him. I tried to remain calm, at least to outward appearances anyway. I had learned that body language counted for a lot and if you look relaxed, preferably unafraid, it may increase your chance of survival. I collected some documents: birth certificates for myself and the girls, but my husband dramatically punched them out of my hands. Remaining calm I tried to distract him by talking as I walked towards the door. By this time he was shouting at me, calling me a slut, insisting I pay for what I had done: taking things from the flat when he wasn't there and taking his daughters away from him. All the time he followed me closely as I attempted to make my exit. I slowly reached for the door handle, aware of the threatening look in his eyes. I got the door open and began walking to safety as he kept on shouting, accusing me of ruining his life. Suddenly, he pushed the door against me, trapping my body half in, half out. I couldn't move under the weight of his body and that of the door. Feeling panic rising I managed to squeeze my body out into the hall, all except my right leg: it remained painfully trapped in the door. I kept pulling desperately until I was finally free, though severely bruised, and fell to the floor.

"All I could see were the huge whites of his eyes as they bulged almost out of his sockets: he looked every inch a madman."

Hurriedly I got up and began running towards the entrance to the building but my husband overtook me, roughly pushing me aside. He stood there blocking my exit as I pleaded with him to let me go and stop this madness, but he only repeated that he would make me pay! Then I remembered another exit via the cellar, down six steps and along a hallway past the laundry room. Trying to stay calm but feeling like a vulnerable animal threatened by a wild predator, I turned towards the cellar. I reached the steps before he jumped me from behind, pushing me against the wall, holding me with one arm and pushing his other arm up against my throat, taking my breath away. I tried to scream but he pushed even harder with his arm. All I could see were the huge whites of his eyes as they bulged almost out of his sockets: he looked every inch a madman. The drink he had consumed diminished his strength somewhat and I was able to raise my leg and kick him as hard as I could. His shocked reaction caused him to loosen his grip and I ran as fast as I could – out of the exit door, not stopping until I reached my parents' house. The sounds of his threats echoed in my ears. I only understood later it was his pride that kept him from running after me. He did not want his reputation as a loving family man to be damaged in the community and still believed he could keep up the pretence that all was well with us.

Later he agreed to the rehabilitation regime only if I returned home first. When I made it clear it was not going to happen in that order, he finally admitted he needed help and relented. I learnt that he checked himself into the clinic for the fourteen day detoxification programme. After that he would be back at home for a few weeks before being eligible to embark on the eight week residential course. To be clean is a long process. There is no cure as such for alcoholism, but treatment therapy and ongoing meetings to help the person remain alcohol free. A lot depends on the individual admitting they have a problem with drink, their genuine wish to get clean and the willpower to see it through. I was not convinced that my husband understood any of these criteria. Whenever I spoke to the girls about their Father I tried to be honest and open without scaring them with too many details, but even considering their limited experience they seemed to have an understanding beyond their years. They knew their Father's conduct was wrong and it frightened them, often to the point they would wet themselves whenever he appeared. Although I tried to ensure I did not speak about their Father negatively all the time, if I'm honest it was very hard, trying to hold it all together, pretending I wasn't terrified when I so obviously was. For the fourteen days he was initially in the clinic our lives took on a rare time of peace. Without worrying every minute what he was planning to do next and not fearing the phone ringing day and night – it was a time of surreal calm, though sadly short-lived. Living with a stalker in our lives had become our daily nightmare.

Chapter 6
JADED HEARTS...

Fourteen days later my husband called, asking me to meet him in the village playground with the girls. He had something to tell me. It was with mixed feelings I walked my two little babies down the road to see their Father. Part of me was still dreaming that maybe our lives would still turn out alright. Maybe, just maybe, my husband would get well and we could be together again as a proper, loving family. The other part of me was paralyzed with fear, remembering all too well his ability to play-act and his frightening, bullying ways. He was waiting for us when we arrived. Of one thing I was sure – the fourteen day detoxification could not have been easy for him; I had been in that clinic, I had heard the cries coming from the wards. But his words brought me back to earth with a bang, making me realise his attempt at getting help was superficial. He explained now he had done the fourteen day detoxification programme just to please me and it was time I went back to the apartment for good. My heart froze. I remembered the doctors at the clinic saying a person could only be helped if they admitted first that they had a problem and secondly were prepared to go through the whole programme. I tried to explain that it wasn't about doing something for me but for himself. Without waiting for me to finish my sentence, he turned around, walked straight to the nearby store and came out with four cans of lager in his hand. I walked back to my parents' house with Taylor and Grace, my short-lived hope in shreds.

"…after two months of hell, we were back to where we started."

So after two months of hell, we were back to where we started. Except that now, I had saved enough money to actually pay for the rental of a small apartment for myself and the girls. At last I had somewhere else to go that wasn't under the terrifying control of my husband or the obsessive control of my parents and their misshapen lives. It seemed that someone was looking out for me as at exactly the time I began to question whether I could do this on my own, I met and made friends with a lovely lady who had recently moved in to the area with her family. We quickly became the best of friends and so did our children. Selma was an angel in disguise. She helped and supported me enormously in practical ways, but more importantly than that, she listened to what I had to say, seemed interested in my opinion and didn't judge me or try and coerce me into doing what she thought was best for me. She gave me some confidence in myself after having been beaten down and overruled by my parents and husband for so long.

Although neither Mum or Dad thought we should move at that time, we did, and my husband's simultaneous decision to go back and live with his Mother for a while gave the three of us hope for much needed peace from the relentless harassing. The relief we felt moving into that flat was indescribable. Just to be able to go outside without looking over my shoulder was good for the soul. Although small with only one bedroom, we felt safe there and able to please ourselves. My parents placed high value on material possessions and they continually reminded me I was foolish to leave so many things behind for my husband to keep but I didn't care; for me the important thing was I had my precious children with me and a degree of sanity back in my life – nothing else mattered. I believed things could only get better.

"From the very day we moved in my husband stepped up his torturous campaign. Every night there were endless telephone calls and the familiar sound of his car screeching past our bedroom window."

I could not have been more wrong! From the very day we moved in my husband stepped up his torturous campaign. Every night there were endless telephone calls and the familiar sound of his car screeching past our bedroom window. Living back at his Mother's house had made no difference as he seemed to spend all his time hanging around our apartment. I assumed he was making calls in a drunken state from a distance when in fact people in the village were asking my Mother why her son-in-law was always standing in the local phone box, yards away from where we lived. Most nights I hardly got any sleep, as the phone would start to ring when I went to bed and wouldn't stop for hours; obviously he could see from his vantage point in the call box when I would put the lights out and so begin his crusade of terror. Initially I would answer the phone innocently, but always there was no voice at the other end, just the sinister sound of someone breathing. It was terrifying. He never answered me when I asked if it was him. I suppose I could have switched off the phone at night but in a weird way I felt safer when it was ringing because I knew he was in the phone box and not trying to break into the flat to reach us. Sometimes I would grab the receiver from the hook and shout into it for him to leave us alone. Often I would turn the volume right down and place pillows over it, trying to prevent it from waking the girls and drown out the continual reminder that my husband was acting like a mad man.

A neighbour on the ground floor alarmed me even more when he mentioned seeing my husband using his terrace and chairs to climb up to our balcony. I lay awake long into the night, listening to the slightest noise outside, remembering threats my husband had made that if he couldn't have me, no on else would either. Deep down I think he suspected I had a lover and was using his problem with alcohol as an excuse to leave him. His irrational thinking would continually place all blame on anything other than the truth. The whole situation had a negative effect on everyday life and even though I constantly tried to encourage my children and tell them I loved them, they were witnessing so much bad stuff around them the principles I tried to teach them somehow didn't seem to match up to my lifestyle. Grace was younger and easier to handle as she didn't argue with me over issues. She was often anxious because of the pressure we were under from her Father, but it was Taylor who clashed with me over many things. I agreed to them seeing their Father at weekends, but obviously he used those times to give his twisted interpretation of the facts and was quick to lay the blame at my door. Taylor would come back after seeing him and question me as to why I had left their Daddy and believed the version that I was seeing another man.

Social Services were involved at this point as a matter of routine procedure as I had filed for sole custody of the girls. I did not want my husband having custody of them as he was so unstable due to the alcohol. Taylor was offered counselling and although it proved difficult to begin with, looking back, I'm glad I agreed to it as I believe it helped her to voice deeply hidden questions and fears. It helped me decide to only allow my husband access to them for a couple of hours at a time, in our apartment. I learned from the sessions that whilst they were in his custody he was frequently too drunk to look after them. When Social Services found out about his excessive drinking from Taylor it strengthened my custody claim for the future.

"The phone calls continued each night and would often begin again at five in the morning, still with nothing but breathing heard on the other end."

Rather bizarrely, during his visits, I noticed certain items of clothing went missing and once I actually caught my husband taking my clothes. I told him to leave the apartment and I no longer trusted him to come back there to visit the girls. I also found CDs were inexplicably scratched and other items broken without explanation, but it was mainly my underwear that disappeared. The phone calls continued each night and would often begin again at five in the morning, still with nothing but breathing on the other end. As I said, it was the silences that bothered me the most by that stage, as I imagined if he wasn't on a phone somewhere dialing my number, he might be attempting to climb up onto our balcony. The tension of lying in bed night after night listening for every little sound had a profound effect on my emotions and general health. Calling the police in on matters like this was pointless. They could and would do nothing unless I or the girls were injured. Domestic situations occur all the time and domestic violence was not considered an emergency in East Germany at that time which is a sad testament to human relationships. Many cases of domestic abuse, whether perpetrated by male or female never even get reported.

In an effort to ease the strain we were all under, a friend recommended I apply to go to a subsidised health resort on the Baltic Sea. We were away for four blissful weeks. It was so beneficial for us removed from the sphere of my husband's influence. We were accommodated in our own apartment with a phone and television, a few minutes walk from the beach, with lovely views across the sands. As it was a resort expressly for single mums and their children going through difficult divorces or in similar circumstances to us, we found it easy to get on together and the girls quickly made friends. Their Father would call every night to speak to them, but would always get angry when they seemed distracted by their new surroundings, not showing enough concern for him. He liked being in control and the distance between us did not sit well with him.

As for me, I could not remember feeling that relaxed in my

entire life. It was as if for the first time, I was not living in fear of arguments and violence and my spirit felt refreshed and free. I neither had my parents around me, forcing me to live my life according to their rules, nor my husband, intimidating me and making me a nervous wreck. The girls had a few hours schooling each day with the other children whilst the mums were free to enjoy some of the various activities available. A different book had been placed by each bedside, mine was entitled 'Stop Worrying and Start Living'. At first I wasn't interested and left it there, but one morning I had the book with me as I waited in the lobby and I began to read it. Immediately I was hooked: here was a self-help book that seemed to know all about the issues I was living through, it seemed as if the book had been written just for me. Every spare minute I had my nose buried in that amazing work when I wasn't making friends with the other mums there.

We talked a lot about our difficulties and speaking to others in the same boat helped me enormously. I think we all found it a great release to talk and encourage one another and know we were not alone in our messed up lives. The time passed all too quickly before I was able to finish the book so I made notes of the main points in my diary and promised myself I would buy it when I returned home. During one conversation, one lady asked me what I would do if I ever had another man in my life who wanted to have children. My knee jerk answer was to say I would never consider getting involved with another man. I felt so let down and damaged by my first marriage, I didn't envisage ever trusting anyone again. Also, I had two adorable little girls to look after, I could not imagine having another human being to be responsible for again.

When we returned home, the kids looked fantastic, like normal children, no shadows under their eyes or fear reflecting in them. I, too, looked the best I had for a long while. But more than that, I felt inwardly renewed, as if I had grown up: no longer the little girl my parents would have me believe I was. I believed in myself: that I was strong enough to make it on my own and generally very positive about life. During our absence my mother had decorated our apartment according to her tastes and ideas, without even consulting me! It was a well-meaning gesture, but all it showed me was her continuing control over my life: abortion, marriage, divorce, everything! I felt stifled by it. I made a pact with myself never to impose my opinions on my children in that way; I always wanted to be there for them, the best mother I could be, but I desperately wanted them to live their own lives and learn from their own mistakes.

"I felt very alone and the loneliness I experienced felt intense and final."

My husband came over to see the girls as soon as we were back and quickly dispelled any hope I harboured that things might be better after our time away. Life slid back to being as hard as it ever was with him drinking, ringing up at all times, pleading and crying to the girls, watching us as we went to school and Kindergarten and the phone calls with the menacing silence on the other end. He was convinced I had another man in my life and wanted to catch me with him. His resumed stalking once again made me very nervous, believing I saw him in every crowd, sensing him walking behind me and hearing his breathing in every silence. I felt very alone and the loneliness I experienced felt intense and final. I filled my time writing things down in my diary and reading the notes I had made at the retreat. It encouraged me to order a copy of the book I had partly read and after it arrived I took it everywhere with me, reading it on the bus, in my lunch hour, whenever I could. I was especially interested in the instructions on how to start your day by asking for your daily bread for that day only – not for any tomorrows. It made sense to me – not to try and work out what was going to happen too far in the future but to live each day as it arrived and put all one's energies into it.

Although the book made references to prayer and looking to

God for help, it by no means forced any religious practices or ideas on me but for the first time in my life I did have the feeling that I was doing something right. I'd had no education about religion but often thought back to the time as a child when I heard about God from old Mrs Becher. I continued to read the book avidly whenever I had a spare moment. My husband's stalking intensified but I began to pray on a daily basis for help to cope. The book instructed me in practical ways to help me stop worrying. It was difficult at first as it was in complete contrast to how I had lived my life up to now, but I found great strength and comfort from those prayers and that book became very dog-eared by constant use as each day brought new challenges. I had lost a great deal of weight, dropping three dress sizes and with broken sleep patterns most nights and working all day I was pretty exhausted.

"But what made my mouth suddenly go dry and my heart beat faster was seeing a hole cut in every blouse in the place where my heart would be."

My husband made it clear he believed the new clothes I bought myself were because I had a new man in my life, preventing me from returning to live with him. The idea that his alcoholism might be at the bottom of it did not even occur to him. I was always spooked whenever I had to use the communal laundry where he had chased me once as he had access to it from the building of our old apartment. One day I went to collect my laundry and noted with suspicion that the door of the washing machine was open and some of our clothes were hanging out. As I began to empty the clothes into the laundry basket, I realised with horror that they were all damaged: torn, zips ripped out, holes in the legs of trousers. But what made my mouth suddenly go dry and my heart beat faster was seeing a hole cut in every blouse in the place where my heart would be. I felt faint, my knees were shaking and sharp tendrils of pain went down my back and arms.

I took my basket of useless clothes back to the flat, an acute nausea rising up in my body. It dawned on me my husband was literally watching everything I did; he had no intention of giving up his irrational behaviour and was overtly letting me know that he could reach me wherever I was, whatever I was doing. I felt exposed and vulnerable. In desperation I went to see my Mother, not because it was easy to confide in her but I needed someone to talk to. I should have known she was the last person I should share my emotions with. In her characteristically detached way, she told me to buy myself some new clothes, there was nothing to worry about, things were only half as bad as they seemed. I wanted to scream. This was not some silly game, I truly believed my life was being threatened. My husband was mentally unstable and I was scared for myself and my children. For many weeks afterwards the once inspirational book lay untouched. I felt I had nowhere left to go and no strength to take me there anyway.

Taylor and Grace were seeing less and less of their Father, although he would try to visit whenever it pleased him. He was still drunk most of the time and when he turned up like that at the apartment, I would send him away, scared to let him anywhere near the girls. My actions were always punished by a night of endless phone calls when I refused him access. On the odd occasion the phone remained quiet at night, I would lay awake anyway listening to every sound, convinced he was trying to get into the flat, or just standing outside on our balcony. I'm not sure now how I managed to function at all during the day as I was always exhausted through lack of sleep and my weight loss continued no matter how much I managed to force myself to eat. Although I had stopped smoking when I was twenty one, I started again after leaving my husband. I was only too aware that this was not good for my health, but was also too stressed to be able to resist the need for a crutch to get me through the nerve-racking days and nights.

With my childhood experiences of a drunken, violent Father and then my husband, I suppose it was a natural progression for me to feel an aversion to men: I was frightened of them. Even though deep down I craved love and friendship from a relationship in my life, if a male figure so much as smiled at me I would have a panic attack. I learned the divorce I had applied for would now take two years to achieve as my husband refused to give his permission and so I was forced to wait. My solicitor at the time confirmed it was all I could do, I could not even report my husband to the police for stalking me because unless he physically harmed me, they could do nothing to help. Fortunately my boss and work colleagues continued to be understanding, which was just as well as my husband continued his vicious attacks and harassment in many more clever and spiteful ways. Despite moving my job location, he managed to obtain the number of the new store where I worked and pretended to call from head office, giving a false name. I lifted the receiver to be greeted by the eerie silence on the other end. Still my Mother insisted things were only half as bad as they seemed. Looking back I do not blame her for being so insensitive, I realise now her reaction then was the reaction she always used in life when she could not control situations. She just chose to ignore them or try and make them insignificant. Domineered by my Father, while always trying to please him she in turn became domineering, forcing her opinions and choices on me.

As the first Christmas approached without my husband, I prepared to make it a joyful time for my daughters. I had always loved the build up to Christmas itself: the streets being lit up, the decorations and lights in the shopping malls and most of all the snow. On Christmas Eve, Taylor felt a little unwell as we went out early with my parents to get the last remaining items we needed. Waiting to pay for my purchases, Taylor asked if she could wait outside as she felt sick. Soon after, I heard her cry out for me and rushing out of the store I discovered she had fainted. I instantly felt guilty for taking her shopping when she was obviously ill. Dad ran to get the car and drove us the short distance to the doctor's who examined Taylor and told me what I already knew in my heart:

that she was emotionally exhausted and at only seven years of age was finding the whole process of our separation and her father's harassment too much to deal with. I wasn't sure how much more any of us could take. At my friend Selma's suggestion I bought an answer machine for the phone. Some days there would be as many as fifty recorded calls on it, relaying only the sinister breathing and still managing to freeze me to the spot. But at least it meant I did not have to actually answer the phone anymore if I chose not to.

I was grateful once more for Selma's friendship; she is a genuinely caring person and very practical. We spent lots of our spare time together and our children always got on. Sometimes, she would come over in the night if things got too awful for me or the girls and her presence was always calming. Unlike my Mother, she never played down events but helped me face our nightmare reality in a strong and positive way. I later discovered that my husband would come to see the girls while I was at work and they played outside. He would always interrogate Taylor as to my comings and goings, never bothering to talk to Grace, considering her too young to supply him with the information he needed. With hindsight I can see why Taylor was so traumatised by everything.

After a year of separation the stalking and harassment, far from lessening, continued just as strong as ever. Further pieces of clothing went missing and sometimes they would be damaged or stolen. I replaced the items without making any mention of the thefts, not wanting to give him the satisfaction that his insane conduct was causing me such heartache, but also because I could never handle confrontation. However, when one particular dress went missing, I replaced it with an exact copy, wearing it when he came to see the girls one day. I was rewarded with his look of shock, which made me feel that at least he wasn't always in control. I began to read my special book again and made an enormous effort to do as it suggested and live each day as it came, not worrying about tomorrow or things I could not change.

Taylor's counselling continued to help her deal with her fears and insecurities. I learned much through her counsellor about my own parents' relationship and how my Mother's need to control my life stemmed from her codependency on my Father's imbalance. She suggested I begin looking for a new husband amongst the rich set. I told her I was not interested in getting involved with another man at this point. I may have regretted not having a loving relationship, but for once I would not be forced to do anything until I was ready. My Mother disliked Selma and constantly criticised her because she was her own woman and would not be controlled by my Mother.

Chapter 7
HOLDING OUT
FOR A HERO...

One afternoon, I excused myself early from a traditional family get-together to go to Selma's house. While we sat outside watching the children play, her four English tenants arrived, inviting Selma and her husband to a barbecue at their place. One of them had a balloon and some chocolate and stood chatting to my daughters, clowning around with them. He invited me to join them for the barbecue and Selma suggested it would be good for me to go. As a fairly young and untravelled girl from a small village in East Germany, I felt nervous and self-conscious spending time with people from another country, who would probably be knowledgeable and worldly-wise. But they insisted and so I went along, totally unaware that my estranged husband was watching me at that very moment, observing everything that was going on.

"...for a brief time I was able to forget my harrowing situation and simply enjoy myself, oblivious to the fact that this night would change my life forever."

Gradually, the relaxed atmosphere at the barbecue and the

enjoyable company helped me to unwind and for a brief time I was able to forget my harrowing situation and simply enjoy myself, oblivious to the fact that this night would change my life forever. The balloon and chocolate guy paid me quite a lot of attention. He was polite and complimentary as well as being tall and handsome and I found it hard to understand why he would want to spend time with me. To my utter surprise at the end of the evening he asked me out on a date. Feeling extremely apprehensive, I asked Selma and her husband Andres if I should go. In the forefront of my mind was the fact that I was still legally married, and if my husband found out I had been on a date with someone it might unleash a whole new episode of harassment. But there was something about this man called Olivier that attracted me. Apart from the obvious physical perspective, he exuded confidence and self assurance. Plus he was funny and entertaining and I was drawn to this different guy from far away. I agreed to meet him the following Saturday.

All week, despite the continuing phone calls from my husband and interrupted sleep, I felt an excitement deep inside. I did not fully appreciate it at the time but I was exhilarated at the prospect of spending time with someone who thought I was interesting and who was not drunk or abusive. My husband continually insisted no one else would ever take an interest in me because I had children in tow. Selma visited me during the week to inform me that Olivier had expressed a genuine desire to get to know me. I learned from her that he was single now but had children from previous relationships whom he loved and spent time with. As a single parent for over a year, I could appreciate his situation and was encouraged to hear he was a good Father. He also worked very hard, often for long hours, as a building constructor. Each new thing I heard about him helped put my mind at ease and settle my phobia of men but each time Selma came round after work for a coffee that week I tried to persuade her and her husband to come on the date with us. She declined, insisting I would be fine.

Unexpectedly, the evening before the date, Selma asked me to look after her children at their house as they were entertaining a large crowd of business associates. Olivier was there too in a professional capacity. He kept smiling at me from his standpoint in the gazebo while I entertained the children. He even managed to join me and spend time with the children, playing with them and giving them English chocolate. I couldn't help thinking that he must be a really good person to relate so well to children, even those he did not know. I watched him carefully, thinking how mature he seemed with good father-like characteristics. Although he had taken a drink he certainly did not seem to be an alcoholic as far as I could tell. I knew enough of the signs. Before leaving, he asked me again to keep our date. Feeling assured by our second meeting I agreed to see him the next evening.

I arranged for my parents to babysit the girls, declining to tell them I was going on a date with a British man, merely implying I would be spending the evening with friends. Firstly I could not tell them I was dating someone they had not met; I knew my Mother would do all in her power to stop me seeing anyone; secondly he was a foreigner and in their eyes that would definitely not be acceptable. My Father had strong racist views along with many people in our village who were critical of foreigners, accusing them of taking our jobs and money, and he would often express opinions in his inimitable bullying fashion. I could not take the risk.

Olivier offered to loan me his car to drive home that night, as Selma's house was outside our village on a new industrial estate. I thanked him but refused, as it was a left-hand drive. Just as I walked away he gave me a quick kiss on the cheek not unnoticed by Taylor, who asked if he liked me and then proceeded to tell Grace and Selma's oldest daughter who was to stay overnight with us and they all laughed together as we walked back home. We passed the open fields and entered the village and I felt a shiver down my spine as I thought about my husband, wondering where he was and if he was watching us at that moment. But somehow, the insignificant small kiss on my cheek seemed to empower me with a strength I did not know I had: strangely I felt protected for the first time in my life which was just as well because the phone rang as soon as we entered the apartment. I picked up the receiver – it was my husband, demanding to know where we had been and accusing me of keeping the girls out far too late beyond their bedtime. He said he had been calling since seven that evening to say goodnight to the girls and would definitely inform Social Services of my behaviour and that I was an unfit Mother. Refusing to engage in his game, I passed the phone to the girls who also showed no interest in speaking to their Dad and they quickly went off to bed. I stood on the balcony long afterwards, listening to music and thinking about these latest developments, unable to get Olivier out of my mind. I sensed my husband was out there somewhere, watching me, stalking me, but for once I actually didn't care.

The next morning I woke refreshed, having miraculously slept the whole night through. I phoned Selma to discover their last guests had not left until four that morning and so her husband did not want to go out again that night. I was in a dilemma, suddenly not feeling confident enough to go out with a man alone; Selma offered to accompany us alone if I wished, but that too did not seem appropriate. The afternoon wore on and evening approached and I felt quite weak and insecure as I got ready and took Taylor and Grace to my parents' house. Finally, after much deliberation and more phone calls to Selma, I drove the car she loaned me to our arranged meeting place. My heart was racing and my hands were sweating as I changed gears. I was torn between totally opposite emotions: fear of the unknown, particularly of exposing myself to the company of a man, yet also an excitement emanating, I guess, from being made to feel like I was a special person. A person worthy of attention; a person in my own right, not my parents' daughter, nor my children's' mother and definitely not the beaten and exhausted wife of my unstable husband.

When I arrived, Olivier gave me a big welcoming smile and once again my confidence soared. It felt like I was in control of a situation for the first time in my life and I suddenly knew I could handle the evening. Whatever his intentions were towards me at that point, I established in my mind that I was going on a date for one evening only. There were no expectations or agendas in my thinking and I hoped there weren't in his. I just wanted to be in his friendly company and relax. We decided to go to nearby nightclub and I chose to drive us there in my friend's car. It gave me something to concentrate on rather than feeling self-conscious and I could talk without having to look at his face all the time. He spoke German ably which was just as well as I had no knowledge of English, but his accent made it hard for me to understand everything he said.

With foreboding, I learned he knew my Father as he worked on the same building site. It would only be a matter of time before the word spread and people in the village, including my parents and husband would know I had been on a date with Olivier, the foreigner. I imagined what the village would make of it too: I would be labelled cheap – a prostitute – and the fact he was not German would make my offence far worse. My own feelings towards foreigners did not mirror that of the village; I had no such aversion to people either from other countries or with a different colour skin, everyone was equal as far as I was concerned. I could only wait and see what people's reaction would be, but I knew in a small community with an inward-looking mentality, it would not be agreeable.

The time at the club passed quickly and we spent most of it talking to each other. Olivier confessed to me that he had two failed relationships in his past and that he had children in both instances. He openly told me he felt blackmailed into marrying one partner because she had threatened to abort his baby and he felt let down by both women. If I'm honest, it was disturbing to discover he had two unsuccessful relationships, but I was pleased he told me about them immediately. I was slightly concerned though when he briefly mentioned he had left his second partner because she became too fat! He soon directed the focus of our conversation onto me and asked all about my life, listening to details in a sympathetic way. I was challenged on two fronts: first because I was not used to anyone paying any interest in my opinions and also because in answering his searching questions, I discovered I knew very little about the real Malaika. So much of what I had done in my life was as a result of being forced to do so or to please others; seldom had my actions been as a result of my wishes or ideas.

"I was captivated by his intelligence and charm and that this worldly man should find a simple village girl attractive…"

Looking back, it's apparent our conversation was far more intense than normal for a first date. I'm not sure why that was – perhaps we were both at a point in our lives where we needed friendship and needed to establish that the other person was sincere in their intentions. Anyway, Olivier soon explained he was not looking for a one night stand, he was interested in a lasting relationship. As a married woman, I was in a tenuous situation: I was not legally or morally available to get involved with another person and I certainly did not want to spend my time dating lots of men, but in my heart I knew that my marriage was over. My husband's alcoholism and behaviour had destroyed whatever closeness we once had. I realised, not for the first time, my marriage had been one of convenience. Not in the usual way a person marries for wealth or nationality status, but I had so desperately desired to escape my family home life and the clutches of my controlling Mother and abusive Father that I had taken the first life line offered to me in order to get away. I had wanted to change my status from that of prisoner to free individual, able to make their own choices and decisions. Rightly or wrongly, I welcomed Olivier's interest in me and hearing he was looking for something long-term was music to my ears. I was captivated by his intelligence and charm and that this worldly man should find a simple village girl attractive and interesting touched my deepest needs.

Declining an invite back to his room I spontaneously asked him to have a nightcap at my apartment instead. I had not drunk any alcohol at the club as I was driving and I knew I had a bottle of wine chilling in the fridge. I thought it might be a lovely end to an enjoyable evening. With hindsight we all have perfect vision. Looking back, perhaps it was folly to involve myself with him so quickly and completely but all my good intentions evaporated as Olivier offered to take me and the girls out to the zoo the next day. He ended up staying the night, calling me his princess and treating me like one, I recall drifting off to sleep believing I had arrived in my own personal fairy tale, convinced it would have the happy ending I had always dreamed of.

The next morning burst in on my dreams as the phone rang. It was Selma wanting to know if I was well and if the date had been good. I bashfully explained Olivier was still there and she swiftly hung up, making me promise to phone later and talk. The girls called too, they had had enough of their grandfather's short temper and were ready to come back home. I panicked, wondering what I would tell them about the visitor in our flat, although they had met him briefly. When they arrived home, Grace, who was only three, just looked up at this tall stranger and smiled. Taylor's reaction was quite different: she had fear in her eyes and it concerned me. Not long after my husband rang the door bell. I had forgotten he arranged to take the girls out for the day. They ran to speak to him through the bathroom window blurting out that Mummy had a new boyfriend in the flat. My breath caught in my throat. I remember thinking boyfriend was a bit presumptuous, but it was too late, the news was out the window and would soon be winging its way around the village. For the first time in ages I hadn't woken up thinking about my husband, however now his presence outside the flat filled my mind and heart with dread. I had no idea what this news would provoke him to do. He left with the girls, and Olivier and I made plans to spend the day together.

Soon the sound of the door bell interrupted our plans. It was Taylor and Grace. I pressed the intercom to let them in and they both came upstairs crying. Taylor explained that Daddy had changed his mind about their day together saying he was busy and had already driven off like a maniac, swearing loudly and calling me as many insulting names he could think of. Thankfully, Olivier took control of the situation and reassured us, saying we would all go to the zoo together. I drove him back to his room to change and waited at Selma's house, updating her on the situation. We ended up taking her oldest daughter with us – an excited little party on an outing to the zoo. I was impressed that Olivier was not phased by taking three children with him and mentally chalked up another point in his favour. We went in his car, listening to music from the seventies. It was not my usual choice, but then he was seven years older than me, so I didn't deduct a point for his musical preferences, just put it down to age!

At the zoo, Taylor was unusually clingy towards me, seldom leaving my side. She did not interact with Olivier at all and still looked fearful. I couldn't understand her reaction, after all, I had spent time talking to Olivier and spent intimate time with him as well, I saw no reason to distrust him or treat him with suspicion so I was a little frustrated that she should behave like that. Hoping that it was just a matter of time before she felt comfortable with him, I played the intermediary while Olivier, to his credit, remained patient and understanding; but Taylor was not won over throughout the day. Personally impressed by my man from far away, I invited him over for the evening and ensured the girls were in bed early. Taylor was normally allowed to stay up later with me, partly because she was the oldest but also from a sense of guilt on my part, I suppose.

Although my husband and I had been separated for over a year, I had chosen not to tell the children the real reason their Father and I no longer lived together. I didn't think it was appropriate for them to try and understand their Dad was an alcoholic and despite his appalling behaviour, I was reluctant to bad-mouth him to his daughters; Taylor's therapist and Selma had both encouraged this course of action. However, I hadn't realised just how manipulative my husband had been in coercing Taylor into believing I was the cause of the family breaking up. Taylor questioned me as I put her to bed. She wanted to know if the reason she was going to bed early was the stranger hanging around her Mother. Would this stranger prevent her parents getting back together? I tried to assure her that whatever happened, nothing would prevent her seeing both her parents when she wanted, but as I tucked her up in bed, I couldn't help being concerned. In an ideal world, my children would have a loving Father with them all the time but there was nothing ideal about our situation.

The following morning I dropped Grace at Kindergarten and Taylor walked me to my bus stop before catching her school bus. I felt happy for the first time in ages. I couldn't help wondering when rather than if my parents discovered I had been out with a foreigner and what their reaction would be, but at twenty nine years of age I felt I should be able to make decisions in my life without them. My work colleagues agreed and were pleased to see me in good spirits for a change. My Mother usually took care of the girls until I returned from work and walked them home to our flat. I rushed home that evening little prepared for the welcoming committee. Taylor and Grace had shared the news of my recent association with Olivier and my Mother was already waiting outside our flat with them when I arrived. Her tone was of one in authority, questioning a child who has broken a favourite vase. She accused me of being selfish and unconcerned about the consequences of my actions. What was I thinking of going out on a date with a foreigner? Had I considered what would happen when he inevitably left town? Was I expecting to go with him? Would I take the girls away from their home to a strange land, far away? She ended her tirade by telling me I had better finish whatever it was I had started before my Father found out and got mad.

My head was spinning – so many questions in thirty seconds! I tried to explain I had no idea where this very new friendship was going. One date and a weekend did not mean I was going to marry this man. I simply wanted to get to know him and take it from there. But my Mother wasn't placated or finished. She demanded I end the relationship immediately. I felt so upset and beaten I had to walk away. I could not believe my Mother was still trying to control my life. I didn't feel as though I had done anything wrong, yet here I was being made to believe I could never please my parents. Not content to bombard me with her demands, I later learned she had also phoned Selma, trying to coerce her into making me do as she wished. I was thankful she was not easily bullied and told my Mother in no uncertain terms to let me live my own life. She slammed the phone down to end the conversation that was not going her way. I am grateful Selma remained a true friend throughout, giving me space to make my own decisions, yet being there with advice and support.

Of course my parents' disapproval had the opposite effect. Instead of pressuring me into ending my friendship with Olivier, it fueled a yearning to know him more, and we spent all our spare time together. He frequently stayed at our flat and smitten as I was, I saw nothing wrong with that, assuming that Taylor and Grace were comfortable with this sudden change in our circumstances, just because I was. I failed to appreciate that for two little girls who had already witnessed such unsociable behaviour from their Dad and were being forced by their grandparents into believing I was a bad mother, these events were confusing and frightening. Often they would creep into my bed at night convinced their Father was standing outside the apartment, or listen terrified as the familiar sound of his car screeched around the block. They both feared their Father so much and in their eyes another male was taking their Mother's attention from them. Olivier tried to deal with them as kindly as they would allow. He cooked English food for us and regularly settled them once they were in bed. He read them stories and left early in the mornings so he was not around when the girls woke up, and I could have some special time with them alone. His patience paid off as the girls slowly became calmer when he was around and more fearful when he wasn't.

My husband's visits increased to the point of madness. Whenever Olivier arrived to see me he would also turn up on some pretext or another. He repeatedly attempted to draw Olivier into his world of bizarre behaviour and did everything he could to antagonise him. Although I had told Olivier much of how things had been since we had separated and he was sympathetic, I don't believe he was aware that he too was caught up in a series of events that would spiral further out of control. The hate and bitterness my husband harboured against me was now also directed at Olivier. Coupled with that harassment, news of our friendship spread through the village and reached my Father. His reaction was to let me know through my Mother that he was displeased. I presumed this would mean he would stop speaking to me. My husband took advantage of the distance in my relationship with my parents to ingratiate himself with them and they became allies in the war against the foreigner. It explained the uncanny knack he had of turning up as soon as Olivier arrived, usually threatening to take our daughters away and fight for sole custody.

I endured relentless phone calls from my Mother, giving me ultimatums to finish with this foreigner then telling me Olivier was seeing other women. His character assassination was perpetuated by my husband, who took every opportunity to tell me he'd been seen with prostitutes and regularly visited a brothel and shockingly, even Taylor was given stories of a similar nature to pass on to me. The pressure on us all was enormous; for me it was more of what I had become used to for so long now, but I doubted Olivier would manage to survive this storm and still be interested in me. Many people in the village passed on their negative opinions about my association with a foreigner to Selma. She always countered their comments with her view that we should be left alone to live our lives.

What I did not appreciate at the time was the full effect all this madness on Taylor. She was eight, old enough to understand some of the charged emotions flying around, and caught hopelessly in the middle, torn by her love for us all. Taylor always looked up to her grandparents but was now confused by all the things they said about me and concerned by their open display of hatred against Olivier – and me. She was still having some counselling through the Social Services but her young mind could not cope being pulled in every direction by those she loved. In her pain and uncertainty, she began writing little notes – cries for help. When I saw some of those notes they broke my heart. I always tried to reassure her but with so many conflicting opinions thrust upon her it is easy looking back to see the damage to her innocent mind and its more serious consequences. Grace did not understand much of what was happening and it was easier to comfort her and put her mind at rest. My Father had publicly declared I was no longer his daughter after discovering I was seeing a foreigner. My Mother took every opportunity to remind me how ungrateful I was after all they had done for me, even resorting to bribery, saying I could have their car when they purchased a new one if I gave up my association with Olivier. Needless to say I did not take them up on their offer and even went to the extreme of returning the pieces of furniture they had given us when we first moved into the apartment.

Things came to a head one day as we sat around the meal table. Taylor asked me if it was true what people in the village were saying about me. When I questioned what she meant, she asked if it was true that I was a slut. My fork dropped out of my hand and my mouth fell open in disbelief. She said her friends had teased her that day whilst playing outside, repeating the poisonous comments initiated by adults. Taylor looked frightened as she spoke, scared that I might smack her for saying such a thing. I gently tried to explain that my friendship with Olivier did not make me a slut, and that people in the village were either jealous or spiteful to say such things, wanting only to hurt me and end our relationship. Their comments obviously caused Taylor a great deal of hurt and I was angry that a young child should be used like a pawn in such a cruel game. She was becoming more confused and continued writing her plaintive little notes, drawn towards those who made the loudest noise. Whenever I attempted to speak to my Mother about it she was characteristically in denial or domineering towards me, but Selma agreed with me that it was a cry for help, and so I persevered. I begged my Mother to stop being so unreasonable, to try and see things from my perspective and most importantly to stop causing Taylor such heartache. Although the Berlin wall had come down, in East Germany the walls of mistrust and prejudice continued in people's hearts. They still gathered on street corners gossiping about things they did not condone or understand, spreading malicious rumours to young and old alike.

Eventually my parents discovered Taylor's notes and took them and her to the therapist without my knowledge. As soon as I found out, I confronted the therapist and she apologised, realising she had violated the trust I placed in her. The confrontation with my parents was not nearly so agreeable. My Mother insisted I was solely responsible for Taylor's instability and they only did what they believed necessary to protect their granddaughter from my unacceptable lifestyle. She told me all the people in the village had predicted I would turn out to be bad, even forecasting I would be the cause of my parents' premature deaths. I couldn't believe what I was hearing. All I had ever wanted was a normal family of my own and to be the best mum I could be. The disadvantage was I had no role model in my life and could never remember my Mum talking to me as a daughter she loved. I had no precious childhood memories of her reading stories to me or cuddling me at night time when I was scared. But when I shared these confessions with her, she did not hug me as I longed for her to do, she merely told me to leave and never come back.

While this maelstrom of events played out, Olivier started to put pressure on me in a completely different way by asking me to marry him and talked about buying me a car. I could not cope with his suffocating attention anymore than I could handle the rejection of my parents. It was too much too soon. I took time to think everything through and then told him one evening that I could not consider marrying him, even if I was free to do so and I did not want him to buy me anything, least of all a car. I gave him the option to end our relationship and was shocked to see him burst out laughing, almost to the point of rolling on the floor. I was hurt at his reaction, only to be told that he was testing me and I had passed his test. He explained how many women had chased him in the past, mostly for his money and he wanted to know if I was different to them. By then I was angry, I didn't want to know about his silly test and I certainly didn't want his money! To reassure me, he explained he had acted like that because we hardly knew each other. Although I allowed myself to be placated, the whole episode left a doubt in my heart I chose at that time to ignore.

"I was hopelessly attracted to this tall, handsome foreigner from far away who was the first person to make me feel important."

We carried on seeing each other as often as possible, more especially when the girls were already in bed so as not to interfere with my time with them. More and more I opened up to him, telling him all about my life, my hopes, my fears. But whenever I tried to direct the conversation around to him, he would invariably change the subject or make a joke to distract my questions. He always needed confirmation of my feelings for him but I did not realise it was because he was insecure. I was hopelessly attracted to this tall, handsome foreigner from far away who was the first person to make me feel important. Even though he was thirty six and I was twenty nine, I was not so concerned as he seemed to be about the difference in age. Though my new-found confidence was shaken somewhat when he announced plans to go back to England to see his son. He was in some kind of trouble with the police and the mother was refusing to help, Olivier needed to be there. From the little I knew, I sensed his son's behaviour might be a way of seeking the love and attention he had not been given. In an effort to support Olivier, I told him I would be happy to have his son live with us for a while.

As he left for England I felt vulnerable, foolishly worrying about the rumours I had heard that he intended to leave me and go back to his wife and children. My Mother was quick to jump on the bandwagon and went to great pains to give me one of his business cards, instructing me to call the number on it and listen to the female voice of his wife on the other end. When I called Olivier for an explanation, he assured me he had no time in his life for such games; either I trusted him or I didn't. Since he had left most of his clothes at my apartment I took it to mean he would indeed be back. Even the girls missed him during his absence, especially at nights when they were anxious in the flat without him. When he returned, he seemed genuinely pleased to see us all and I took that as a sign that, like me, he wanted us to be together, no matter what odds were stacked against us.

Chapter 8
KEEP THE FAITH...

"I don't think either of us was prepared for the continued onslaught of disapproval and opposition to our relationship."

I don't think either of us was prepared for the continued onslaught of disapproval and opposition to our relationship. The more time Olivier and I spent together, the more the campaign against us accelerated to another level. At his workplace, Olivier was accused of causing trouble for my Father and although he tried to laugh it off, saying it was only a small matter, it culminated in his transfer to another building site in Berlin, a two hour drive away. The way the men conducted themselves at work always shocked Olivier: he saw them drinking to excess, even during their lunch hours and instead of going home straight after work to be with their wives and families, they would continue their binge drinking often to the point of passing out. He could not understand the mentality that governed most of the local men. For me it was nothing unusual, I was used to seeing drunken men around me, my childhood was marred by alcohol abuse and my life since had been ruled by its prominent place in our community. I was angry and felt responsible for the trouble Olivier was having, but he passed it off and we made plans for him to visit me on weekends after the transfer.

"Looking back, I know I was blinded by my feelings for Olivier, I was infatuated with him and knew with our deepening friendship, I was falling in love with him and everything he represented. For the first time in my life I felt alive, loved, cherished."

A surprise invitation to visit the house he owned in France filled me with an unfamiliar excitement. In my rationale it proved he cared about me enough to include me in his life. This naive girl from a small village in Germany was about to travel to the far away, to fulfil her dreams, to escape the shackles holding her captive to a life she did not want. I could hardly contain my delight as I told the girls about our proposed trip. Grace was fine – as long as I was with her she was happy. Taylor's reaction pulled me up short, as she flatly refused to go. She made the excuse that she couldn't leave her grandparents, they were suddenly her responsibility and priority. Looking back, I know I was blinded by my feelings for Olivier, I was infatuated with him and knew with our deepening friendship, I was falling in love with him and everything he represented. For the first time in my life I felt alive, loved, cherished. Perhaps my blinkered vision kept me from seeing any flaws in the relationship or his plans, which became more adventurous each week. He spoke of us possibly living in France together, full time, fulfilling his own personal ambition. I didn't really take the time to talk to Taylor in detail about her fears, I was too caught up in my own fairy tale, presuming she would come round to agreeing eventually.

My husband had stopped taking the girls out, but continued to turn up at the apartment to discover all he could about my plans. Often he would come when I was at work and Taylor was back from school. He continually bombarded her with questions, always trying to stir up trouble, feeding her scraps of gossip, trusting it would either influence her opinion of me or be passed on to cause more stress. I cannot begin to understand his thought processes, but he went to great lengths to emulate Olivier, dying his hair and getting a tattoo. His fabricated stories to Taylor included Olivier sleeping with many other women while he was seeing me and that he had a wife back in England. The onslaught had been relentless since I had begun my friendship with Olivier and as well as losing a lot of weight during my husband's stalking episode, I was exhausted by the endless attacks. I desperately wanted to escape – to go far away and hopefully lead a quiet, but most importantly, normal and happy family life.

There was an unexplained spate of damage to cars, Olivier's being the main target, but also those of Selma and her husband Andres; it was mainly scratches, but noticeable ones. It was embarrassing and frustrating for me and all the time I was scared Olivier would suddenly leave because he was fed up with it all. Clothes continued to go missing from the laundry room, including the children's. One day I arrived home from work to discover Olivier's watch was missing. He had forgotten to take it that morning and I had placed it on the kitchen table but it had mysteriously disappeared. I searched everywhere before asking Taylor and Grace as they played outside. Taylor denied any knowledge of the watch but I sensed she was not telling me the whole truth. I asked her to be totally truthful with me and assured her no matter what had happened she would not be in trouble. She sat on the table, her head down looking so broken and forlorn. Her Father had been waiting at the flat when she arrived home from school. The girls had strict instructions that he was never allowed in the flat if I was not there, but he asked to use our toilet. Taylor agreed, not seeing the cunning that lay behind the innocent request. While she waited in the stairwell with her friends, my husband obviously used the opportunity to grab the watch, assuming it to be Olivier's and making excuses, left immediately.

My heart ached for my baby – for that is what she was. Taylor was being used by her Father and grandparents to get to me and her great love for me was placing too heavy a burden on her tender shoulders. But there was much more she carried deep inside I would only uncover as time passed.

When Olivier came back that night we decided to go to the police station to report the theft – for that is what it was. We stopped at the house where my estranged husband now lived with his parents and his Mother let us in, making her disapproval of Olivier very obvious. However when she heard why we were there she became very angry with her son, who was drunk and verbally abusive. I had warned Olivier not to react, no matter how provocative my husband was. His Mother searched his room and demanded he empty his pockets and rucksack but the watch was not found. She gave me his car key and I left to search it followed by a tirade of swearing and insults from him. The watch was not there either. My husband was doing his best to trigger a reaction from Olivier, perhaps hoping he would start a fight. As I turned from searching the car, my husband was at my side and all of a sudden put his cigarette out on my face. Olivier immediately pulled him away from me, insisting this was no way to treat a lady. My husband laughed saying I was no lady, but a slut, a prostitute, all the while, inviting Olivier to take a punch at him. I begged him to leave with me immediately and we walked back towards the car, hoping to diffuse a tense situation.

My husband was not finished. He followed us swearing and shouting further abuse, still hoping to get a reaction. Then, without warning, he ran towards Olivier and jumped him from behind. Knowing my husband to be both physically strong and capable of anything, I screamed as I saw him approach from the corner of my eye and Olivier jumped aside telling him to stop. But he did not stop, instead he kept attacking Olivier, kicking and punching him like a rabid dog. Olivier fought back and although he was tall and a good build, it took all of his strength just to defend himself. I watched in disbelief at the insane scene being played out in front of me. My husband gave me a look of satisfaction, between his onslaughts. He was bleeding from his mouth and nose and I wondered where his strength came from as I knew he was seriously drunk, but each time Olivier managed to extract himself from the fray, he was attacked again, until finally we made it to our car and hurriedly drove away to safety. Olivier held my hand in the car to pacify me, assuring me he would never treat me in that way. It seemed an odd thing for him to say as I had not even thought about him in that way. I suddenly realised I still had my husband's car keys in my hand. Convinced I had the only spare one at the flat, we stopped at a lake on the way home to calm down and I threw them as far into the water as I could before heading for my friends' house to collect the girls.

To our complete amazement my husband appeared close behind us as we arrived back at the flat. Getting out we hid behind the other parked cars but he soon found us and continued taunting Olivier trying to goad him into a fight. By now he was making such a noise that Taylor and Grace were watching from the window; they must have seen their Father's face covered in blood and wondered what on earth could be happening. Olivier insisted he stop as the children were watching but my husband was not listening to any reason. His blind rage was fueling him to continue. He shouted to me, asking if this was what I wanted, if this made me happy. All at once, Olivier pushed him to the ground, pinning him down. He forced him to take a deep breath and observe his children crying at the window. My husband stopped struggling and looked, then got up and left but his expression told me he was still furious; he would have carried on if his daughters had not witnessed his madness.

We went inside to calm the girls. Olivier was very gentle with them but they were terrified. They had only seen this last assault and had no idea the provocation had come from their Father. Taylor was really scared and did not want to go back to our flat with Olivier; it certainly didn't help their relationship as she blamed him entirely. Selma and Andres suggested she stay with them for the night and so we went home with a pacified Grace. That night I slept with Grace and Olivier slept on the floor beside us. Not too long after we had gone to bed, we heard a car driving around the apartment at full speed, screeching as it turned the corners. Olivier and I looked out of the bathroom window at the front of the building to see my husband and his friend driving dangerously outside. It was after midnight and dark as the street lights had been extinguished, but we saw their car heading, at full speed, towards where Olivier normally parked his vehicle. It suddenly screeched to a halt inches before hitting another car as they realised it was not Olivier's car. The crazy speed driving continued until the early hours and when it was time to get up for work, Olivier left the flat without saying anything and I couldn't help worrying it might be the day he wouldn't be coming back.

Selma arrived just before school time having left Taylor at her house for the day. She did not understand what had happened the previous evening but was still disturbed by events and Selma felt she would be safer there. I knew nowhere was safe while my husband was on the rampage. Before she left I went to get my washing from the laundry and discovered more clothes were missing and what remained was thrown on the floor. Obviously I had no proof it was my husband doing this, only my gut instinct to go on, as there was no sign of breaking and entering. I knew he hated me enough to damage and steal my clothes but I failed to understand how he could do the same to his daughters' things. To my complete surprise and relief, Olivier came back that night. I told him I would understand if he wanted to finish our relationship but he gave me a big hug and said there was no way he would be leaving. He ensured his car was hidden, parked away from the flat but the scratches increased so he parked it in our friend's garage. I was not even sure it was just my husband doing the damage – perhaps my parents were also involved. I was grateful for Selma's loyalty and help, I don't believe any of us would have survived that time without her and her husband.

The summer holidays came around and the day finally arrived

when we were to leave for France. I was tremendously excited, not just to be finally going to another country, crossing the border, but also because we would be away from the nightmare situation we had endured for so long. When everything was finally packed and we were ready to set off, I called the girls to get in the car. We had not told them our planned departure time just in case my husband appeared but now we needed to get on our way. Taylor suddenly began screaming hysterically refusing to get into the car, insisting she had to remain because of her grandparents. We assured her they would be fine for a week and we'd be back before she knew it but she would not be reasoned with. Reluctantly I called my Mother to come over and talk to Taylor. It was difficult for me to do as neither of my parents had spoken to me since I began seeing Olivier, except to demand I end the friendship.

My Mother arrived promptly, voicing her fears that we planned to leave for good and take the girls out of the country, never to bring them back. Although it was something I longed to do, leave my country and the mess that was my past life, I explained I would never do that without telling them first. Even though Olivier and I had discussed moving permanently to France, now was not a good time to discuss it. Eventually Taylor was reassured that we would come back to Germany and she got in the car. I was baffled as to why she had such a huge mistrust of Olivier, as far as I knew he had done nothing to deserve that opinion. What I did not know then, was, the web of lies and hatred that had been subtly fed to Taylor would cloud her opinion of Olivier and lay dormant in her mind, causing her to fear and mistrust him.

"It was extremely challenging but with Olivier by my side, I felt strengthened, almost invincible."

Our journey was not without its dramas. We were involved in an accident when a driver in France ran through some red lights, driving straight into us. Fortunately we were all unhurt, but Olivier decided to divert to England first to have his car repaired. We caught the ferry to Dover. I was terrified of big ships and the sea, having almost drowned once in the Baltic Sea when I was young. I had to confront my fear as I did not want to make the girls anxious or allow Olivier to think I was weak and useless. It was extremely challenging but with Olivier by my side, I felt strengthened, almost invincible. On the return to France, I even managed to sit outside on the deck, watching the other ferries sail past. We stayed a week in England and for me it was an amazing time. I had never been out of Germany before and I could not believe all that I saw. Driving through France had been an adventure, but England was something else again. I was so enthralled by everything I barely noticed how tense Olivier was, presuming his quietness was due to being reminded of his past. He did not want to talk about it and I respected that and did not pressure him. As soon as we were back in France, his mood lightened and he looked happier than I had seen him before. Although we could not spend the time in France we planned due to the accident, I felt sure we would all be back, and looked forward to happier times.

The girls were pleased to arrive safely back in Germany and see their grandparents, though they seemed to have enjoyed our little holiday. I was less enthusiastic about our return as Olivier had to leave for his job in Berlin that same day. Although I found it hard to deal with I remained positive as he left, concentrating instead on his return. Almost before his car had disappeared from sight my husband appeared like a bad penny with his malicious tales of Olivier's infidelity and the double life he lived. He gloated when he told me Olivier was only using me until he left for good but as he had already kept one promise to me to take me to France. I had no reason to doubt his feelings for me were genuine. I had Selma, Andres and my work colleagues to reassure me and my beautiful daughters to care for as I waited eagerly for his return.

He arrived every Saturday but had to leave again on Sunday. It meant we had precious little time together, but I saw it as only temporary and tried to get on with my life. Invariably my husband would miraculously appear at the flat almost as soon as Oliver arrived. He was like some fierce animal trying to prevent a rival taking his territory. Whenever Olivier was with me I felt stronger but as soon as he left I would feel quite alone and vulnerable. At least the menacing phone calls stopped as I had changed the number again and it was only known by very few close friends. I had not even entrusted it to Taylor in case she accidentally told my Mother when they visited her. My Father and others in the village would cross the street if I approached so I felt they didn't deserve to know my new number or anything about my business. I tried to hold my head high and pretend it didn't bother me but deep inside I felt ostracised, punished like a naughty child, My weight dropped even further as the anxiety took its toll. Each time I went out it felt as if I was being followed, sensing my husband's presence nearby.

Had it not been for Selma's amazing unconditional friendship and wise advice, I'm sure I would have suffered a breakdown. Despite being targeted and having cars damaged, she was a great source of strength. The children and I were still unsettled most nights and often at dawn as well by sounds of my husband's car screeching around outside. It was with horror I discovered he had once shown the girls a rifle he kept in the boot. I began to wonder if he was mad enough to shoot me but more than that I was angry he had irresponsibly shown his daughters. Olivier suggested I think about moving to a place where my husband would not find us, perhaps even to England. He offered to help me but my lack of confidence in myself made it impossible to consider I could survive. So I stayed put, enduring a worse kind of survival. The thought of being in a foreign country alone, without Selma, and my girls without their friends, was scary enough, but I also knew that Olivier was not close to his family either. I had no burning desire to swap one set of family disputes for another. It was kind of him to care enough to want to help, but I declined his offer, after all we had only known each other for a relatively short time, too soon to be planning long term commitments.

My decision to stay in the village had of course sentenced us all to a continuation of abuse from my husband. The fear I and my daughters lived with during that time may seem irrational beyond belief but when you are actually in that situation, you cannot envisage change – there is no way out and absurd as it may seem to an outsider, you continue blindly crashing in to each day ill-prepared and feeling totally isolated. Added to the stalking was my fear that the authorities would actually listen to my husband and I would lose custody of my children as he kept threatening. That was something I knew I could never survive. My entire life had been lived under the shadow of a dictatorship. Authority was everything and the ordinary man and woman on the street had no freedom or rights. Officially the regime was over but the widespread concepts and fear of officialdom remained, deeply scarring every area of our lives.

"...my husband's absurd activities continued to dominate our lives..."

As my husband's absurd activities continued to dominate our lives, I feared for my own sanity and that of Taylor's. Night after night during the week I would lay awake, listening for sounds on our balcony, believing him to be there, waiting for an opportunity to break in. Sometimes I would stand in the flat, motionless, holding my breath with fear believing him to be just outside on the balcony, peering through gaps in the venetian blinds. With knowledge of the gun he possessed, I imagined he planned to use the weapon against me. I never once had the strength to pull the blinds up and look, instead remaining there frozen to the spot like some hunted animal. My work colleagues worried about about my physical and mental condition, convinced I would suffer a complete breakdown if the situation continued in its intensity. I reduced my working hours to be with the girls more but I too worried I was becoming paranoid. They suggested I move to the city, keeping it secret from my husband. Although it sounded a good idea in theory, I wasn't sure the girls would be able to cope with another move, away from their friends and familiar surroundings.

"My biggest hindrance by far in all decisions I had to make was my own lack of self confidence…"

My biggest hindrance by far in all decisions I had to make was my own lack of self confidence; at twenty nine I was unused to making choices of my own, having always been controlled by my parents. My husband's drunken outbursts against my ability as a mother continued unabated; he insisted I was unfit to look after Taylor and Grace and as I was hanging around with a foreigner it proved I was a prostitute and a slut. His accusations threatened my hope of sole custody of our children. My fear of the establishment supplanted even the fear of my stalker. In East Germany during the dictatorship, the authorities and police were very brutal and harsh, speaking down to individuals, demanding you always toe the line, insisting you have no worth or rights. Widespread effects of that regime would be felt for a long time as the system had been ingrained into the very foundations of our society.

A hearing for custody was set at court and Social Services planned to visit both parties before coming to a decision about the girls' future. In a small way I felt relieved, trusting that their findings would dispel any accusations about my inability to be a good Mother, but I dreaded the actual visits. When the woman from the welfare department arrived, she concentrated mainly on questioning Taylor, insisting on speaking with her privately. Racked with doubts and fear, I listened at the door as this stranger spoke with my daughter. After a few questions, asking Taylor how she felt towards her Father, the woman focused the conversation on my relationship with Olivier. I listened for a short time but could not resist opening the door and expressing my disapproval at what I considered unreasonable questions. The woman disagreed, insisting everything about my new relationship with Olivier was very relevant to Taylor's future welfare. It seemed Social Services were more interested in Olivier than their Father who was an alcoholic, subject to outbursts of unstable and dangerously threatening behaviour. They ignored the fact I had left him and filed for a divorce before meeting Olivier. In an uncharacteristic show of strength, I asked her to leave our apartment.

"...I was horrified to learn someone had cut his petrol pipe and interfered with the brakes of his car."

I looked forward to the weekend when I could talk events over with Olivier and was disappointed when he rang to say he couldn't make it back. He sounded a little strange but when I asked if anything was wrong, he explained he was behind schedule with work. Not convinced, I persisted until he told me the car had broken down. When I offered to drive over and fetch him, he said he would try and get the car repaired and get back as planned. I still did not feel comfortable, sensing he wasn't telling me something. Fears jostled in my head fuelled by rumours that he had found a new girlfriend within weeks of working in Berlin. Or perhaps he had been threatened by my husband? Eventually, he did arrive back and I was horrified to learn someone had cut his petrol pipe and interfered with the brakes of his car. He only become aware of it on the motorway to Berlin the previous week. From then on he would hide his car whenever he visited, but the incident had obviously shaken him as he showed signs of nervousness and always seemed unsettled at the apartment, eager to leave the village. At my insistence we went to the police station the following weekend but, as before, they showed little interest in something that had not yet caused actual harm to anyone, dismissing it once again as merely a domestic incident. I was shocked. Would a murder have to be committed for us to be taken seriously? I was sure the girls' lives were not in danger, but seriously feared for my life and now Olivier's, too.

Enraged himself, Olivier seemed to be taking the matter one step further and was even considering harming my husband. I was disturbed when he asked me if I could stand up to police questioning if anything happened to my husband or whether he should move us out of the country altogether. In desperation I asked Selma and Andres to talk some sense into Olivier, to make him see this was not the way to handle things. Eventually he calmed down, but having lived with this strained situation myself for so long, I could sympathise with how he felt. Each time we said goodbye, I feared he would not return, unable to endure the pressure. Once his eyes were full of tears as we parted and I was convinced I would not see him again, so I was relieved when he called to say he needed to take his son away for a week but would see me in a fortnight. I had agreed to let Taylor go away with my parents for a holiday and Selma and her husband also left for the summer, leaving me alone with Grace.

Not wanting to be at the mercy of my stalker, I called another friend who lived an hour away and made arrangements to visit her for the weekend. I was concerned when she called a few days later to cancel our plans. She had received a strange call from a male asking about my proposed visit. I was sure it had been my husband and it was confirmed when my friend said the name he had given: it was the surname of my brother-in-law! My friend apologised, explaining she did not wish to become involved in any trouble but now that my husband had her number, he could find out where she lived. I was intrigued as to how my husband had got her number, until I suddenly remembered I had given it to my Mother in case of an emergency with Taylor. All those who opposed my actions were, it seemed, prepared to form strange alliances in their pursuit of controlling my life. When questioned, my Mother vehemently denied any involvement. Still perturbed I asked Taylor if she knew anything.

Once more she sat at the kitchen table, hiding her adorable little face in her folded arms. At first, she was reluctant to tell me anything, but eventually I convinced her I was not angry, that I loved her no matter what and she opened up. With tears filling her eyes, it all came spilling out of her tormented little soul. Apparently, my husband had convinced her something bad would happen to me and she would lose me so she had been persuaded to give my friends' number to her Father. I hugged her tight and explained her Dad was using her to gain information about us so that he could control our lives. I prayed she understood without causing damage to her impressionable young mind. After everyone left, I locked Grace and I into the flat and shut all the blinds. We did not leave for the entire weekend and I again prayed there would come a time when these horrible events would fade into the past and we would no longer be ruled by fear.

Throughout the next week I left early each morning to drop Grace off at Kindergarten before hurrying to catch the bus to work. At the end of the day I would rush home to collect her before returning to the flat to lock us in for the night. All the time I was haunted by an overpowering sense that my husband was never far away, stalking me, watching my every move. One afternoon I discovered to my horror that our washing had been vandalised again. What remained of our clothes were all over the floor and the machine itself had been trashed. Regrettably, not one of the other residents reported having seen or heard anything suspicious. They considered it more important to gossip about my liaison with a foreigner than to observe the crazy behaviour of my husband. I was an outcast in my own village. I grabbed Grace's hand and ran upstairs sobbing at this latest violation. I dialed the emergency number, determined someone should listen to my predicament. I must have sounded distressed as the operator dispatched two police officers who arrived within minutes. I explained briefly what had happened in the past months and showed them the damage to our clothes. For what was perhaps the first time in this nightmare, I was taken seriously and a forensic unit called to the scene.

"I would force myself to remain awake, listening for sounds of an intruder, praying with all my heart for the God I wasn't sure was there to rescue me from this hell on earth."

They took fingerprints of every conceivable surface inside the flat and on the balcony and asked me to make a statement at the police station of all the previous incidents as soon as was convenient. The case went before the Prosecutor, who analysed all the evidence, including fingerprints. For elimination purposes they took fingerprints from Grace and me too. I was advised by the police to keep all the doors and windows locked and call them if I noticed anything else suspicious. I wasn't sure how much more I could take. This was not living, merely existing in fear. I did not know what each new day would bring; I barely slept at night, I was so terrified. I would force myself to remain awake, listening for sounds of an intruder, praying with all my heart for the God I wasn't sure was there to rescue me from this hell on earth.

Taylor called me twice every day during the holiday with her grandparents. I tried to reassure her anxious little mind that everything was fine with us and we looked forward to her return home, but when our laundry was vandalised again, I asked to speak to my Mother on the phone. I told her everything that had happened since they left but she was very short with me, insisting things were only half as bad as they seemed and there was nothing I could do. She cut the conversation short with the excuse that she must stop talking to me because my Father would be angry if he found out. It was devastating not to receive one word of sympathy or comfort after everything we had endured. My heart cried out for the mother I'd never had but reality made me accept I would have to do everything for myself in this world.

Talking again to Taylor I learned that my husband also experienced problems: his car had been broken into and the radio stolen. A nagging thought in my head warned me it may have something to do with Olivier and despite Selma's reassurances that he wouldn't retaliate in that way, my instincts suggested differently. Try as I might I couldn't shift the thought that Olivier may have paid someone to break into my husband's car, knowing he had the perfect alibi as he was in another country with his son, but jumbled thoughts remained just as I was absorbed in providing the police with details of all the previous incidents. Although they had obtained my husband's fingerprints, the process of analysis and elimination could take up to a year. I realised I could not expect a rapid outcome but welcomed a result nonetheless.

Chapter 9
PIECES OF
A DREAM…

Although Olivier continued to drive all the way from Berlin every Saturday just to be with us for one night, the lies about his dual life continued unabated. The girl he was allegedly involved with in Berlin was supposedly pregnant with his child. It was inconceivable that he should drive all that way to be with me for such a short time if he was involved with someone else, nevertheless my mind was tortured by my insecurities, fueling seeds of doubt. He tried to keep things light and made humourous comments about the gossip but we were from two different worlds and our language differences made it hard for me to understand and accept his flippant approach. A sense of humour could cost you your freedom in the former East Germany and we remained reluctant to express ourselves freely in that way. Making jokes about your personal situation or mistakes simply was not part of our psyche. Olivier did not like being in the village anymore; each time we ventured out together, curtains would move, people avoided eye contact with us and it was generally difficult to ever feel relaxed.

My heart missed a beat when he called me at the end of

September to tell me his contract would be finished and he would leave his job in Berlin at the end of October. Again my lack of self-esteem made me believe this was his way of finishing our relationship; I was convinced he would be leaving his job and me for good. So it was with much surprise I heard him ask me to go with him to his sister's fortieth birthday celebration in England in November. I was speechless, realising he still wanted to be with me and I was touched by his invitation to be introduced to his family as his girlfriend. My own family had never welcomed him, instead they had ostracised him and me and gone out of their way to destroy our friendship.

"Finally, the penny dropped: this man actually liked me!"

Finally, the penny dropped: this man actually liked me! I was ecstatic as he talked about us going to see his house in France again as soon as his contract was over. We talked for ages on the phone that evening. Eventually, I asked him where he was and he said on the way to his accommodation in Berlin. I could hear him getting out of the car and walking along the street. He asked me to keep him company on the phone while he walked, explaining it was some distance. As we chatted and he spoke loving words to me I could hear him mounting stairs. Still asking me to stay on the line, I could hear the sound of keys and him saying he was finally home. Then all of a sudden my front door opened and I saw him through the glass door standing in the hall! I could not stop myself shrieking with delight as I ran and hugged him. All my anxieties vanished as I basked in the joy that he had driven for hours just to be with me for one night before returning to Berlin the next morning.

The following night, Olivier drove back from Berlin once more and stayed for four whole weeks; we enjoyed the most special time. He would pick me up from work or surprise me by turning up there with flowers often preparing a meal for us all to eat in the evening. It was so good. He planned to stay until the end of

October then we would go together to France to see his house there before going on to England for his sister's birthday. As the invitation did not include the girls, I spoke with Taylor and Grace about our plans, giving them the choice to stay with their grandparents or with Selma and Andres. My Mother intervened, insisting they were not to be allowed to stay with my friend as she did not approve of her. As we drove away, it was hard leaving the girls who were sad not to be coming with us, but I knew they would be well cared for and, frankly, I was desperate to have some time for myself – especially away from the narrow-minded village life. In my mind I was running through the possibilities of a new life in France, a new start for us all. I hadn't mentioned my plans to anyone except Selma, terrified in case my parents or husband persuaded the authorities I was unfit to care for my children.

"I felt a sense of peace I could not recall having before."

Despite desperately missing Taylor and Grace we spent a magical week together at his French house. It required an enormous amount of work to convert what looked to me like a very old barn into a suitable home but with Olivier's expertise I believed it would happen. We did simple things together, like planting trees and buying building materials for the renovations. I felt a sense of peace I could not recall having before. Although we discussed the possibility of me and the girls moving to France with him, I did feel somewhat overwhelmed by the prospect, after all we had known each other for less than six months. I called the girls twice every day and was alarmed when Taylor told me there had been a fire at our apartment, but everything was alright. I learned from my friend her story was a fabrication, possibly to get my full attention. What I did not know at that time was Taylor's Father had convinced her I would go away with this foreigner and never return.

Towards the end of the week Olivier suggested we forego attending his sister's birthday and stay in France for a few more days, but I insisted we keep our commitment though I was nervous of meeting his family, and so we journeyed once more to England. The ferry trip was very different to my first encounter. This time I felt confident of Olivier's affection for me and away from the oppression of my husband's presence, I was at last optimistic that life was changing for the better. During our talks, Olivier asked me if I would ever consider having another child but I replied two was perfectly enough for me. He explained that people in England often had larger families, something we did not consider routine in East Germany.

As we left the port, our car broke down and its repair delayed us in arriving at his sister's party until well into the celebrations. Speaking only a few phrases of English made it difficult for me to communicate and as I was tired by then, I sat down while Olivier chatted to his brother and sister. When he eventually joined me, I realised I was sitting next to his parents. Although he had introduced me to his seven brothers and sisters, I knew he was not on good terms with his parents and the atmosphere was a little tense. I felt very much the outsider, a foreigner unable to understand what these people were saying and it frightened me. But I didn't need to understand every word spoken to realise his family had their differences. I made a mental note that I did not want to get involved in their family politics any more than I did my own, but it made me sympathetic towards Olivier, as I thought I understood.

I was surprised when the closing bell rang in the pub. It was different in Germany, where bars stayed open late and celebrations would go on well into the early hours. We stayed overnight at a sister's house but I could not sleep: everything was strange and I did not feel comfortable. I got up early to shower and make myself a coffee, finding it difficult to negotiate my way around. Olivier eventually found me crying and tried to reassure me all would be well. We were due to part soon – I to go back to Germany and he to go to France but he said it wouldn't be long before we were together again and he wanted me to be his wife. Thinking I had misunderstood, I asked him to repeat it and was overjoyed when he did. I remember feeling so safe and happy. This man actually loved me and wanted to share his future with me. It was arranged I would fly back to Germany and when he dropped me off at the airport he entrusted me all his credit cards for his German bank accounts containing his life savings. I was overwhelmed at this gesture of trust and was certain he intended to come back for me. It was my first flight and it was with a mixture of fear and excitement that I boarded the plane. The little village girl from East Germany was extending her wings and it felt good but my feelings of joy were overshadowed by the prospect of returning home to the unknown. I was desperate to see my girls, but unsure about the reception I would get from my parents and my husband.

Immediately I arrived at our flat I called Taylor and Grace and waited excitedly on the balcony for them to arrive. Olivier called to check I was safely home, repeating this separation was necessary but only for a short time. He was going back to France to begin renovations on the house and he would be back with us for Christmas. At the mention of Christmas, I suddenly realised our future was not going to be as straightforward as we hoped. It was not just our wishes to be considered but those of the children, their Father and grandparents. At least I had the assurance that Olivier actually wanted us to be together and it helped me resume my normal routine and patiently wait for changes to come. The days passed slowly but I busied myself with the girls and work. The nights were difficult as we were still unable to sleep properly having had our sleep patterns interrupted for so long.

During phone conversations with Olivier he again brought up the subject of children, expressing a desire to have a child together. I was unsure. I had thought I would be able to say an emphatic no, I had Taylor and Grace and they were everything I could ever wish for, but when you meet someone and become involved with them emotionally it is not easy to be so certain. Part of me still dreamed of that fairy tale life with a loving husband and family. I would have to wait and see. But at least I was no longer plagued by doubts about Olivier's feelings towards me. Despite fresh rumours of his infidelity and slights against his character at the building site where he worked, I was convinced his intentions were honourable and I concentrated my energies on passing the two months before I would see him again rather than give any time to the petty gossip that raged around me. Although I did not actually see him doing so, I was sure my husband still continued to follow me everywhere and the phone calls to the flat continued constantly, sometimes producing as many as fifty messages a day.

"During that break I fought and won the battle for sole custody of my daughters."

The lead up to Christmas meant the store where I worked was very busy but my boss gave me time off until the new year. During that break I fought and won the battle for sole custody of my daughters. Selma accompanied me to the hearing, and although the social worker I had asked to leave my flat gave evidence of my new relationship, the judge, miraculously, did not consider it relevant to the case. When Olivier finally arrived I couldn't stop hugging him, believing all my troubles were about to become history. Originally, we planned to leave for France after Christmas day but Olivier did not feel safe in the village anymore and was concerned about further vicious attacks on his car and so he asked me to leave with him earlier. I sat down with the children to tell them of our revised plans. Grace was acquiescent but Taylor was adamant she could not leave her grandparents before seeing them for Christmas Day. Believing I had another battle on my hands, I was surprised when she agreed to go as long as we could see the place where Princess Diana had been killed in a car crash that summer. Olivier agreed to this odd request and after packing all the presents in the boot of the car, we finally set off.

The journey was long, all the way from East to West Germany, then to Brussels before reaching the north of France. It was midnight by the time we reached the outskirts of Paris where an accident caused a serious traffic jam. Becoming impatient, Olivier started swearing at the delay and suggested we take the next exit and forget the detour to Paris. I agreed as it seemed the most sensible thing to do, but Taylor was deeply hurt by what she saw as the latest in a list of broken promises by Olivier. She hardly spoke for the remainder of the journey except to say that grandma and grandpa had been right all along, Olivier only cared for me and wasn't interested in the children.

When we arrived I was impressed by the amount of work Olivier had already completed, the house had been transformed though it was not quite habitable. For the time being we were to live in the caravan standing in the grounds. It felt extremely odd to be spending Christmas in a caravan, but I got a sense of how wonderful the house would be when it was finished, and so a small sacrifice seemed worthwhile. The world I came from put such value on material things and it was certainly a shock for the girls who had been brought up to expect the best money could buy. Even in our small village I knew that people who lived in caravans were considered as 'trailer trash' but I considered the joy of being with a man who loved me far outweighed any discomfort I might endure in a caravan for a couple of weeks.

The following morning we drove to town to buy essentials and stock up on food. Olivier quickly got on with work around the house while the girls made friends with the neighbouring farmer's children, and I adjusted to a very different life than the one I knew. The girls called their grandparents on Christmas Eve, which is the big day of celebration in Germany but our enjoyment was marred somewhat by my Father declaring I had made another big mistake with our lives. As the girls happily played with their presents, a telephone call from England shattered our peace with news that Olivier's Father had been rushed to hospital suffering from a heart attack. While we were still in shock, a further call twenty minutes later informed us he had died. Finally letting go, Olivier broke down in tears as I held him in my arms, devastated because I knew he had not made peace with his Dad before his death. He spent the rest of the day working on the house, not speaking to me about anything. I knew him to be a rather private person when it came to his feelings and so did not force him to communicate, but found it disturbing that he sought sex that night as a release. It was not the first time he had acted that way after difficult news and though reluctant to discourage him, it did make me feel uneasy.

By morning his mood had lightened and he offered to take us to town to buy some more presents for the girls. He intended to go to England the next day to be with his family and offer financial help to his Mother. We hoped the funeral would be before the year's end but it was scheduled for the first week of January – the day I had to be back in Germany for work and the girls for school. Circumstances always seemed against us spending more than a couple of days together at any one time. Olivier arranged for us to fly back to Germany from England, and although I was grateful for the time together on the ferry and journey over there, I felt helpless to comfort him as he was very withdrawn. I offered to fly back to be with him after the funeral, once I had arranged care for Taylor and Grace. He seemed consoled by that. I was sad to leave him, even though it would only be for a short time. Selma met us at the airport and it was good to have someone I could talk to. I was not comfortable back in Germany as I was anxious about what my husband might do and an expected barrage of criticism from my parents.

The prospect of New Year's Eve alone with the girls sent me out to buy fireworks to cheer us all up. After lighting them on our balcony the patio door remained open as we went from the front to the back of the apartment watching everyone else's display through the windows. Taylor was thirsty and went to the kitchen to get a drink but returned within seconds demanding I close all the windows, venetian blinds and patio door. Her face was pale and she was shaking and obviously terrified by something. I asked her what she had seen to frighten her in the flat, but she just shook her head and stood rooted to the spot. Shivers of fear spread through my body as I ran to close the patio doors. As well as seeing the fear in my daughter's eyes I instinctively sensed my husband's presence: I knew he was close by, but calling the police would be futile: we were not physically harmed and there was little they would do for harassment. What I did not know at the time that only became apparent much later was my husband was actually inside the flat when Taylor saw him! Trying to protect me, she had not wanted to let me in on her terrible secret.

"Olivier called the next morning to wish us a Happy New Year, insisting that it was going to be the best one ever. His reassuring words made me feel safe and happy."

Olivier called the next morning to wish us a Happy New Year, insisting that it was going to be the best one ever. His reassuring words made me feel safe and happy. My boss agreed to give me yet more time off work, and Selma agreed to look after the girls while I went to England to support Olivier after his Father's funeral. My Mother was not happy with this arrangement; she still blamed Selma for my involvement with Olivier, and managed to persuade the girls to stay with her and their grandfather whilst I was away. I was somewhat concerned about Olivier's obsession with exactly what I should wear during my visit to England; he always expressed strong views about disliking fat people and although that could not be applied to me as I had lost so much weight, it was as if he would be showing me off. Dismissing my doubts, I reluctantly said goodbye to Taylor and Grace and headed once more for England.

Direct from the funeral, Olivier met me at the airport. His dark suit making him look every bit the handsome prince of my fairy tale. We chatted and he kept asking me how much I loved him and had missed him. Even driving the car he continually kept touching my hand. I felt as if nothing could take away my happiness. We drove to his sister's house only to collect his bag before leaving to catch the ferry immediately for France. He explained he wanted to go to get away from everything for a few days. The renovations on the house had progressed even further since my last visit. Olivier had enlisted the help of another English man living in the area who was there when we arrived. My lack of confidence about speaking a foreign language made me slightly uncomfortable in the company of Olivier and this stranger, but as they both worked hard on the house during the day I also lent a hand with the painting and overcame some of my shyness.

"As we all worked on the house I took in more of the beautiful surroundings, hardly able to comprehend that this might one day be my new home."

As we all worked on the house I took in more of the beautiful surroundings, hardly able to comprehend that this might one day be my new home. Each evening we would finally relax with dinner and a glass of wine, just enjoying the peace and tranquility. On the third day there I received a call from Selma to tell me that Taylor and Grace were now staying with her until my return. They had apparently gone there from their grandparents' house after a disagreement. My Mother had continually spoken negative things about me, Olivier and Selma and they did not want to stay there any longer. I was horrified but after speaking to them realised they were both fine and I totally trusted Selma to take care of them until I returned.

Later that week Olivier said the house would be ready within a couple of months, and I would be able to move into our new home. I was a little shocked. Having a date seemed to make everything more real. There was still much that needed finalising: I had to find a tenant for my apartment in Germany and I wanted the girls and I to be able to speak at least some basic French. I needed to investigate immigration requirements and whether I would be able to place them in schools in the area. I wanted to do everything the right way round, but to Olivier, these were all matters of small importance. He offered to pay me for looking after the house once we moved in. I thought this a little odd, after all, if we were to be living together as a couple, why would I need to be paid for doing work around the house? He explained he wanted to help me out with my finances and didn't want me trying to manage on the maintenance I received from my husband.

I was concerned about the girls' reaction to this imminent move. I would be taking them away from everything they had known in their young lives, away from the only family they had and bringing them to a foreign country to live with someone who was not related to them. Although Olivier had spent some time with them, children do not like major change: they like continuity, it makes them feel safe. It was one thing to have Olivier stay with us in the flat in between his work contracts, but I knew it would be another thing entirely to expect them to live in his house in France and go to a strange school where they would not even know the language. As much as I was falling in love with Olivier, I was afraid of this enormous step I was about to undertake. It was no surprise that we had our first disagreement during that week in France, as I was desperately trying to get my head around this proposed change of lifestyle. What was a surprise was Olivier's behaviour during the fall-out. He took on a very domineering role that I had not witnessed in him before, and I realised I still knew very little about him. The focus of our conversations would inevitably be me as he always seemed reluctant to open up about his past life and feelings.

One night, we lay in bed talking, and I kept probing him for some insight into his innermost thoughts, but he cuddled me trying to change the subject. The next morning when I expressed my concern to him about his reluctance to talk about himself, his mood changed instantly and he became quite aggressive. He told me to get dressed as he would take me home to Germany immediately. He insisted his life was very straightforward, and I could either accept how he was or leave. He left the caravan and went over to the house for a coffee. I felt very vulnerable, like a child that has been reprimanded by an adult. I stood there holding back the tears. My initial reaction was to try to please him, to maintain harmony and I realised I had to change if we were to remain together: I had to accept the private person he was. I joined him in the house but he pretended to be busy, not even looking at me. This felt just like being at home with my parents. Whenever I had done something they did not like or disagreed with, my punishment was always that I would be ignored.

It took all my inner strength to walk over to where he sat. I put my arm around his neck, perched on his knee and with gentle wisdom beyond my usual understanding, I told him I didn't want us to part like this and I needed him to understand that because my childhood and adult life had been so entrenched in pretence, lies, hidden motives and agendas, I craved an openness from him I had never had before. What we were planning was a huge step for me and my children, I needed to be absolutely sure that it was right to go ahead. I needed assurance that I wasn't leaping out of one complicated situation into another. When I told him I loved him very much and wanted to be with him, his manner softened and he hugged and kissed me. Then, as if everything was settled and normal life could resume once again, he got up from the table saying he had lots to do that day and needed to get on with the work as the house would not get finished by itself.

"I chose to listen to the child in me searching for the fairy tale ending, I chose to believe Olivier would be different – my hero…"

It is only with hindsight we can clearly see the warning signs of danger approaching, and then it is often too late to alter the course of our lives. We can only hope that hindsight will equip us to make better decisions next time and learn from our mistakes. My love for Olivier and craving for the perfect family life blinded me to seeing the similarities between his personality and that of my Father and my husband. Instead of trusting my instinct, I chose to listen to the child in me searching for the fairy tale ending, I chose to believe Olivier would be different – my hero –

and together we could accomplish anything and overcome any obstacles. How little I knew of the fragile scales that balanced his volatile mind.

Chapter 10
DYING OF
LONELINESS...

With the week almost over, I telephoned Selma to let her know I would be back later the next afternoon to pick up the girls. But Olivier had other plans. Instead of making an early start the next morning, he did some small jobs around the house before leaving to buy more building materials, giving his friend instructions of what needed to be done while he was away. By lunchtime I realised we would not be back in Germany as I had promised. I felt bad letting Selma down, but Olivier seemed unperturbed by his tardy timekeeping. We eventually set off after midday and I had to call and advise her of our late arrival. It was agony making excuses for his behaviour and Selma was understandably not very happy, after all she had already taken my children in when they ran away from my parents and was unaware of the difficult circumstances I was experiencing. When we finally arrived late at night, I made my apologies and went home with the girls. Something about Olivier's eyes made me think he had changed his mind about us and as he left to go back to France I couldn't help thinking our relationship was over.

Once more I got on with our daily routine. I continued to

collect Olivier's mail, but when he didn't call during my first week back I convinced myself we were finished. Regardless of their earlier disagreement, Taylor visited her grandparents briefly everyday. She always came home asking me the same question: were we about to move to France to live? She was very worried this might happen. I knew this suggestion had come maliciously from my Mother and eager not to cause Taylor anymore anxiety, even though my own stomach churned as I did so, I denied it would happen. I hated lying to my child but in truth, although Olivier had wanted us to move as soon as possible, now I wasn't sure if that would actually happen. Although he telephoned, the calls were always short and he never talked about love, instead enquiring about his post and whether I had decided to move in the next couple of months or not. I was distraught, torn between wanting to make our relationship work and balancing that against uprooting my children from their familiar surroundings. I made excuses about the things I needed to achieve before leaving but Olivier found the details all unimportant. He kept insisting things were different in France, registrations were not necessary and the best place to learn a new language was by living in the actual country. I felt under so much pressure but still my instinct did not win over. My emotions were telling me I loved and trusted this man and wanted to be with him no matter where that was, whilst my instincts were erecting all kinds of delays and excuses that I chose to ignore.

"I would sit by the phone waiting for him to ring, continually lifting the receiver to check it still worked."

As Olivier's interest seemed to decline, so too did his calls. I would sit by the phone waiting for him to ring, continually lifting the receiver to check it still worked. Taylor sensed something was wrong and mentioned it to my Mother and husband, who made the most of every opportunity to make me feel alone and insecure again. Collecting his post one day I noticed a personal letter from

Russia. Suddenly all the past rumours crowded back into my head and I convinced myself they must be true and he really did have someone else in Russia. Normally he would ask me to open the letters when he called and I would tell him the contents. This time I didn't wait for his call, instead I asked Selma to come over. I was shaking as I opened it – and a picture of a woman fell out on the floor. My world crumbled. Though written in English I understood enough and the words cut into my heart with such pain. This woman introduced herself as Olga and said she would love to live in England. She loved to cook and had no problems keeping a house clean. It seemed she was answering an advert. I was numb. How could Olivier possibly do something like this? What was I to do with the information I now had? My choices screamed out at me, I could either destroy the letter and pretend I had never seen it or I had to confront him. I felt sick in my stomach – how could I keep silent about this and continue a relationship with him?

Olivier called soon after to check if he had any mail. I revealed the usual business then mentioned there was a letter from Russia. When I questioned him about business contacts there he denied any but asked if I could forward the letter to France. I could not pretend any longer and apologised, explaining I had already read his letter. But when I asked if it was the reason he had distanced himself from me, he denied anything was going on. He suggested it must be his work colleagues playing a joke on him, as they had before by searching for women for him by placing adverts in newspapers. Even to my love-blinded mind it seemed a weak excuse but wanting to avoid confrontation I chose to accept his explanation. I chose to ignore all the alarm bells going off in my head and preferred to believe this 'man from far away' was the one I had been waiting for all my life. Somehow sensing he had the upper hand he confidently told me he would never play games. Everything he had done on the house in France had been for us, he still loved me and I could either believe him and get over this or we might as well finish right now. Panic flooded my world –

that was not what I wanted. He quickly went on to tell me what work he had completed on the kitchen, saying he had bought a bed for us too. I agreed to drop the subject, but I could not forget it and knew it was not yet laid to rest.

Although his calls continued, they were either late at night or early in the morning and I felt he remained distant. The whole situation played on my mind, worrying me constantly, making me very weak and needy. All I knew was I couldn't bear the thought of losing him. Life at home remained at a high level of stress. Because Taylor's therapist breached her confidentiality by discussing details with my parents, I was forced to stop her therapy, leaving no outlet for her fears. The rumours about Olivier's secret life multiplied. I could choose from a number of permutations, all geared up to cause me to finish our relationship. Olivier had finished with me and returned to his wife in England or conversely we were together and about to move to France to live and take the girls with us.

By the end of January our situation had obviously become too much for Taylor. As I finished the dishes one Sunday I noticed her sitting on the kitchen floor ripping a newspaper to pieces as she talked. She was obviously traumatised. She said she couldn't stand this life anymore, it was too bad, too painful. She wished she could be like the newspaper, ripped to shreds. She sobbed and asked me to let her die! I was horrified seeing my child in this state. It seemed our Mother-daughter relationship had been eroded away by all the poisonous lies but I loved her with all my heart. I immediately stopped all contact between her and my parents and her Father. They were using an innocent child to perpetrate their campaign of hate against Olivier and ultimately me. It would be some time before I discovered the extent of the damage they caused to a little girl who believed she needed to protect her Mother from being hurt and lured away.

I called our doctor, apologising for calling on a Sunday. I briefly explained what Taylor had said and the doctor asked me to bring her immediately to the surgery. After examining her, she thought it necessary to send Taylor to see a psychologist friend of hers who ran a clinic. I phoned Selma to ask for help; I needed her to take care of Grace and loan me her car. She did not hesitate with either request. I also called Olivier, not expecting him to answer but when he did I blurted out what had happened and how frightened I was for Taylor. I wanted him to know I still loved him and needed him so much. He told me to remain calm saying he was on his way to be with us. I felt a huge wave of relief sweep over me. On the way to the doctor's, I decided we would leave as soon as possible with Olivier to go back to France, as far away from my village as possible. I would do anything I had to in order to escape to the peace and tranquility I had known there. I hoped the doctor would understand the situation and agree with my solution.

When we arrived she gave Taylor her full attention. Taylor explained she was tired of always being told what to say to me by her Father and Grandmother. She did not want to listen to her Grandma complaining that her Mother was doing wrong all the time and she was scared in case we moved away to France. I was amazed at the doctor's response to Taylor. She explained there was nothing wrong with me dating Olivier, and even if we did move to France there was nothing to be frightened of: she would always be able to keep in contact with her family here in Germany. She even added it might be better for us to live somewhere else as it may help to solve some of the problems our family was experiencing, living too close to one another. I felt like jumping over the desk and kissing the doctor. She spoke gently and wisely to Taylor, and seemed she was giving me the go-ahead to finally move. I dreaded telling Taylor my plans from the beginning but now she had a smile on her face as the doctor put into words what I could not: I would always have my children's best interests at heart and I would never knowingly hurt them or make them unhappy.

The doctor finished by saying I could take Taylor home but she advised I return the next day and see her colleague. I explained Olivier was on his way from France to offer what support we needed, and I was sure he would not mind if we returned back there with him for a time of rest together. The doctor agreed it was the best idea and offered to take care of informing the school, kindergarten and my work. Before we left she encouraged Taylor by reminding her that Olivier was coming to fetch her. Taylor visibly grew in stature in her chair. Everything seemed to be working out for good for the first time in my life. I was not expecting Olivier to arrive much before midnight as it had been noon when we had spoken on the phone, but he miraculously arrived at nine o'clock, immediately giving Taylor a huge hug before greeting me. Taylor was so pleased to be receiving such special attention. I told him all the doctor had said and what I had suggested. He was very happy and we decided to leave early in the morning for France.

We set off and I was relieved to be leaving everything behind for a whole month. Any problems that Olivier and I had before seemed no longer to be there. As soon as we arrived I called my boss to explain in more detail what had happened. She was incredibly understanding. How I longed for a mother like that. In contrast the call to my Mother did not go well. I told her what the doctor had said and asked her to accept Olivier and I were together and stop involving Taylor in her personal vendetta to split us up. I did not intend to hurt anyone in our family but I desperately wanted my Mother to let me live my life and make my own decisions. She denied ever putting thoughts or words into Taylor's head and said she was offended by my accusation. As far as she was concerned, I was mistaken about her intentions and she had no time for me in her life anymore; she had to concentrate on her husband for once. She insisted she had always been there for me and for all her care I repaid her by going against her wishes in seeing Olivier. Her scathing words made me cry. I realised any further conversation with my Mother would be futile and so I called my boss again, desperate for some words of comfort.

The days that followed were good for the girls. As Olivier and I continued to work on the house, they spent all their time playing with the local farmer's children, helping to feed the animals and having fun jumping in and out of the haystacks in the barn. Seeing them so happy, I took the opportunity to tell them we would be living here permanently soon. The weather had been warm and we sat outside the house discussing it. The bedrooms were finished and so we were already sleeping in the house and the girls had their own bedrooms and separate bathroom. On hearing the news Taylor got up and ran off saying Grandma and Grandpa had been right all along and I had lied to her. I let her go, satisfied she could not get easily lost in the open fields all around us, understanding she needed some time on her own. Grace was absolutely fine with the news, but then she was only four and did not fully comprehend what was happening in her life. Eventually Taylor arrived back and sat on a big rock outside the house. She agreed to move to France with us as long as I promised if she did not like it, I would let her move back to Germany when she was fourteen. Even as young as she was and despite all the conflict, Taylor always felt responsible for her grandparents and now needed to know she could return to look after them if she chose. I gave her a big hug and promised her she could do that, hoping in time she would come to love our new life and my new man. The girls went back to play with the farmer's children and I believed we had overcome a huge hurdle, but life is seldom that simple.

I was worried because Olivier hardly took any time off from the arduous schedule he had set himself to finish work on the house. He would work all day and only stop late in the evening. On his birthday I bought a cake and we called him in after lunch to blow the candles out but he seemed unable to relax. Reluctantly he agreed to go for a walk with us along the beach but the atmosphere in the car was heavy during the thirty minute drive there. He made it clear he would rather be back at the house working than out with us, but when we arrived, the beach was beautiful and the sun was shining. I held his hand as we strolled along behind the girls but when Taylor turned around and saw she immediately pushed herself between us, took my hand from Olivier and held it tightly. Only much later did I learn that she was terrified at that moment as she believed it was the moment her Father had warned her about, when Olivier would abandon her and Grace and run away with me. I encouraged her to rejoin her sister but she would have none of it, gripping my hand for all she was worth and refusing to say anything in answer to my questions. Olivier turned and walked back to the car, his attempt at time-off over.

"Bringing the conversation to an end, he said it would be better if he took us all home that evening."

Back at the house, the girls resumed their play with the farmer's children and Olivier went and lay down on the bed. Not wanting to harass him, I sat downstairs alone. When I eventually went to see if he was alright I found him staring at the ceiling. Unsure about what to say but feeling I needed to make amends I apologised for Taylor's behaviour but he did not look at me. When he chose to speak it was to tell me he couldn't take the responsibility of anyone else, it was never worth the pain. I tried to find words to express just how much he meant to me; he was the reason I had the strength to live through each day. There had been so much disappointment in my life, this was the first time I felt things were improving. I couldn't believe he would give up on our dream over something so trivial. I walked over to the window, my eyes filling with tears and stood watching the girls playing happily outside. Although I opened my heart to him and exposed my true feelings, it had no effect on his mood. Bringing the conversation to an end, he said it would be better if he took us all home that evening.

My mouth dropped open, I couldn't believe what I heard. He was dumping me – just like that – and now he was literally going to dump me back on my doorstep in Germany. I could see by the look on his face there was to be no further discussion. I was now convinced he had wanted to end our relationship before and had given so many signs, but I had chosen to ignore them and desperately hung on to my dream. I called the girls and told them we were going home almost immediately. Their young minds did not understand, they were simply enjoying themselves with their new-found friends. I had no explanation to offer them for Olivier's change of heart that they could understand, I wasn't even sure I understood myself. Without having time to collect our things we were bustled into the car and set off in silence as I fought back the tears. Olivier tried to raise the girls' spirits by mentioning they would soon see their grandparents, but they too sat in their seats utterly confused and downcast.

After a few miles and without any warning, Olivier suddenly turned the car around, took my hand, said he was sorry, and headed back in the direction we had come. As soon as we arrived at the house, the children went out to continue their games as if nothing had happened but I was unable to switch back into happy mode. I was dumbfounded and confused. From the first day we met we had encountered so many problems with my parents, my husband and everything that had gone on I couldn't believe that Taylor's actions on the beach could tip the scales so drastically to make Olivier want to take us home, but neither could I understand his complete change of heart by bringing us back. Not for the first time I felt wary of this volatile man and kept my distance. He opened a bottle of wine and poured two glasses, then took me in his arms and held me tight.

"...why did I choose to ignore all my instincts and believe I was special to him?"

He explained how his past experience with women had hurt him so much he had toughened up, mistrusting people's motives. His first marriage was a total disaster and he felt used. All he wanted was to be loved for who he was but was scared of the love I showed him and cautious of being used again. Worryingly, his explanation did not reassure me. Then he said something I found very disturbing. Whilst holding me tightly against him he looked me right in the eye and told me if anyone crossed him again, they would never be happy. He must have felt my alarm as my body stiffened and I tried to pull myself away from him. Why could I not believe him when he said he would never hurt me, though? Why did my flesh creep when he told me I was different from all the others? And why did I choose to ignore all my instincts and believe I was special to him? We stayed as planned until the end of the month when Olivier drove us back to Germany before returning the same day to France, saying he did not feel safe in our village anymore.

Chapter 11
ADDICTION
DENIAL...

After Olivier's return to France he kept phone calls short, mainly asking when I would be joining him. He insisted he'd renovated the house promptly because of our need and didn't understand why I was delaying moving there. I felt very pressured, worried about finalising things in Germany and how we would get our belongings to France, but he dismissed my concern over possessions saying he had everything there we could possibly need and even offered to pay the rental on my flat for six months in case I couldn't get another tenant, although he later retracted that offer. I saw again how he viewed life as either black or white, very straightforward, you either did something or you didn't. He informed me I would not need a resident's visa to live in France and I chose to believe this well-travelled man of the world.

The matter came abruptly to a head when he called during the night to tell me he would not be coming to Germany any more to see me unless it was to take us to be with him in France. Although I was feeling shocked having been awoken from sleep, my brain clicked in instantly and I understood everything he said. My heart was pounding with the fear of losing him and when he hung up I could hardly breathe. I slid out of bed and knelt on the floor still clutching the phone, crouched over like a baby. I had been in this place before. I had felt this kind of fear before, the familiarity was frightening. This was the way my Mother always spoke to me when she wanted to get her own way: either you do as I say or you will be punished. I don't know how long I stayed there, scrunched up in a ball but I did not sleep again that night. I smoked cigarette after cigarette until I felt physically sick trying to understand why he would force my hand in this way if he loved me as he said he did.

"…there was a faint nagging voice in my head warning me I would regret this one day."

I didn't expect him to call again and I was too confused to call him. I asked Selma for her thoughts on Olivier's actions. She advised me to sort out the basis of our relationship before making the move to another country. She said he should be prepared to wait until I was happy with all the arrangements or he would lose me in his impatience. That was all very well but I had all these strong feelings for Olivier. What was I supposed to do with them? I couldn't switch a button and turn them off; I was in love with the guy. But even in the midst of all those feelings of love, and despite spending all my time making arrangements for this proposed move, there was a faint nagging voice in my head warning me I would regret this one day. I became quite ill with migraines and so much weight loss I looked skeletal and very unhealthy. I had already quit my job as part of my preparation for the move, in fact I had not worked since Christmas, as Olivier had convinced me I didn't need to work now I had him.

Spending all day in the flat made me even more sensitive to my surroundings, my paranoia picked up on each tiny detail and sound. One morning after the girls had left for their schools I heard noises outside. I had not pressed the entry buzzer but stood paralyzed with fear imagining my husband was stalking me again

– standing just outside our door. Gossip had spread about me quitting my job so I guessed my Mother would speculate on my plans to leave Germany. When I summoned enough strength to finally open the front door, I found my little nephew kneeling on the floor. He had been pressing his ear up against it to listen. In defence of being caught in the act he said he was checking to see if I was all right. I loved my nephew very much and was incensed that a young child should be used in such a way to spy on me. Whatever people's intentions were, this action had the effect of pushing me to phone Olivier and tell him I would be ready to leave whenever he came to collect us. He told me to pack but not tell anyone; he would call to tell me as soon as he was on his way.

"…despite all the persecution and unhappiness, it was all I knew and anything else suddenly became the frightening unknown. Too terrified to leave yet too exhausted to stay…"

After hanging up the phone all my insecurities came flooding back. What had I done? I had agreed to leave all the familiar things I knew and go with my children to a foreign country with a man I did not know extremely well. Despite my husband's irrational behaviour, despite my parents' continual rejection and control, despite all the persecution and unhappiness, it was all I knew and anything else suddenly became the frightening unknown. Too terrified to leave yet too exhausted to stay, caught between a rock and a hard place. It occurred to me then that Olivier was pleased I had agreed to go immediately as that was what he wanted; he had got his way but I was too tired to fight anymore. I think I made excuses for his behaviour in my mind by reassuring myself he was not an alcoholic nor a violent man, he was neither a bully nor a manipulator, he seemed generous, loving and kind; he was my knight in shining armour from far away. He was under stress from all the renovation work he had been doing on the house in France – which after all – was for our future as well as his.

Having convinced myself I was doing the right thing, I began to surreptitiously pack our belongings ready to leave. Not telling anyone our plans was like being eaten alive from the inside. I was longing to talk to Selma but Olivier had advised against anyone knowing, even my best friend, as he said rumours had their own insidious way of spreading unseen like gas. Every day I waited for the phone to ring, for Olivier to say he was on his way to pick us up, but it didn't. I hated the secrecy and desperately wanted it to be over so that we could get on with normal life – whatever that was. As the waiting turned from days to weeks I thought I would lose my mind. On top of the mental pressure, my financial situation was worsening as I had no salary coming in. Four weeks passed and March was almost over. The first day of April was my birthday but I didn't feel like celebrating, instead I prepared to go to my bank to arrange an overdraft to cover my rent arrears. Just as I prepared to leave the flat, the phone rang. I answered it automatically with little thought of Olivier now. When I heard his voice I was too exhausted, too drained to feel excitement; every last drop of vitality had been drained from me so remaining cool I did not reveal my state of mind to him. I didn't want him to know how much I loved him and needed him – how weak I was without him.

I asked him where he was and what he'd been doing for so long. He explained he had been really busy sorting everything out at the house but I was unable to speak, I had no strength to overcome the disappointment and depression I felt. I told him I needed to go as I had an appointment with my bank manager and missing an opportunity to talk further, I hung up. Convinced I would never see him again I did not want to make myself any more vulnerable. I dreaded the reaction of my parents, who would be sure to let me know how satisfied they were that things had worked out just as they had predicted. Coming back from the bank later that afternoon, I was surprised to find Selma waiting for me outside the apartment. Excitedly she told me Olivier was at their house, collecting his belongings. I felt sick and faint, my knees were shaking. This was my D-day: he had come to collect us as he promised. Watching as he drove up to our apartment building I was confronted with the reality of what I was about to do; deep inside turmoil reigned, outside I didn't know whether to smile or cry. Selma returned home, leaving us together while the girls continued playing outside.

Olivier went straight upstairs to bed: he was tired after his long journey in the van and asked me to wake him for dinner. Before he slept though he made it plain that he expected to have sex with me. He didn't ask, just presumed it was his right. I felt used, dirty, yet unable to protest, almost as if I was trapped inside my own body. It was a weird feeling and not one I wanted to have repeated. Here was I, about to make the biggest move of my life not having told my daughters for fear Taylor would refuse to go; terrified my husband would discover our plans, estranged from my parents, unable to say goodbye or even talk to my dearest friend and all he could think about was satisfying his sexual desires. Where I was felt very close to the edge of sanity. I moved around like an automaton, not daring to delve too deep into my feelings, scared of what they might reveal.

Later that night as the girls prepared to go to bed, the doorbell rang. I heard my estranged husband's voice on the entry phone. I could tell he was very drunk. He insisted on seeing the girls and challenging Olivier, the loser he tauntingly called him, to another fight. I told him to go away but he stayed for ages, ringing the bell incessantly. The girls did not want to see their Father, his behaviour unsettled them. I even went outside to try and reason with him but he shouted abuse at me, calling me a prostitute and Olivier the foreign cowboy. He made it clear he would do everything he could to stop me leaving the country and taking his girls with me, and planned to visit Social Services in the morning. I told him to go home and sleep as his drunkenness was upsetting Taylor and Grace. When he eventually left, I called Selma and she agreed to have them for the night in case he came back causing further trouble. To my surprise Olivier started to leave too, saying he could not cope with any more of this fiasco. The fragile coping mechanism that had been holding me together seemed to snap at his reaction. I asked him why he had bothered to come, telling him I did not need to be rescued out of pity. I told him if that was his motive then he should leave me to sort out the mess that was my life, maybe it would ultimately be calmer without him. After all, the troubles were far from over: I still had to convince Taylor to leave with us and not insist she stay because of my parents. I was determined not to leave her behind, she was my daughter, I loved her with all my heart but sensed I would have to fight to keep my Mother from stealing her away from me.

With hindsight I can see Olivier wasn't committed to my daughters. I fitted into his plans for a future but he could take or leave the girls. Alarm bells rang faintly when he spoke easily about me leaving Taylor with my parents for a while but there were so many things screaming for attention in my head, I am ashamed to say they went unheeded until it was too late. When he asked me if I wanted him to leave, I was immobilised with panic: I didn't know what to do. Feeling like a doll that has been stretched too far in opposite directions until broken, I wasn't sure whether I could cope with any more and although he stayed for the night, we did not speak then or in the morning. Selma arrived with Grace to wish me a happy birthday after taking Taylor to school with her own daughter. I walked to the kindergarten with Grace, sure Olivier would take the opportunity to leave for good. My heart was pounding as I hurried back to the flat but he was still there, himself unsure as to whether he should go or stay and wait for me.

With an inner confidence I did not feel I challenged him about his behaviour asking why he had built me up to expect so much, only to dash my hopes by constantly changing his mind. I longed to be with him permanently and was prepared to make big changes in my life to achieve that, but I didn't want him to do anything for me out of pity. With the baggage I had in my heart and mind and two children it was never going to be effortless to make our relationship work. I wasn't asking for a Father for my children, but I was asking for a lover and friend who would support me as I cared for them and who would make every effort to get along with them and love them because they were part of me. He sat on the windowsill listening all the while I spoke, then as I finished he stood up and told me to collect everything I needed so we could get out of there.

We arranged he would drive ahead, meeting me and the girls at a stop on the motorway, to deter anyone following us if they saw us leaving together. As I waited for Taylor to come home from school, Grace played in the garden and I called my lawyer who would be acting on my behalf at the upcoming divorce hearing. She was genuinely happy for me and wished me a better future. All that remained was for me to write a letter as soon as we arrived in France with my new address, the rest could go ahead in my absence. I was relieved deep in my soul to know by moving away I would no longer to be harassed by my husband's stalking. Then the only remaining call I knew I could make without being shouted at, condemned or bullied was to my most precious friend, Selma. I just couldn't leave without saying goodbye. Before I spoke she realised it was me and told me she already knew I would be leaving. Neither of us could express our love for each other with words, they were grossly inadequate. She had been my confidante, my rock and a truly kind, compassionate and noble friend. She never judged me as most people in my life had done, but was always there whenever I needed someone I could trust – with my emotions, and most importantly, with my girls. She was unable to come to say goodbye in person, it was too painful for us both.

Somehow receiving her blessing made me feel better. I called for a taxi and waited with Grace for Taylor's school bus to arrive at the stop close to our flat. Before Taylor had alighted from the bus she noticed the taxi and, cleverly assessing the situation, asked if we were actually leaving. She asked me not to make her go, saying that she just couldn't come, couldn't leave her grandparents. I asked her to do as I requested and get into the taxi, but she started to cry hysterically, upsetting Grace. Terrified of being discovered by my parents or my husband before we left, I grabbed Taylor's school bag and bundled them both into the cab with me and slammed the door. I can't imagine what the taxi driver thought, but to me it felt as if I was kidnapping my own children. I told the driver to take us as fast as he could to the first stop on the motorway, but it seemed we were travelling in slow motion. I felt like a twelve year old running away from home, petrified I would be found out and made to go back home where I would be in serious trouble. As we drove I saw images of our village life slowly pass my eyes. Our escape wasn't happening nearly fast enough for me: I was convinced my husband would suddenly appear chasing us in his car, forcing us to return. When we passed the building site where my Father worked, I glimpsed him working on the roof. I shut my eyes willing him not to recognise us in the taxi. The girls cried all the way to the rendezvous point with Olivier.

Resembling a getaway scene from a bad movie, we piled into Olivier's van but as only three people could sit in the front, one of the children had to sit in the back amongst the hurriedly packed black bin liners thrown there. I had only packed bare essentials for us in the rush, including a few of the children's toys, but most of our belongings had been left behind. I knew the journey would take us a long time in Olivier's old van. It was around midday when we left and at best we could only hope to reach our destination in France by nine the following morning. The experience was made much worse by Olivier issuing lists of rules as he drove. He told me I would have to put some weight on as I was skeletal. As regards Taylor and Grace, they would have their own bedroom and would be expected to undertake certain tasks around the house, receiving pocket money only if they were completed satisfactorily. I couldn't believe what I was hearing but felt so weak and drained from the morning's farce I was unable to interrupt with any of my own thoughts. My head was crammed with doubts and fears about our departure and everything surrounding my relationship with Olivier. Oddly, it even occurred to me he had forgotten to mention it was my birthday. I felt overlooked and unimportant but secretly hoping he had remembered and planned a surprise for our arrival in France. How silly our thoughts are sometimes: how self-centred, and how wrong!

During the journey Olivier received a phone call and conducted it in English. Although I did not speak much of the language, I could understand enough to glean from his conversation that it was his sister asking whether he would be at an imminent family celebration. He reassured her he would be there, explaining he was on his way back to France from Germany taking me with him as I could no longer cope with my home situation there. At no point did he indicate we had planned this move together and I would be living with him in France, just that I couldn't cope and he had helped me out, almost implying by his tone that he was stuck with me. It struck me then, how much he had changed since we met almost a year before. Even the way he looked at me was different. Gone was that unmistakable look of love in his eyes, replaced by a condescending look of tolerance – or at least that was my perception.

Both girls had fallen asleep on top of the black bin liners in the back of the van. As I looked at them, my heart broke. I wondered what their young minds must be making of this mess that I had made them endure. I prayed silently for them, all the while wanting to scream at Olivier to turn around and take us back home but I chose to remain silent. Finally I too fell asleep, exhausted from trying to make sense of Olivier and his volatile moods, unable to look at his face I felt so low. I woke as we pulled in to a petrol station in France in the early hours of the morning. He got into the van after paying but his only conversation was to comment on me being awake at last. When we arrived at the house later, he went straight upstairs to bed without saying anything.

"The thought that grieved me more than anything was the decision was not theirs, they had no choice in the matter."

I stood for ages with the girls in that house, immobilised with shock, scared to move in case we woke Olivier. The last two years I had been to hell and back. Persistently harassed by my estranged husband, alienated by my family and now without a job or money, I was in a foreign country with someone who acted as if they couldn't bear the sight of me. Looking down at my young, vulnerable children all I could think was I had made the biggest mistake of my life so far; my fairy tale had broken into thousands of pieces. I left our clothes untouched in the van. Although the building work was finished on the house, there was no furniture inside except beds and a kitchen. There were no wardrobes or places to sit or eat. It was hard for Taylor and Grace too, coming from a home where they had everything, leaving their friends and grandparents for this strange place with only their Mother and a man they did not know well. The thought that grieved me more than anything was the decision was not theirs, they had no choice in the matter.

At that point I wanted to drive the van back to Germany myself, but I did not have a penny in my pocket and no bank account; we were stranded in the middle of nowhere. The thought suddenly occurred to me that this was my thirtieth birthday, supposedly another milestone in my life. It felt like the continuation of a prison sentence, only the surroundings had changed. I could hear my Mother's voice in my head, taunting me, telling me I had made another big mistake. It was then I knew I couldn't go back to my life in Germany; my pride would not let me. I wanted to prove to everyone they were wrong and it was possible to have a normal happy life and loving relationships.

"I immersed myself in denial, pretending there was nothing wrong in our relationship and trying desperately to regain the love I believed we had once shared."

Hours later, Olivier reappeared downstairs, asking why we had not emptied the van of our belongings. I quickly rushed to do that, keen not to do anything to upset him and cause further tension between us. Looking back I can see that time as the point at which our relationship changed drastically, although I was oblivious at the time. I became obsessed with doing everything I could to prevent his displeasure or anger. I immersed myself in denial, pretending there was nothing wrong in our relationship and trying desperately to regain the love I believed we had once shared. The shift in my manner, however subtle, must have registered on a deeper subconscious level with Olivier. The more acquiescent I became the more aggressive he was towards me and the girls, swapping his considerate and affectionate ways for those of a controlling tyrant.

He ordered the girls to sleep in their separate rooms. Sparsely furnished with only a bed in each, I could see the anxiety on their faces. Taylor was eight and Grace only four and they had always shared their beds growing up together. Not daring to cause trouble I secretly countered his instructions, suggesting they sleep together once he had gone to bed. I sat each night reading to them as I had always done before, but it was not long before he made it plain he was not happy with that routine either. He told me everything was different now and we were to get on and make the best of our new lives. What he seemed unable to comprehend was we all needed time to adjust to our new surroundings and the changes. Just because we had left our past life behind in the physical sense did not mean we had left all our fears and emotions behind too.

Lying in bed next to him at night felt all wrong, but I could not put my thoughts into words, his moods were unpredictable and I did not wish to upset the fragile peace. He made it very clear that life would be lived his way and I thought of him as a volcano bubbling away under the surface, but ready to erupt without warning. After a week of endless cleaning and chores, I opened a bottle of wine one evening. When Olivier enquired as to the occasion I said it was nothing important, merely to acknowledge my birthday on the day I moved in. He apologised and said I should have mentioned it before and happily drank to a new start in my life but nothing more was said about my birthday or this new chance at happiness he believed he offered us.

Aside from the challenge of adjusting to our new surroundings, it was, as I had predicted, extremely difficult for the girls to settle. They were continually frightened by the idea that their Father would find out where we were and suddenly appear, in a rage, demanding we all go back to Germany. I was no less stressed by panic attacks and found myself more than once running to the window, convinced I heard his car screeching up the lane announcing his arrival. Night after night my dreams were dominated by images of him dragging us into his car and taking us back, all the while screaming angry abuse at me. One night the the sound of thunder caused me to break down in tears as I slid onto the floor in front of the bedroom window. My nocturnal activities woke Olivier, but I dared not share my fears with him, and excused myself by saying I couldn't sleep. I knew his advice would be to get on with this chance of new life we had been given or leave. I was scared to arouse the unfeeling stranger lurking within. Tragically, my actions reminded me of my Mother who would do anything to prevent my Father from exercising his anger. Grace was having frequent nightmares and Olivier's patience with her was short-lived. He would continually tell me to control them as their behaviour could not continue. We were not allowed to adjust to the changes, merely accept them. Even though the girls were missing their friends and grandparents, he decided it was best we did not contact them for a few months giving the situation back home chance to calm down. I could not disobey his instructions: I was convinced I needed to please him in all things in order to get our relationship back on track.

Chapter 12
BROKEN PROMISES, SHATTERED LIVES...

As the weeks progressed neither Taylor, Grace nor I seemed to adjust to our new home, although I pretended all was well to Olivier. I missed Selma's wise words and friendly love tremendously. Too late I remembered her good advice about making sure I arranged schools for the children in advance, as well as investigating the immigration status for us all before we left. Arriving at the beginning of Easter made it impossible to achieve anything immediately. Not speaking French and having no idea where to go to get help exacerbated my situation. Olivier refused to get involved, thinking it had nothing to do with him; when I asked for his help he told me in no uncertain terms that he had given us a new start in life and could not take on all our responsibilities, the rest was up to me. He spoke down to me, telling me off, reminding me of being rebuked by my Father, and his tone became increasingly more aggressive. He used intimidating, abusive language I was not used to nor fully understood, though the sheer venom with which it was delivered said it all. It was the first of countless times I would hear the 'f-word'. Any swearing was forbidden by my parents, its use swiftly punished and although I had occasionally been exposed to it at work it was not considered acceptable for women to hear such language where I grew up.

With no help forthcoming from Olivier I called the German embassy in Paris for assistance but they did not offer much in the way of practical aid. Secretly I cried, feeling our circumstances were desperate. Finally Olivier stormed off to the local council office with his French dictionary to get further information about schooling. He was still of the opinion none of this was his affair and refusing to understand this was one reason I wanted to delay moving from Germany until everything was organised. He returned home informing me a teacher would get in touch, but for the time being the schools were closed for the holidays. I was especially concerned that neither Taylor or Grace could speak French, and Grace had only attended nursery in Germany. Already her anxieties were manifesting themselves by her wetting the bed. In the beginning I was able to hide it from Olivier but he made matters worse by forbidding them to snuggle with me in my bed every morning as they had always been used to. He used the excuse that it would be considered inappropriate behaviour and he could get into trouble if Social Services found out, but I knew it was another way of controlling us and our natural expressions of love and affection. Every time he discovered the girls sneaking into each other's bed at night, he would become angry and they were even forced to ask permission to enter the bedroom I shared with him.

I lay silently awake each morning, waiting to hear sounds from the girls' bedroom before joining them there, but this practice only lasted until Olivier decided he'd had enough of it. He made it plain his preference was to have sex as soon as he woke in the morning – to satisfy his own desire – and I was expected to comply with his demands with no thought for me as a person. I felt so cheap, like the prostitute I had been labelled back in Germany. He used me as he pleased, taking what he wanted, enjoying the power he exerted over me.

One night, Grace woke from a nightmare and called out for me. Olivier forbade me to go to her, saying I had to leave her to get over it alone otherwise she would always control me. I refused and went to comfort her, testing his scant patience. He followed me, shouting, calling us abnormal and telling all of us we could get the hell out of his house. Now he always spoke to me in English, never resorting to German, and though I did not understand every word, I was able to gather the gist of his message by the anger in his voice. Placating the girls who were now both wide awake, I told them everything would be fine and got back into bed hoping to avert further outbursts. Olivier meant business, and having worked himself up to a state of outrage, continued shouting at me, insisting I take my brats and leave immediately. He kicked me when I refused to get up and persisted in doing so until I could bear it no longer and went downstairs. I locked myself and the girls in one of their bedrooms holding my stomach which hurt from kicks that had found their mark. Determined not to allow me the satisfaction of my silent rebellion, Olivier followed with a spare key trying to gain access to the room.

"I did not know then that I was pregnant, carrying the child of the man whose behaviour was causing us all to be terrified."

We pushed the bed right up against the door and all sat tight on it preventing him from reaching us, but could not escape from his barrage of anger and abuse. I did not know then that I was pregnant, carrying the child of the man whose behaviour was causing us all to be terrified. All I knew was I didn't know this man! We sat trapped in that bedroom for ages as he tried to gain access. I knew I had to keep him out at all costs – for the sake of the children and myself. I don't know how he wasn't able to get in, only that all the past experiences of my life with my husband and Father gave me a superhuman energy to keep the bed and door between us. Taylor put my thoughts into words when she said her

Grandma was right. I knew we should not have come, but had no idea how on earth I would sort this mess out. Olivier continued to shout through the door insisting he had given us a new life and this was how we repaid him. If we didn't appreciate his efforts he told us, in no uncertain terms, to leave. Finally he went back upstairs to bed and we fell asleep, exhausted on the single bed pushed up against the door.

Loud music blaring throughout the house woke us all early the next morning as Olivier began removing the hinges to the bedroom door. He continued his tirade of verbal abuse interspersed with orders to get out of the house. We hurriedly got dressed and I took the girls outside, desperately wanting to walk away from the house and the mess. But where on earth could we go? We were in the middle of nowhere in northern France with no money, no friends and unable to speak the language. Nonetheless, with our passports, some biscuits and a bottle of water, I grasped the girls' hands and we began walking towards the small nearby village. Shortly afterwards, Olivier followed us in the car, asking me to get in, apologising as he had not meant any of this to happen. I ignored him, holding Taylor and Grace's hands tighter and kept walking; there was no way I wanted to get into his car.

Reaching the village we managed to get away from him, hiding behind a small shed. When he drove off, we hid for some time in a big field near the house. But Olivier knew I had no real way of escaping and gave up searching for us. Refusing to give him the satisfaction of knowing I was beaten, we remained in the field until midday, watching him coming and going from the house. The girls were unusually quiet, still traumatised by recent events. Captive to my thoughts I reflected the course of the past year. There was so much to regret and yet I couldn't bring myself to regret falling in love with him, wanting the happiness of a normal family, desiring the perfect fairy tale life. I was only sorry for what I had done to my children, for what they had to endure. But how could I have known that all my hopes and dreams would end like this?

Sometime after noon, Olivier drove away from the house with his caravan in tow. It occurred to me he might be running off and leaving us behind. The thought shocked me that he could do that but my main concern was what to do next. Both girls were hungry and so we approached the house cautiously, watching in case he returned. The door was open and we went inside and made some sandwiches and stayed there, not really knowing what on earth we should do next. I was only half surprised when Olivier arrived home later. Neither of us spoke and for the next week we shared only the same house. I slept each night with the girls on a single bed in one of their bedrooms. It was behaviour I was entirely used to, both from my parents and the home I had shared with my husband. That was how we dealt with everything: not communicating, not seeking solutions to problems, merely ignoring them until they hopefully went away. I remembered too that my Father had not spoken to me since my first association with Olivier, and had forced my Mother and the whole family into behaving the same way.

Olivier made no attempt at reconciliation, showing no remorse for his conduct. He reminded me of my Father making me feel vulnerable by prolonging the dispute for so long that I would forget the original cause of the disagreement. The side of my character that emulated my Mother sought to make things right or plaster over the cracks, and so I agreed to make an effort in the faint hope that our relationship would improve, revert to how it was in the beginning. Often I discovered Olivier listening at the door when I spoke to the children in German. He understood my language very well and like a small child, tried to discover information by covert means rather than asking questions outright. For my part, although the pressure we lived with was immense, I did not want to return to Germany. I did not want to give my parents the satisfaction of being able to say they were right all along and the foreigner was no good, his intentions towards me were never honourable. Despite only knowing dysfunctional family life, I still naively believed in a better life in this world.

Despite Olivier's appalling conduct, I still hoped it would all come good in the end and my hero would reappear.

Soon the teacher visited from the nearby school, bringing with her a friend who spoke perfect German. Consequently the meeting went well and the girls could start school at the end of the month. I was concerned for both of them and especially Grace. Everything would be new to her, including a foreign language and she was still my little baby. Olivier showed no interest at all in the arrangements. He disappeared as soon as they arrived leaving me to handle everything as if we were no longer a couple. The survivor deep inside me made a decision then to make the best of our situation. I would prove to everyone I was not a loser; I could cope with whatever life threw at me and survive, and I promised myself I would never give up. The struggle to achieve that was fraught with frustration and without Olivier to confide in and rely on I would secretly call Selma, asking for her advice. Some days I would not have been able to get out of bed if it had not been for her unconditional encouragement in the face of constant trials. I'm not sure how much Olivier enjoyed watching me strive to achieve my goals but he never once took me lovingly in his arms and made me feel cared for.

"Taylor, Grace and I had to make do with our single bedroom surrounded by black bin liners full of our clothes."

Without warning he fixed the phone to receive calls only, which meant I could no longer turn to Selma for help. I was reluctant to ask him for anything, even food, but as I had no money of my own or means to get any, I did use the food he bought for himself because the alternative was my children would starve and I would not let that happen. Whenever he went out he always locked the phone and television in his bedroom Taylor, Grace and I had to make do with our single bedroom surrounded by black bin liners full of our clothes. My heart broke anew for my children when I considered what I had done in taking them away from everything they had before. In my blinded state, I sometimes forgot the emotional roller coaster they endured in Germany. Now, there didn't seem to be much difference between the two bizarre situations. Olivier took himself away from the house most days leaving us completely alone and if he forgot to lock his bedroom door, we would sneak in there and watch the television to pass the time. On one occasion, I even locked myself and the girls inside, remaining in there after he came home, just to let him know what it felt like not to be in control.

"No matter what terrible things happened, no matter how irrevocable the circumstances, just like my Mother, I began making excuses, convincing myself things were not as bad as they seemed. I was living in denial."

In time Olivier made small moves towards reconciliation, phoning when he was out and leaving messages of apology. But he had awakened in me a stubbornness inherited from my Father and I am ashamed to say I prolonged the disharmony far too long, wanting to punish him for treating me so badly. I had trusted this man: trusted his good intentions towards me and my daughters and he had betrayed that trust and damaged our relationship by making me feel worthless. He implied everything he did for us was out of pity, with him as the good guy and me an inconvenient burden he couldn't get rid of. Deep in my heart I craved for a return to how things were between us in the beginning, and I think that desire led me to replicate my Mother's pattern of servile behaviour with my Father and cover over the cracks without ever addressing the issues. No matter what terrible things happened, no matter how irrevocable the circumstances, just like my Mother, I began making excuses, convincing myself things were not as bad as they seemed. I was living in denial.

Unaware of these things at the time, it is only now, looking back, I can see clearly how my thought processes were shaped by my parents and how I made some disastrous decisions as a direct result of imitating their behaviour and rebelling against their need to control my life. Coupled with a need to survive the devastation of my marriage, I built a hardened, impenetrable wall around my heart and it has taken considerable time to repair the damage suffered by myself and my children and remains an ongoing journey. Similarly, the demolishing of the Berlin Wall was momentously begun in November 1989 but the aftershocks reverberated throughout Germany for many years afterwards. People are still living with the consequences of life before and after the chains of control were smashed. There are many survivors of that tragic time of division but many lost the battle to break free from oppression and even lost their lives in the process.

I was a product of my life's experiences, shaped by the only role model I knew. Copying my Mother I became a slave to Olivier's demands. During the day I waited on him at every opportunity, cooking for him, keeping house and generally doing anything I could to persuade him to love me and stop the aching hurt inside. Each night and morning I was his cheap prostitute, purely used as a means of sex for him, yet despite feeling sick to my stomach and hating the person I had become I made no complaint. Instead I would torture myself with imaginings of past infidelities and would suffer his verbal abuse if ever I felt strong enough to confront him about my fears. He frequently accused me of losing the plot laughing at me directly or choosing to vent his offence as anger against the girls. If I ever disobeyed him or expressed my dissatisfaction at the way things had turned out, he would abusively tell me to go back to Germany if I didn't like the arrangement. Of course, he knew as well as I did, it was not an option for me any longer. I had burned my bridges by moving with him to France, and would never be able to face living anywhere near my husband or expect sympathy from my parents. Olivier cruelly reminded me I had nowhere to go saying he was the best thing that had ever happened in my life. He would sometimes hug me and say how lucky I was to have a boyfriend like him.

Boyfriend! I didn't even consider us a couple after the hideous month we had just spent together in France.

When it came time for the girls to go to school after Easter all three of us were desperately unhappy. Despite the kindness shown to us by the teacher we had met, Grace was terrified, not speaking any French. Taylor was incredibly brave in front of her sister but I knew deep down she too was scared and unhappy. Convinced I had ruined my daughters' lives all for a man, I barely managed to leave the school grounds before breaking down, crying tears of guilt. Financially, Olivier made it clear he did not consider it his responsibility to provide for my children, even though I left Germany with nothing to live with him. Desperate for companionship, I felt utterly friendless and whenever he was out and the phone left connected, I would take the opportunity to phone Selma and spill my heart out to her. Left in charge of my finances and the flat in Germany she sent some money as soon as she could. I was hoping my estranged husband would agree to pay maintenance for school fees but none materialised. The staff there were very kind and understanding, knowing a little of my circumstances. Nevertheless I couldn't help feeling like a silly little girl again who had messed up. I ran off with a foreigner whose promises turned out to be nothing more than empty words and finding myself a stranger in a strange land I was suffering for my bad choices.

"I was at the mercy of Olivier's mood swings yet he seemed unaware he was continually messing with my head – calling me his girlfriend one minute when it suited him, changing his mind the next."

I was at the mercy of Olivier's mood swings yet he seemed unaware he was continually messing with my head – calling me his girlfriend one minute when it suited him, changing his mind the next. I lived in a perpetual state of anxiety. I couldn't wait for the girls to come home after school each day, concerned they would not understand any of their lessons. The teacher suggested I go to help out during their lessons which came as a welcome relief, and I hoped it would enable me to acquire a basic vocabulary in French, too. Far from being kind and understanding, Olivier was totally against this idea, saying I had to let my daughters do things for themselves instead of stifling them by constantly helping. Torn between him and my children I displeased him further when I agreed to go each day. He unexpectedly announced one day that he was going to England for an indefinite period. My desperate begging and crying made no impact on him at all and within a week he had made his travel arrangements. He departed in the middle of the night, seemingly deaf to my uncontrollable crying, leaving us stranded in the middle of nowhere, without a backward glance. Even Taylor implored him not to go and leave her Mummy crying.

Hearing my daughter's touching request jolted me out of my self-pity. After all, I was the adult, I should be taking care of my children, not the other way around. I stopped crying and started acting like the mother I so desperately wanted to be. Getting to school each day was not a problem as it was within manageable walking distance. Shopping for food supplies would prove tricky being miles from the nearest town with public transport non-existent. The only possibility was the old van we arrived in from Germany. I could drive but had never driven a big van like that and the gear stick was so worn, it was impossible to see the markings on it. Undeterred, I practiced on the driveway and when I felt confident enough, I told the girls to get in and we set off. Looking back we laugh because I drove in second gear for ages until I could change the stick only to find ourselves in reverse, travelling backwards on the road. At the time I was terrified and the girls were screaming for me to drive forward!

Walking through the town that day, something inside gave me strength and determination to go on: to climb this new mountain, no matter how hard it would become. Selma sent us some money, which was just as well as Olivier left none, so we were able to buy food. I realised in order to survive I would have to improve my language skills but found French extremely hard to master; it certainly helped that one of the teachers spoke fluent English. Olivier found work with a travelling circus in England and phoned several times during the first week, trying to make contact with me, but I was so hurt and angry with the way he had treated us, I refused to answer his calls. His absence gave us all a peace as we adjusted to our new routine. I was no longer in fear of arguments with Olivier, stalking by my estranged husband or spiteful village gossip. Taylor and I were getting along really well, warmer weather was around the corner and I began to relax at last. Our days were spent enjoying each other's company for the first time in ages. My history seemed to be repeating itself, though I would not make the connections until a long time later.

It was a huge shock to discover I was pregnant! Too much of a shock to appreciate I had managed to drive into town again and actually purchased a pregnancy test kit from the pharmacy without any help whatsoever. Although we had spoken about another child and I had stopped taking precautions, I now realised how foolish my actions were and understood too late how wise was my friend's advice. It was too early in our relationship to consider having a child together – there were many complications in my life before we met without considering all the nagging doubts that had arisen over the past weeks. Then irrational thought kicked in and I imagined that if he actually knew I was pregnant, things might change and everything would turn out perfectly. I called Olivier and told him my news. Hearing his voice did nothing to reassure me, only make me panic even more and so I hung up, saying it was all a mistake and I needed time to think. He quickly rang back, but all I could suggest was for me to have an abortion. My heart froze as I said the words. I had not yet told Olivier about that part of my life and my two previous abortions. Their effect on me was still profound, I wasn't sure I could share it with anyone.

Early in the morning two days later he called again, asking me to marry him. Oddly that was the last thing on my mind and it caused me panic as I remembered him telling me his first wife had threatened to terminate her pregnancy if he did not marry her. That episode had definitely coloured his judgement of women. I explained we couldn't conduct those aspects of our relationship over the phone, something that important had to be discussed face to face. Besides, I was still legally married to someone else; marriage to Olivier wasn't an option. I decided with or without him I wanted this child and concentrated on my girls, spending all our time together, laughing and bonding like never before. My immediate concerns were for my unborn child. Newly arrived and with scant knowledge of the local services and language, I wondered how I would make all the arrangements for the birth. Also, shortage of money meant I could not afford to go to the doctors immediately as you had to pay for visits as a foreigner in France. Selma informed me my estranged husband had been banned from driving after being caught driving whilst drunk when he crashed his car during a chase involving the police. He had also lost his job, so I reckoned on no further maintenance forthcoming from him, but at least we were away from any possible harassment from him if he found out about my condition.

Chapter 13
RUNNING UP THAT HILL…

"The three of us spent the most wonderful months I can ever remember that summer in France. For the first time in my life I felt free of burdens and fear."

The three of us spent the most wonderful months I can ever remember that summer in France. For the first time in my life I felt free of burdens and fear. I was no longer under the oppressive control of my parents, nor terrorised by the aggressive behaviour of my husband. And though I had not then come to appreciate it, I was also free from Olivier's strange and volatile ways. It was like a never-ending holiday; we went to school together, shared meals together and indulged in endless laughter and fun. The storm, it seemed, had abated and I believed I could conquer mountains. We were invited to visit the farmer's family opposite who became good neighbours. Olivier meanwhile seemed to revert to the man I met in Germany, calling me every couple of days, though I had not forgiven him for his treatment of us. If I'm honest, I enjoyed the renewed attention he paid me. He seemed far more caring since learning of my pregnancy. He even asked if the girls and I would like to join him in England as his contract with the circus still had some time to run. I was not eager to leave my comfort zone for more unknown territory, but he persisted until I agreed. I hoped by being face to face we could talk about the future more easily. I explained I needed to see a midwife sooner rather than later and he made an appointment for me in England. I was forced to trust him again and when the arrangements were complete we joined him. The girls were more excited to see him than me; I was unsure of my feelings for him. He noticed my aloofness and in turn gave me vexed looks and spoke to me like a parent dissatisfied with a child.

"For the next few endless hours, Taylor, Grace and I sat outside the caravans in the middle of a field somewhere near Birmingham."

Arriving by ferry, we travelled from Portsmouth to Birmingham where the circus was based, all the while I was preoccupied with a need to talk things over with him. He had arranged our accommodation in two caravans, one for us and one for the girls, but I was not happy with that idea even before we reached our destination and I was shocked to see just a few caravans in a field with no sign of a circus! Nevertheless, Olivier ordered the girls into their caravan and prepared to go to bed himself, saying he was tired after driving all night to collect us. We slept on the ferry and so the girls were soon outside playing while he made it very obvious I was to go to bed with him. I suppose I could have refused but I feared the consequences and arguments that would follow so I suffered the disgrace and disgust I felt inside, afterwards lying silently in the bed while he slept, desperately wanting to join my children outside. When he finally awoke, he dressed for work, brushed aside my request to talk and told me not to make a scene as he was already late. For the next few endless hours, Taylor, Grace and I sat outside the caravans in the middle of a field somewhere near Birmingham.

Things didn't improve with time. Our relationship, strained at best, was tested over every small detail and only made me distance myself even further from Olivier. A visit from some of his work mates made me uneasy. I quickly sensed they were all heavy and continual drinkers and it worried me. I had experienced the bad effects of alcohol enough to know I did not want it in my life ever again. Olivier made an appointment for me to see the doctor, but insisted the girls remained in the caravan while he drove me to the surgery. I would not hear of it – they were eight and four years old. He forced me to do a lot of things against my will but I would not leave my daughters alone in a caravan parked in a field outside a strange city. Besides, I desperately wanted the girls to be involved in the pregnancy, I believed it was important for all our futures to include them, make them feel that they were not being cast aside in favour of the new baby.

When he arrived to take me to see the midwife I refused to get in the car and walked away from him with Taylor and Grace. At first he followed, telling me to get into the car, then his tone changed and he began shouting, using abusive language, telling me to leave. He mentioned my distant mood, insinuating the baby probably wasn't his anyway as his friends in France accused me of sleeping around while he was absent. I could not believe what I was hearing, his words were incredibly hurtful but mostly they confirmed how little I knew this man whose child I was carrying. Once again fear took over and I took the girls into one of the caravans and locked the door. He kept banging on the door throughout the night, promising to send us all back to Germany. Finally he gave up and went to sleep in the other van, returning the following morning threatening to book our flights. The girls were hungry by midday, so we came out and I prepared food for them. I called Selma. She rightly reasoned I had two choices: either to stay and stick it out with Olivier or return to Germany, but suggested seeking a refuge for us rather than going back to where my estranged husband was, which could prove dangerous. When she called back with numbers for refuges I panicked, afraid to take that step, afraid to face the future completely alone, responsible for three children. Distrust in my own ability to cope alone in the world did not so much make me decide to stay but rather decide not to go – anywhere.

The following months travelling with Olivier and the circus were awful. I suffered from severe migraine headaches and constant cystitis. He treated me merely as something to satisfy his needs, never once attempting to talk about our relationship or future. Instead he would get into bed every night insisting I accede to his demands for sex and disappear the next morning to go to work. I lost all self respect but not my childish dream of a better life. I persisted in looking for the good in Olivier, declaring my love for him again and again, despite his indifferent attitude towards me, hoping he would change and everything turn out as I originally hoped. One concession he made was to allow the girls to visit the midwife with me as I showed no sign of relenting on that issue, but I was not happy to be referred to as his wife for those purposes. When I questioned him on that point he said it was necessary as I would have no insurance cover otherwise. I was uncomfortable as what I was doing was tantamount to fraud. He simply told me to shut up as I did not speak the language. I had no idea of the way things were and should not get involved in things I did not understand. When I persisted, saying it did not seem right, he told me to forget it or he would leave.

Those words struck terror into my soul. Of all the things I could not bear was the thought of being left alone. Since my Mother had left us alone as young children to go out night after night to look for my missing Father I had this inherent fear of being abandoned. I told myself to remain calm, do as I was told and everything would be alright, just as I had told myself over and over in the dark bedroom as a child. Doing as I was told did not alter the misery of the next few months as we travelled through England. There were constant arguments and fights and we never did have time together to talk over our future as he promised. From seven in the morning I would be alone in a field with my girls until Olivier came home late at night. I would serve the meal I had prepared and then provide sex for him, like some kind of dessert. I did not know anyone and could barely speak the language. We remained with him but I felt totally abandoned.

We all missed the beautiful surroundings and freedom of the house in France and Taylor and Grace were missing their home in Germany by now along with their grandparents. We visited the nearby town and I gave the girls five pounds to make a phone call, forbidding them to mention my pregnancy, terrified my Mother would persuade me to have an abortion even from that distance. With my pulse racing I dialed their number, immediately passing the receiver to Taylor. My Mother was relieved to speak with them both and told them my Father had suffered a breakdown after our departure, and had been in hospital. They informed the police of our departure, supposing we had been kidnapped by the foreigner. She still would not accept that I was forced to make the decision to leave because of the treatment I received from them and my estranged husband. I did not know how much of my Mother's news to believe, it was not beyond her to lie or exaggerate in order to control my emotions. Afterwards the girls sat outside the telephone box and sobbed. They felt responsible for their Grandfather's distress and were severely homesick for all their friends. I hugged them close to me racked with guilt, wanting to wave a magic wand and make their lives perfect, but how could I do that? I believed I had done the best for them by leaving Germany but all I had brought them to was more heartache.

"I had always been told I could do nothing on my own by my parents, reinforced by my husband and Olivier over and over, until it was truth to me."

When Olivier found out we had contacted home he was angry. We had left Germany at the beginning of April and it was August, according to him, plenty of time for us all to adjust to our new lives, without hankering after something in the past. In order for him to control me, it was essential I had no ties with another place and no one to turn to except him. At the time I could not see his intentions or understand his thinking. All I knew was a complete lack of confidence in myself to take charge of my own life. I had always been told I could do nothing on my own by my parents, reinforced by my husband and Olivier over and over, until it was truth to me.

"…I agreed to stay, naively thinking things could change. I truly believed I loved Olivier and hoped that love and perseverance would be enough to solve our differences. Now, I understand some lessons have to be learned the hard way."

Arguments always simmered under the surface ready to erupt on a daily basis. On each occasion Olivier would blame the children or my condition saying once the baby was born the old Malaika would be back. Fed up with his comments I could not wait for the summer holidays to be over so we could return to France without him. He must have sensed this and could not accept I should want to be away from him, I was even surprised myself. Time-wise we had been together for more than a year but in reality much of that time was spent apart, conducting the relationship by phone. Out of the blue he asked me to stay with him in England until November, promising he would change if both me and the the girls did too. Frankly I failed to understand how much more changing we could do to comply with his wishes. However, I agreed to stay, naively thinking things could change. I truly believed I loved Olivier and hoped that love and perseverance would be enough to solve our differences. Now, I understand some lessons have to be learned the hard way. Was it love or another escape route from the marriage I embarked upon to escape from the frying pan of my loveless childhood? Everything we are is the end result of all we have experienced and the choices we make when faced with each situation.

"Life ricocheted around our heads: we lived in a tension of short-lived peace and outbreaks of arguments and abuse."

Life ricocheted around our heads: we lived in a tension of short-lived peace and outbreaks of arguments and abuse. If I did anything to upset the delicate balance of Olivier's equilibrium, I was told to leave immediately, and take my kids with me. Sometimes he would raise my hopes only to dash them again. Whenever I made gestures of togetherness in public he would pull away as if ashamed of me. By the end of September the girls had missed the beginning of their new school year due to my decision to stay and I was feeling bad for them. After searching for him one night when he failed to show up as he promised I shouted at him. I'd had enough and wanted an end to this impossible situation, demanding he book a ferry crossing for us to go back to France. I went back to the caravan, which had become our latest prison, followed by Olivier accusing me of losing the plot. He berated me for speaking to him like that in front of his friends, telling me I was a drama queen and attention seeker before driving off in his car. I was awake most of the night, waiting for him to return but he didn't. By seven the next morning I was more than alarmed. I was twenty four weeks pregnant, stranded in England with a travelling circus believing the unthinkable had happened and we were abandoned.

By midday his employer had visited our caravan several times to enquire as to his whereabouts and I had no choice but to say I did not know. As the day progressed I made frantic plans, contacting the German Embassy, asking for assistance to get back to France or Germany. Late in the afternoon Olivier turned up insisting I hear him out. He realised it was not working with us in England so he planned to quit the circus and take us back to France promising it would all be better once we were there. His intention was to remain in England and work until he had enough money to retire, then we would live happily ever after. Apart from feeling guilty for causing him to quit his job, I told him I did not want to have a relationship whereby he lived in one country and me, his child and my daughters lived in another. Seeing each other once a month was not my idea of a close and stable family unit, and his proposal did not bode well for our future but he insisted it was the best solution or he could lose the house in France.

Mental exhaustion and tiredness from the pregnancy caused me to be violently sick during the rough ferry crossing. Pains in my stomach were so severe I feared I was losing the baby. Even Olivier showed concern and a rare compassionate side, holding me and stroking my belly to calm me. Nevertheless, he decided before we even arrived at the house he would leave again for England in just a few days. Busy organising the girls' return to school and settling us back in the house I was surprisingly unaffected by his pending departure. He seemed more troubled, accusing me of being cold towards him and not caring. During the ensuing weeks, he called regularly to check how I was. Little concerned about Taylor and Grace, he never asked how they were, only mentioning them to insist they were not to sleep with me as it was unacceptable. He even went as far as to say I should watch out for Taylor as she was a trouble-maker, influencing Grace's opinions. I am ashamed to say I listened to his twisted view of my children and found myself clashing with Taylor more and more.

"The more time we spent together trying to work out our relationship, the more I became concerned."

By the end of October, Olivier decided it would be better if I returned to England to have the baby there and came to collect us. We would spend much needed time together as a family returning to France after the birth. I hoped his theory would work in practice! He disliked leaving his dream house behind, but I comforted him with the knowledge that we would return as soon as possible after the birth. He had secured a flat for us for a few months, but when we arrived I could barely hide my disappointment at the arrangements; it was a dump by any standards. True I had enjoyed a relatively good standard of living in Germany, but this was not about money or material possessions, I could endure any hardship as long as I felt loved but the continual upheavals were unsettling for the children and me and I realised I was going along with Olivier's plans purely to please him and cater to his wishes. None of these arrangements were my choice and I was unsure of his true feelings for me. The more time we spent together trying to work out our relationship, the more I became concerned.

Chapter 14
LOVE DON'T LIVE HERE ANYMORE...

Soon after arriving at our new temporary home, the arguments began again. Mostly they were due to the sleeping arrangements for the girls as Olivier demanded they sleep separately. Considering everything they had been through in their short lives, I sympathised with their desire to share the same bed. They had endured a good deal of trauma and change, it seemed perfectly normal they should seek solace in each other's presence, especially at night when fears and insecurities surface. Their love for each other was one absolute in a world they found hard to understand or trust. Olivier's nagging continued unabated until I told him I could bear it no longer: I would rather leave him and bring up three children alone than stay and subject us all to his incessant bullying. He was skilled at turning situations around, drawing sympathy, taking the attention away from his own shortcomings whilst highlighting the faults of others. Wearing a permanent pained expression as if all this was our doing, he begged me to help him change. I was confused – on the one hand, blinded by the love I felt for Olivier, I believed he could change and everything would work out well in the end. On the other hand

I feared his words were just empty promises and I had fallen for them yet again. Two opinions were at odds with each other, trapped inside a body that became paralysed at the thought of being on my own.

Rows were frequently about money because I was dependent on him for everything. Olivier gave me twenty pounds to do the week's shopping. Despite not knowing the value of English money, I soon realised it was an impossible task and mentioned it. He accused me of wasting money and walked out. My dilemma was the girls were due to start school and I needed to buy their uniforms. I had no choice but to wait for him to come back. Four days passed with no sign or news of him! I began to panic as we now had nothing left to eat. Desperately, I searched the flat and found a foreign note in his suitcase. Relieved, I took it to the bank but was shattered to be given only four pounds for it by the cashier. I bought some bread and bottled water and used precious coins to call the German embassy in London to ask for help. I could not use the phone at the flat as Olivier had set it as usual, to prevent outgoing calls.

"I felt dirty, a vagrant, cast off, but forced myself to go through further humiliation and briefly explained my situation..."

I felt dirty, a vagrant, cast off, but forced myself to go through further humiliation and briefly explained my situation. The person on the other end said they would call me back at the flat within twenty minutes. I can't explain how comforting it was to speak to someone in my native language again. Later I explained I wanted to go back to Germany but learned it was not possible as it was already November, and with the baby due in January the airlines would not permit me to fly at that stage of the pregnancy. I was bitterly disappointed having finally found strength to leave our unbearable situation and return to Germany, no matter what the consequences.

With the last of the money, I called Selma who was horrified to learn of our latest predicament. Sensing my desperation, she even suggested I consider having the baby adopted as alone, without income, I would find it difficult to provide for Taylor and Grace, without the added responsibility of another baby. The thought of giving my baby away was agony, but Selma had always offered practical, wise counsel and in my hopeless circumstances it seemed like a solution, however painful. I finally plucked up courage to take the girls to school without their uniforms, crying and explaining to their teachers that my partner had left me stranded without money. I felt depressed and friendless, hoping against hope they would not view me in a bad light. Dream-like, I walked into town to find the local Social Services centre. By the time I found the place I was in a terrible state. I had been crying uncontrollably, screaming silently to heaven, asking why this was happening to me. With little English and using pathetic gestures I tried to explain I wanted them to take my baby for adoption as I could not look after it. I somehow needed them to take it from me there and then – to save me from the waiting, living with the pain of my appalling decision. A lady took me into a separate room and gently spoke with me. She asked me to consider going back home to the flat and thinking about my decision for another week before making the final commitment. It was not what I wanted to hear, but I agreed and went back to the flat.

"Entreating him to stay would not change his heart towards us: I was completely alone."

The next day Olivier walked back into the flat and our lives. Characteristically, he completely ignored us initially, making us feel we were worthless and didn't exist. That behaviour continued as he came and went at his convenience. I was too scared of him to say anything and spent the time he was there in fear of upsetting him. It was bizarre getting into the same bed each night, without a word passing between us except for him repeatedly telling me my pathetic life was worth nothing. He rescued us in Germany and offered us another chance but I had blown it and I should sort my brats out. One day I humiliated myself further by falling to the floor, clinging desperately to his leg as he was about to leave for work. It had no effect on him whatsoever. Entreating him to stay would not change his heart towards us: I was completely alone.

The week passed and I knew I could not put my baby up for adoption. No matter what the circumstances were for us, I could not give my baby away. I explained things in simple terms to Taylor and Grace. They were amazing – so strong and insistent I keep this brother or sister of theirs, declaring they would leave, too, if I went ahead with adoption plans. The power of their words, coming from such young hearts gave me the strength to believe we could face whatever hardships Olivier inflicted on us. When I returned to Social Services, the lady there was really pleased with my decision. She made phone calls and arranged a translator for the following day when they accompanied me to another office. I explained my circumstances and reasons for being in England; they explained I was not eligible for housing but organised some benefits for me and made preparations for the birth. I learned financial help could take up to six weeks, which was worrying as Christmas was approaching. They advised me to stay where I was, not to make myself homeless unless my life or that of my children was in danger. If such an emergency developed I was to call 999 immediately. Somehow I could not believe things would ever get that bad. I still nurtured a foolish dream that my hero, in the guise of Olivier, would turn up one day and we would live happily ever after!

Reality did not dance in tune with my dreams. Olivier continued to ignore me most of the time, getting on with his daily routine without a care in the world. I had no money whatsoever, but for the sake of my children I demeaned myself by using his food. My heart bled for my girls, they had no choice in their circumstances, they were at the mercy of their Mother who was responsible for this unacceptable situation but could do nothing themselves to change it. One day I was called to the school as Taylor was unwell. Very pregnant but trying hard to run to get there I was shocked to see an ambulance by the entrance. Taylor was lying on the floor of her classroom attended to by paramedics: she had fainted. The teacher and paramedics told me she would be fine but I was to take her home for complete rest. As I cared for her, I tried to talk to Olivier hoping he might realise what our conflict was doing to her but he accused her of attention-seeking like her Mother; we were both drama queens. His words stung like a slap on the face. I could not believe he could be so cruel. He continued to come and go during the week and at weekends he did not stay in the flat at all.

Shortly before Christmas during a routine visit to the midwife's surgery, I mentioned I could not remember the last time I felt the baby move inside me. Unable to trace a heartbeat, she consulted with the doctor and they insisted I go immediately to the hospital with my partner. Embarrassed, I briefly explained that my partner was no longer interested, although we still lived together. In the end I was taken to hospital in an ambulance after collecting Taylor and Grace as I could not disappear to hospital without them. By now I was terrified that my unborn child was dead inside me and tortured myself with recriminations that all this was my fault: I had not wanted my baby enough; had even considered its adoption and now I had paid the ultimate price. My daughters were wonderful, caring for me in their child-like way and it was with immense joy that I finally felt a small movement of the baby. I knew beyond any doubt then that I wanted the precious child I carried.

Having no way of getting back home and no contact for Olivier, I reluctantly gave the midwife the number for his sister. I did not want to burden her but had no other choice. She arrived and took us home and I learned that she had called several times but received no answer. I later discovered the reason: Olivier switched the button on the phone to silent mode. I was not even aware such a facility existed but it frightened me to consider he could plan such an action. We found him in the kitchen, eating his meal as if nothing untoward had happened. He merely chastised me for keeping the girls out so late on a school night. When I explained where we had been and why, he did not seem unduly bothered but simply finished eating his meal.

"One day, my paranoia caused me to believe I saw my estranged husband waiting on the corner opposite the flat."

My mental condition declined drastically in those weeks leading up to Christmas. I spent most days in the flat by myself, just looking out of the window or watching mindless television. I began smoking again, which was something I was vehemently against, but too weak to stop. One day, my paranoia caused me to believe I saw my estranged husband waiting on the corner opposite the flat. My throat constricted in panic as I questioned how he came to be there. My Mother knew where we were living so I could only imagine she had told him. Irrationally I continued to torment myself; he had no money, no car so how was it possible? Terrified I jumped back from the window. I wanted to call Olivier – to scream to him for help but having no contact number I called his sister again in desperation. Her husband came over immediately and did actually see a man standing outside, though he later disappeared after getting in to a car with someone.

When Olivier arrived home that night, I told him what had happened. He seemed concerned at the prospect of my husband knowing where we were but he immediately blamed it on Taylor, accusing her of calling her Father to tell him whereabouts. I could not believe Taylor would do such a thing but in a moment of irrational thinking I dialed his number in Germany. His Mother answered the phone and with hands shaking, I disguised my voice, asking to speak to him. She informed me he was asleep. Relieved I replaced the receiver but it dawned on me the extent of my paranoia. Olivier's mood turned to full-on aggression. He accused me again of being a drama queen, always seeking attention with my pathetic games and told me I was a gold-digger, just like his ex-wife. Oddly, his last remark hurt the most. I had no money, I had given up everything I owned to be with him including my secure existence and my children had sacrificed their familiar lives. When I reminded him of that he simply said our lives were completely worthless and if it hadn't been for him rescuing us, I would be dead by now. I should thank him for everything he had done for us. Incredulous as his accusations were they sank into my very being and took hold of my spirit, causing me to feel lower than the ground on which I walked.

"His response was immediate and shocking: he punched me hard in the face and went to bed."

Throughout Christmas, Olivier made an effort to pretend everything was fine between us as his daughter, who was the same age as Taylor, visited. Unlike him I could not easily switch moods after his daily assassination of my character and my attitude caused even more arguments. Each time he punished us by walking out the door with his daughter, leaving us behind like filth to be scraped off his shoe. He blamed everything on Taylor. If there were disagreements between the girls, it was always Taylor's fault, his daughter was never to blame. It was frustrating to watch as I could see they were all just being children and blame was too harsh a word to apply to any of them, but Olivier would not listen to my reasoning. His daughter had been sleeping on the sofa in the lounge but he decided she should sleep in his bed and I had to manage on the couch. I protested as the pregnancy was too advanced for me to sleep there. His response was immediate and shocking: he punched me hard in the face and went to bed.

I got no sleep that night, my body was in shock and my mind in turmoil. I was scared but foolishly my overriding emotion was guilt. If only I had kept my mouth shut and done as I was told he would have no reason to hit me. All I could reflect on was my status as a foreigner, pregnant, stranded in a country with two young children, with no rights. My lip bled badly and remained very swollen the next morning. From his continued animosity towards me I knew I could expect no change of heart from Olivier, so I called the embassy and told them to go ahead with arrangements to get us back to Germany as soon as possible after the birth, which although estimated as weeks away could occur at any time. Olivier carried on with his life, ignoring me, only returning to the flat to change before going out again. It was in desperation I asked him to take me to the hospital one day as I experienced bleeding. He relented after the girls went to school.

Present during the examinations, Olivier asked countless questions about my condition and that of the baby. The answers he received disclosed to him for the first time my history of abortions though he chose to say nothing then. Although checks revealed all was well with the pregnancy, the doctor wanted me to stay overnight for observations. I could not trust Olivier to look after Taylor and Grace, his whole attitude towards them caused me to doubt he would take care of them in my absence, and so I discharged myself. He was extremely angry, threatening to hold me totally responsible if anything happened to his baby.

"I don't know why but perhaps I hoped he would understand something of the pain I still felt terminating those earlier pregnancies."

I don't know why but perhaps I hoped he would understand something of the pain I still felt terminating those earlier pregnancies. Perhaps he would appreciate I had made terrible mistakes in my past and understand how precious this new life was to me. How wrong I was. He drove me home from the hospital embarking on a tirade of spiteful abuse, fuelled by the fact that I would not trust Taylor and Grace to his care and my decision not to tell him the circumstances of my past abortions. He accused me of being a prostitute, sleeping with countless Russian soldiers during their occupation of the former east Germany. Deeply wounded that he could hold such an opinion of me and exhausted by his barrage of abuse, I refused to be drawn in to any conversation with him and remained silent.

At the end of January the midwife was concerned as, according to her calculations, I was considerably overdue, but still I refused to go into hospital. My own intuition and maths convinced me my baby would be born in February. I planned to take the girls to a film evening at school on the first of that month and was dismayed to feel familiar pains as we prepared to leave the flat, but trying not to show alarm, we went anyway. I did not want to let the girls down as I had promised them this treat. It was about nine in the evening as we walked back home and I shared my conviction with them that their new brother or sister would arrive soon. They were very excited as I put them to bed. Olivier did not arrive home until after ten and went straight to bed. I covered myself up and sat on the sofa, hoping I could delay the birth until daylight but it was impossible and a little later I was forced to wake Olivier and tell him the baby was on its way. His accused me of seeking attention again and told me to leave him alone, so I went back to the lounge. By now the contractions were every twenty minutes but I remained calm, checking my timings and breathing steadily.

"Taylor tried to tell me repeatedly that Olivier was only interested in me, not them, but I chose to ignore her intuitive input reluctant to face the painful truth."

Some time later, Olivier came into the lounge. When he realised the baby was definitely on its way, he suddenly galvanised into action asking what he should do. I was upset we had not made these arrangements together like any normal couple preparing for the arrival of their child, but it was too late for regrets. He called his sister to come and be with Taylor and Grace. They would not go to school, and before leaving for the hospital I promised them I would be home as quickly as I could that day. I intended to make my hospital stay as short as possible, but babies have their own schedules and following an extended and painful labour, I finally gave birth to our daughter Summer in the early hours of the next day. Surprisingly Olivier stayed with me, leaving later to collect the girls. He took the following week off work but if I thought it was in any way to help out, I was deluded. He did not get involved in looking after the baby or doing anything around the house. I was expected to do it all while he used the time to catch up on sleep. I chose not to confront him or ask for the help I so desperately needed. I know I was still frightened of him but also secretly, if somewhat foolishly, believed in the possibility of a future for us all together. I hoped tolerating all his moods might prove my love for him and he would revert to the man I met in Germany. With hindsight of course I can see the foolishness of my thinking. Taylor tried to warn me repeatedly about Olivier, but I chose to ignore her intuitive input reluctant to face the painful truth.

It soon became apparent the flat was too small for all of us and although our relationship was almost non-existent, I decided not to go back to Germany at that time. I'd had enough of moving around and Taylor and Grace had been in their new school for less than six months; it was not fair to expect them to be uprooted again. Olivier wasn't happy with this decision, accusing me once more of being a gold-digger, telling me crudely to get out of his life, taking my pathetic possessions in black bin liners just as I had arrived. I was trapped, it seemed I had nothing to look forward to yet I could not go back. Eventually we moved to a bigger house with a small garden in the same town. I spoke to my social worker who was as confused as me at the outcome of my situation but she advised me to stay with Olivier and not make myself homeless as it was by no means guaranteed I would be offered any help from the local authorities. Knowing I was in touch with Social Services, Olivier continued to verbally express his low opinion of me but seemed cautious about actually throwing me out on the streets.

Summer was unsettled as a baby. She would cry constantly day and night. When I walked Taylor and Grace to school, she would cry all the way there and back again, only quieting when I held her. I was soon exhausted, having no help from Olivier, who always demanded the house was clean with meals and laundry provided when required. A mother from school offered to look after Summer for a while on the condition I slept and did no washing or housework. Taylor would often get up in the night to help me with Summer as Olivier remained asleep or away for days at a time. It was his way of punishing me for not obeying his rules. Sometimes after feeding and changing, I would leave Summer with Taylor and Grace watching her. Observing this, Olivier accused me of being a terrible mother, threatening to call Social Services. On one occasion his anger was so violent he threw the games Taylor and Grace were playing onto the floor and smashed them. The girls were terrified of him but I dare not confront him, I feared the punishment that would inevitably follow if I ever questioned him or complained. For much of the time I would sleep on the sofa in the lounge, with Summer in my arms, or share a bed with Taylor or Grace. It disgusted me to get into his bed as he would invariably satisfy his sexual needs without any exchange of feelings.

"I was so desperate for his love and approval, I would repeatedly tell myself he could change and the anger and violent outbreaks were the exception not the rule."

Whenever his daughter came to stay Olivier would put on a pretence that everything was fine between us. At first I went along with this facade, believing he wanted reconciliation, though he seldom apologised for his behaviour. Taylor would always tell me he was playing games with me. Even at nine, she had an awareness beyond her years but there was always a part of me living in denial of reality: hoping for a change of heart, not wanting to give up. I was so desperate for his love and approval, I would repeatedly tell myself he could change and the anger and violent outbreaks were the exception not the rule. He kept us all living in a tension dictated by his moods. Perversely, the more he withheld his love and attention, the more I chased after it, but he continued to abandon us overnight and also for whole weekends, not disclosing where he was going or when I could expect him back. It proved another blow to the foundations of my self esteem as it dawned on me his desire to have a child together in a loving partnership was nothing more than a sham on his part.

"I loathed my status: a cross between Cinderella and sexual plaything…"

I was sick to my soul of the daily round of arguments, fights and pretence. I loathed my status: a cross between Cinderella and sexual plaything, but if I dared to challenge him on any issue he was quick to crush me both physically and emotionally. He did not like it when I mimicked his swearing; he would threaten me by standing with his face right up to mine telling me I was a slut and prostitute, worthless, not even entitled to breathe the same air as him. I should take my pitiful black bin liners and go back to where I came from. I hated what my life had become but as soon as he walked out the door, with no assurance of when or if he would come back, all my phobias rushed in to haunt me with fears of being alone.

When my indignation surfaced I would confront him whenever he deigned to return home, even though I knew my questions would bring retribution. While I was changing Summer on the bathroom floor during one such encounter, he turned and kicked me in the face. The metal toe cap of his boot cut my lip and caused bleeding but his only comment was I deserved everything I got. Taylor witnessed what he had done and shouted at him saying he was no better than her Father. Olivier did not like that at all and went towards her as if to strike. Holding Summer in my arms I placed myself in his way and told him he would have to kill me before laying a finger on my children. He left the house immediately. Remembering the recommendation of Social Services, I phoned the police and informed them of the incident. They called at the house and took all the details preparing to return later and speak to Olivier but he did not come home until the following day.

"Once again my seesaw emotions caused me to panic when I considered the thought of him leaving us for good."

That time he apologised for the way he had been acting and offered to move out of the house leaving me and the girls alone. Once again my seesaw emotions caused me to panic when I considered the thought of him leaving us for good. Why did I feel like that? Why would I even consider staying with someone who continually shunned me and used physical violence against me? Looking back I can see how the events caused my emotional instability. From as far back as I could remember I was on a quest to find a perfect partnership that would dispel all the distorted images of tainted love I carried with me. I wrongly believed relational success depended largely on me doing things right because I had been conditioned to think everything bad that happened to me was my fault. I could not see the child within, desperately wanting to be loved, fearing to be left alone, being made to suppress emotions and put up with every blow life dealt me because things were never as bad as they seemed.

I knew I needed to take some time out and told Olivier I would like to go back to Germany for a break. I was exhausted and though I didn't understand at the time, I was suffering from post-natal depression as I struggled to feel normal maternal instincts and bond with Summer. Part of me associated her arrival with the rejection from Olivier. I needed time and space to to recharge my batteries; I wanted to see my friend and the girls needed to see their grandparents. My final request was as much a surprise to me as it was to him, but I asked him if he would take care of Summer while I was away. To my absolute surprise he consented and booked tickets for our flight. I arranged to stay with Selma and she met us at the airport. Taylor preferred to stay at my parents' house but Grace chose to remain with me. It was wonderful to be with someone who was kind and caring and it was an enormous relief to tell her everything without feeling judged. It compensated in some way for the rejection I experienced again at the hands of my family. None of them spoke to me, apart from one cousin who had the decent manners to acknowledge us and ask how we were coping in a foreign country.

"My hopes were high that the short separation had helped Olivier appreciate us more but I was in for yet another shock."

Selma was sure I had made the right decision to leave Germany, to escape the pressure of my family's narrow-minded speculation and rejection as well as the ordeal we suffered at the hands of my estranged husband. However, she was shocked when I shared some of the awful things we had lived through during the past year. My arms were still covered in bruises from the latest violence and although I did not elaborate on that, as an intelligent woman I'm sure she was able to fill in the gaps. Olivier called every day and often several times to see how we were. I think he found looking after his daughter for the first time since her birth quite demanding, and was keen to reassure himself I would return and take over that role. The week passed all too quickly, and our plane touched down at Heathrow to an anxious Olivier, waiting to greet us with Summer. He gave us all a hug and welcomed us home much to the astonishment of Taylor and Grace. Not once, in all our travels had he ever welcomed us home! We stood watching the planes while he smoked a cigarette before driving us home. Both girls were trying hard to hold back their tears, sad to be away from Germany once more. Summer had learnt to crawl during my absence and I immediately felt guilty for going away without her.

I told Olivier that Selma and her husband planned to visit us in the coming half term. He seemed pleased with that, liking them both. My hopes were high that the short separation had helped Olivier appreciate us more but I was in for yet another shock.

"…I chose to betray her trust in me, swayed by Olivier's warped and twisted opinion of my innocent child."

Within a matter of days the arguments resumed. He was forever blaming Taylor for every disagreement, accusing her of being evil and vicious, wanting to break us up. After all he had done for us he said we should be grateful and I must smack her bottom or put soap in her mouth for causing so much upset. I do not condone smacking children for any reason due mainly to all the physical punishment I endured as a child under the strict authoritarian regime of my Father. When Olivier walked out on us again I was so distraught I, too, blamed Taylor and actually pulled her towards me and put soap in her mouth. I am ashamed of what I was reduced to. Under no circumstances did she deserve that kind of treatment. All along she had only wanted my happiness and safety. She always supported me, helping me in so many ways – both by loving me unconditionally as well as looking after Summer. Often Taylor would get up in the night when I was feeding Summer just to keep me company. She had become my surrogate partner and best friend and though only ten, was seldom free to be the child she actually was. Taylor knew how much I was hurting and wanted nothing more than to ease my pain and yet I chose to betray her trust in me, swayed by Olivier's warped and twisted opinion of my innocent child.

When he condescended to come back to the house, he demanded major changes. I was to be much more strict with Taylor, giving her clear rules to stop annoying him. He didn't like the fact that she always helped me with Summer – probably because he never did and it pricked his conscience – but I see now he was also jealous of the closeness they shared. I was on income support by then and Olivier worked pretty much to provide for his own needs, never considering we were his responsibility, even his own daughter. I bought food with my allowance but if ever there was a lack of items in the cupboards he would shout abuse at me, asking what kind of woman I was, answering his rhetorical question by declaring I was incapable of doing anything right. He was not surprised my husband got drunk and hit me: only a drunk person could bear to live under the same roof. In an outburst of bravado I told him my income support would only provide food for my children and myself and he could go to hell. That only served to make him angrier, shouting and swearing abuse at Taylor. She was ultimately the one held responsible: it was always her fault.

"Olivier's frequent rages led him to destroy the children's dinner…take the fuses out of the washing machine …and even take the key out of the electricity meter when he went out…"

Olivier's frequent rages led him to destroy the children's dinner I had prepared, take the fuses out of the washing machine when I refused to do his washing and even take the key out of the electricity meter when he went out, leaving me unable to obtain a top up until he came back. As an additional punishment he would refrain from speaking to me for days and ignore Summer. The rest of the time he came and went in the house as it suited him only making an effort to control his temper and irrational actions when his other daughter came to stay. It was customary for him to take her out for the day, leaving us all behind, including Summer. She was not a content baby, crying all the time and only calm when I held her in my arms. It grieved my heart to see all three of them ostracised like that, and then I would fall into the trap of blaming myself, wishing I had consented to his ridiculous rules if only for their sake. Over and over he would tell me to clear out with my kids and my black bin liners, playing on my fears of returning home and admitting to my parents I was wrong to leave with the foreigner.

"…I was learning to obey Olivier our of fear not love, as to do anything else was social suicide for me and the children…"

His son came to live with us for a while. I did not mind, in fact I enjoyed having him around. He had problems in his relationship with his Dad but I was convinced love and attention would make a huge difference in his life. Olivier told me to mind my own business as I did not understand English enough to comment. I was used to him criticising my language skills, after all, my knowledge of English was only through practicing with the girls and other mums at school, but my maternal intuition told me the boy was desperate to be loved and accepted by his Father. However, I was learning to obey Olivier our of fear not love, as to do anything else was social suicide for me and the children, so I withdrew even more into my own world where you didn't complain about anything you just kept quiet and put up with the hand you had been dealt.

Chapter 15
TRUE COLOURS...

Despite my ten year old daughter constantly telling me things were not going to improve and that Olivier did not love me, I chose to live in passive acceptance of my fate. It was a nightmare existence, not just for me but for the children as well, though I doubt I fully appreciated that at the time. The greater nightmare though was the prospect of returning to Germany, so I hung on desperately hoping for change. Olivier meanwhile continued much as he had before. He frequently switched off the electricity to prevent me using appliances, and fixed the phone so I could not make calls but it was on a mental level he chose to wear me down until I had no self-esteem and suffered from depression. The verbal abuse was a daily occurrence as he constantly reminded me everything in the house belonged to him and we had no possessions or rights. Only his generosity and our black bin liners stood between us and destitution. He called me a German bitch, gold-digger and ungrateful slut, telling me no one was twisting my arm to remain, and I should remember, were not for him I would probably have been killed by my ex-husband. He even sympathised with him, understanding his need for drink to make it possible to live with me. I couldn't pull myself out of the worthless pit in which I lived. Even my favourite book that inspired me so much when I was stalked by my ex was no longer an inspiration; I could not even open it. I couldn't understand how I could be a gold-digger when I was surviving on money from Social Services and not from him, but as soon as I opened my mouth to protest, Olivier would relentlessly bulldoze more life out of me.

Shortly before Selma and Andres arrived, Olivier decided to move again. I checked with the council who advised me I was still not eligible for housing so I had no other choice but to move with him. It was a breath of fresh air to have my friends' company, and as Olivier knew them well he did not feel threatened. They helped us decorate the new house and when we were alone, Selma patiently listened to my questions and offered as much advice as she could, all the while making it clear she would not be able to endure the life I chose. Assuming I would not have the courage to tell them about our problems, Olivier put on a front that all was well between us. Unable to keep up his act, he walked out on the day they were to return to Germany. Though they knew everything, they were shocked at his behaviour and I was acutely embarrassed. He returned just in time to take them to the airport acting as though nothing had happened but immediately they departed he accused them of being gold-diggers like me. He hired a people-carrier to transport us around and being self-employed, lost a week's work due to their visit. When I attempted to defend them, reminding him they had paid their way during their visit, he simply continued his insults. I could bear it no longer and lashed out at him, slapping his face. He retaliated immediately by punching me full-on in the face with his fist, catching my eye which instantly swelled up, telling me not to mess with him. I was a parasite and troublemaker who would do well to get out of his house and follow my friends back to Germany.

Reluctant to draw attention to myself, I stayed indoors for the next couple of weeks. No matter how I tried to disguise my injured eye with make-up, the bruising was very apparent. I denied Taylor and Grace the pleasure of having friends over to play, I was ashamed people would discover what really happened in our house. Without seeing the comparisons, I was now living exactly the same life as my Mother. Momentarily a revelation would hit me as Olivier shouted at me or called me a filthy name, reminding me of how my Father spoke to my Mother but mostly I was oblivious to the similarities. Taylor spent more and more time at friends' houses unwilling to be in Olivier's company. I took her to see several therapists in the hope that she would be able to talk about her anxieties but they made no headway with her. Olivier and I did not speak properly from October to Christmas that year and whenever his daughter came to stay, it led to further arguments and accusations against my children, causing him to walk out time and time again.

"The effect Olivier's relentless character assassination had on me was total. On a conscious and sub-conscious level I believed I was valueless…"

The level of self-debasement to which I had sunk immobilised me completely. I did not consider myself capable of doing anything on my own or for myself. Even though I was the only one caring for my children, I did not see myself as able to accomplish anything. The effect Olivier's relentless character assassination had on me was total. On a conscious and sub-conscious level I believed I was valueless and each time he abused me, instead of stirring me to act against his bullying, it reinforced all the negative things he was instilling in my mind. Summer was very close to Taylor, much closer than she was to me or her Father because Taylor looked after her almost entirely then. She would come home from school and take Summer with her to do the shopping, while I was often in bed suffering with migraine headaches and stress if I had been unable to contact Olivier during the day. He continued to victimise Taylor and I now understand he was jealous of her bond with Summer. Although I knew in my heart she was not to blame for our problems, I was too weak and vulnerable to confront him anymore, and I shamefully let Taylor compensate for both incapable parents.

Both she and Grace desperately needed a break from the daily strain, and so I swallowed my pride and made plans for them to go to stay with their grandparents in Germany for the upcoming half term. To my complete surprise, my Mother asked if she could return with the girls and stay with us for a week as she had never laid eyes on her youngest granddaughter. I agreed, although Olivier was not at all happy at the prospect. Then, on an impulse, he booked a week's holiday to Majorca for me, Summer and him while the girls went to Germany. I hated the idea of going away somewhere without them, as if I was off to enjoy myself the minute they were out of the way, but it wasn't like that. Once Olivier made up his mind, opposing him was futile and deep inside I harbourbed the thought that it might turn things around, even at that late stage, and we could continue as a happy family. His whole attitude changed as he looked forward to the three of us going on holiday together, and it reinforced my opinion that he did not consider Taylor and Grace as part of that family.

In a climate of hope and still living in denial of our fractured lives, I bought Olivier a ring for his birthday and Valentines Day. Untypically, Olivier also bought me a present – a ring, and presented it to me saying we were now officially engaged. Despite craving a reconciliation, there was no way I would consider getting engaged or married but he kept talking about it as if it was decided. Characteristically, after a couple of days, he reverted to his old grumpy and abusive self. I was constantly tired because Summer was still waking every night crying and I would have to get up, give her a bottle and hold her until she finally went to sleep. Unable to participate in sex at his whim Olivier would punish me by staying in bed all the next day, leaving me to entertain the baby alone. His only interest, apart from sex and eating, was shopping so we trailed around after him all day and endured sleepless nights. I called the girls every day concerned about them, and worried what might happen if they bumped into their Father or even be taken to meet him by my Mother.

Finally, the week was over and we flew back to England to await the arrival of Taylor, Grace and my Mother. I had not spoken to her, other than to discuss arrangements for the girls, in almost three years and the time she spent with us was awkward to say the least. I found it difficult to be with her – our dysfunctional past and her need to control everything made it impossible to bridge the divide in one week, so our contact was punctuated with long silences. Olivier, on the other hand, took advantage of my Mother being a captive audience and made the most of every opportunity to berate her for causing him so much trouble, demanding an apology from her. Although Mum pleaded with him to leave the past behind, his incessant bullying upset her and she spent much of the time crying. Taylor and Grace would sit with their Grandmother, comforting her, and for the first time, Taylor opened up about much that had gone on before we left Germany.

She said it was not all her Grandmother's fault: her Father had caused much of the mayhem, even threatening to kill me on occasions. He instilled in Taylor that Olivier was only interested in me and as soon as it was convenient he intended to abandon the girls in a forest somewhere. All stuff of sinister fairy tales perhaps, but to a young child the effect of his malicious intent was profound; it explained Taylor's reluctance to go out anywhere with Olivier in the early days. She shared with us for the first time she had seen her Father standing in our flat the night we were watching the fireworks. My blood ran cold. It was as I had believed all along. My husband had actually been on our balcony spying on me and even in the flat while we were there. During the time my Father refused to speak to me, he would circle the block around our apartment every night as he knew my husband continually tried to break-in. Although Taylor's revelations brought back the horror-story element of our life back then, it confirmed to me that my intuition then had been right. All those times I had imagined I was going insane, with images of my husband stalking me was in fact a survival instinct kicking in and warning me. We all ended the evening crying, except Olivier who walked out, angry he had received no apology.

"Somehow the verbal abuse was worse than the physical violence. I had no defence against it, no fight in me to deflect his damaging words. I just accepted them and they hung over me like dark, oppressive clouds."

To cap it all, he refused to take my Mother back to the airport for her flight home and it was only after I pleaded with him he relented. My Mother said she would never visit us again and I knew my Father would bear a grudge for an indefinite time. Afterwards I sat with the girls, sharing their tears. Despite everything in the past, it upset me to see my Mother treated so badly. I knew it would only be a matter of time before I was punished because an apology had not been forthcoming from her and true to form, Olivier resumed his incessant verbal abuse to me. He insulted my family and friends, accusing them all of being worthless gold-diggers and especially me: I was the worst offender, not deserving to breathe the same air as him. When he spat in my face before walking away, I just stood there like a little child, accepting everything he said. Taylor shouted at him, saying it was no way to treat a woman. In response he shouted back at her saying her Mother was nothing like a woman, only a pathetic piece of shit with a shit life. I was nothing more than a slut, just as Taylor would be too. When Taylor begged me to say something – to fight back, I am ashamed to say I did nothing, not even in defense of my beautiful little girl. Somehow the verbal abuse was worse than the physical violence. I had no defence against it, no fight in me to deflect his damaging words. I just accepted them and they hung over me like dark, oppressive clouds.

Olivier's insidious campaign against Taylor continued, but I was unaware of the insane level of his hatred of her and too damaged to fight back. The bond between Taylor and Summer continually incensed him, arousing new jealousies and spitefulness. Whenever Olivier posed a physical threat to any of the children, losing my apathy, I would immediately spring into action, placing myself firmly in his path. If he attempted to hit any of them he would have to seriously injure me first because I would fight like a lioness protecting her cubs. He was cunning and chose the seemingly less aggressive path of derogatory assault, verbally inflicting wounds that would not be immediately apparent. He blamed me for being too soft in the discipline of my children, failing to appreciate I wanted to behave differently to my parents. I chose to show my children unconditional love first and out of that, instruction that guided without condemnation. Irritated by the fact that I never backed his type of authority, Olivier barked orders at everyone but especially Taylor, insisting she was out to destroy our future together. He warned she would kick me in the teeth one day, leaving me behind, making nothing of her life and probably becoming pregnant by the time she was fourteen. Summarising his contempt he declared he would not piss on her if she were on fire. Such appalling input for a tender young soul to receive.

In contrast to Olivier's childish approach, Taylor's insight was mature. She constantly challenged me to see what I was doing with my life by staying with this man. I remember her vowing she would never allow a man to treat her the way I had been treated. Her body was still that of an immature young girl, but she chose to adopt the mind of an adult, ahead of her time. Her innocent childhood had been stolen and replaced by the pressures of life in a big bad world. Taylor became increasingly frustrated with our situation, wanting to run away; she suffered terribly both at home and falling out with her friends due to the stress. I think she only remained out of loyalty to me, hoping I would wake up soon and face reality. I was no help, wanting us to suppress emotions for the sake of peace and all the while living with extreme paranoia: where could I go if I left, what could I do? My self-confidence was at its lowest point, or so I thought. Convinced I could not speak or understand English properly, I expected no help in my adopted country but neither could I return to the country of my birth. I never went out apart from to and from the school and the supermarket. I was afraid to meet people in case they discovered anything about me or failed to understand my pathetic attempts at their language.

One week, one of the mums from school invited me to join a 'mum and toddler's' group held in a church hall nearby. I was surprised to see one of Grace's ex-teachers running the group. She was a lovely lady and there was something very calming about being in her company. She was always smiling and genuinely friendly. She reminded me of Selma, and I eventually plucked up courage to share something of my background when we met after the group for a coffee. It was the first time I talked about my past with anyone other than my closest friend but it felt right and she was always keen to listen. I looked forward to our meetings because apart from the toddler group I had no outlet of any kind.

Olivier was hardly around now, merely coming back to the house to sleep and change before going out again; at weekends he did not come home at all until late on Sunday nights. I did not dare question where he was during his absences, and rather innocently did not suspect he might be seeing other women. Whenever I saw an opportunity I would entreat him to stay in with me but it seemed he flicked a switch and was not even interested in sex. I should have read the signs but my paranoia filled my waking thoughts, squeezing out any rational thinking. He did occasionally imply if I changed and sorted my children out he might consider reconciliation. Otherwise he punished me for not obeying his rules and I believed every word he said. He managed to turn the financial support I received into a weapon against me, accusing me of not trusting him to take care of us, suggesting I pay him back all the money he had spent on us. I was constantly told to improve my English and forbidden to teach Summer any German words, which I had difficulty remembering, afraid for so long to speak my native tongue in his presence, apologising if I ever reverted back.

"Still dependent on my pathetic situation, addicted to the adrenaline rush I experienced when I had done something wrong and awaited punishment."

When the school summer holidays arrived, I again arranged for Taylor and Grace to spend time with my parents which made them very excited. I dreaded being alone with Summer at the mercy of Olivier, but did not feel strong enough to go too. Still dependent on my pathetic situation, addicted to the adrenaline rush I experienced when I had done something wrong and awaited punishment. Almost as if the attention and the punishment it brought was better than the despairing loneliness suffocating my heart. After the girls left, Erin, the lady from the toddler group, came round to the house for a coffee. She was due to go to Australia on holiday for the entire summer and wanted to see me before leaving. She brought such a sense of peace with her and I was overwhelmed by her concern and kindness. She mentioned her and her husband attended a church every Sunday and said I would be welcome to join them when they returned from Australia but only if I chose to. She briefly explained people met there to share their stories, have coffee and sing and I promised her I would consider her offer. It was strange to be given a choice. I was used to being told what to do by my parents, my husband and Olivier. As she left, she said she loved me lots and 'God Bless'. I felt very confused: how could she love me – she hardly knew me? I presumed it must be because she went to church. I had heard about people like that, mostly from a negative point of view, but she did seem genuinely nice and promised to send me a card.

In the girls' absence I put a great deal of effort into getting along with Olivier as I continued to deceive myself things could be fixed. It was exhausting trying not to upset him, carefully choosing my words so he would not walk out on me. Summer was missing her sisters but by now she was sleeping through the night and talking, it was pure joy to be with her during the day. In the morning she would get up to have breakfast with her Daddy for ten minutes, as she was always in bed when he came home at night, and he never wanted to spend time with her at weekends. Olivier's son came to stay with us again. He was a few years older than Taylor, and he and I got on well, but he did not stay for long. Olivier had no patience with him, punching and hitting him if anything was wrong. He did confide in me of his love for his Dad but added he feared him so much and respected me for being strong and standing up to Olivier. That was laughable: I was never strong, merely deluding myself I could fix the impossible. When I discovered his son was drinking excessively and taking drugs I told Olivier hoping he would reach out to help him. I was mistaken; it led to further violence and his son left, for which I felt sadly responsible.

The holidays passed too slowly for me as I seldom went out, and apart from my daughter I had no company but my own. I was looking forward to the girls coming back from Germany, but the excitement was short-lived. One morning, Summer came in and gave me a hug in bed and when Olivier asked her to hug him she pushed him away calling him a skunk. He swore profusely and blamed Taylor – my slut of a daughter – for Summer's reaction, accusing her of teaching Summer to speak to him like that. He told me Taylor was no longer allowed in the house until she changed her behaviour. At first I laughed, thinking this must be some kind of joke, reminding him he swore in front of them all the time, but Olivier had a set of rules for my children and a set for himself. He told me Grace could come back but not Taylor. I could see by the look in his eyes that he meant what he said. I was devastated, what on earth was I supposed to do? I couldn't bear to leave Taylor with her grandparents but I was faced with an unthinkable choice: either my daughter or Olivier. The thought of the consequences, whatever choice I made, filled me with dread.

I reluctantly called my Mother and told her what had happened. She wasn't surprised by my news, as Taylor had been talking about her home situation all the time and declared she had no intention of coming back to England. I spoke with Taylor on the phone, dying inside. How could I choose my wretched life with Olivier over her. However, she explained she was tired of all the fighting and being blamed for everything and she wanted to escape. I tried to reason with her, for my sake and that of her sisters. I asked her to be brave and make one enormous effort to get on with Olivier but she was adamant. Apart from being unable to imagine life without Taylor, my fears increased as I considered what she would have to endure staying with my parents. She did not know them as I did, they were able to put on an act for a short time but long term it would be horrendous for her to live with them. I couldn't agree to it and I begged her to reconsider but nothing would persuade her to change her mind. The final blow came when Grace declared she wanted to stay with Taylor. My chest felt so tight I imagined I was having heart failure.

"I was torn apart. I knew I could not lose my children for this man, no matter how much he controlled my life."

I was torn apart. I knew I could not lose my children for this man, no matter how much he controlled my life. Olivier had given me his credit card to purchase something for him on the internet. Without asking I also purchased tickets for Summer and me to fly back to Germany the following day. I did not want to go back to Germany to live, but how could I remain in another country without my two daughters? I called my Mother back and told her to expect me; she agreed to accommodate us all until I found somewhere to live. Waiting to leave seemed endless and I was so stressed I could do little else but cry. When Olivier arrived home from work that night he saw the pain I was in, and in an unusual expression of compassion offered to pay for me to fly out to Germany and stay with the girls for a while. He even volunteered to financially help me settle back there if that was my ultimate decision. I felt so bad for stealing from him to buy the tickets and once more harboured thoughts that perhaps it was possible for him to change and for us all to be a happy family.

When he left for work the next morning it was all I could do not to throw up in front of him. I paced around the house, overcome by weakness and fear of the consequences when he found out what I had done. Finally, I could bear it no longer; I knew I could not deceitfully leave him. I called my Mother and lied to my own children saying I could not find Summer's passport. Though relieved at not going back to Germany I was petrified of telling Olivier what I had done. I told my Mother to put Grace on a plane straight away and then called Olivier, asking him to take a break as we needed to talk. We arranged to meet and go to the airport together to meet Grace from her flight. He only broke the silence during the journey to ask if we really were picking Grace up or whether it was still my intention to return to Germany making him suffer as he watched me leave with his daughter. His anxiety was apparent as he kept looking at us in the rear view mirror. For my part, I was only too pleased to have a breather from his displeasure.

Grace arrived, none too pleased to be back in England. She was happy to see me and Summer but had her own agenda as far as living with Olivier was concerned. She refused to speak to him until her older sister was allowed to come back to live with us. I could hardly blame her for her attitude though I knew it would bode trouble for the future. My body was exhausted and my brain was numb; I felt weak, unable to take a stand and do the right thing for myself or my daughters. In desperation I visited the doctor for the frequent, severe migraine headaches and was referred to a therapist regarding my depressive state. Sadly, I could not afford the sessions and only attended for a short period of time. The general essence of the advice was to walk away from my relationship with Olivier; it was never going to work if he did not want it to, however much I hoped it would.

In a matter of days Olivier sensed Grace's animosity towards him and took up his relentless attack on my pathetic life and family again. To escape the daily abuse I decided to return to Germany for a few days in the hope I could convince Taylor to come back to England. I needed to see her face to face and hold her, telling her of my love for her, my first-born child. She needed to hear her life was precious to me, not discarded like some old rag doll. When I arrived I was unprepared for the level of resistance from Taylor. Even my Mother was surprised by her Granddaughter's determination to stay, though she quickly used it as ammunition against me, accusing me of being a negligent Mother. Looking back I can see how deluded I was, thinking the relationship with Olivier would ever be transformed into my happy-ever-after dream. Believing I had no choice but to return to England, I said goodbye to my child, desperately praying she would change her mind when the summer holidays were over. As the plane took off headed for England and Taylor remained behind of her own free will, a part of me died inside.

Chapter 16
WHIRLPOOL...

Olivier met us at the airport actually welcoming us back home. I could not understand why he should use language like that when he had never really welcomed us into his home. Taylor had given us a CD of the song *Girlfriend* by 'N Sync and I put it on in the car. Music had become such an important part of my life, lyrics especially spoke to me, sometimes as a reflection of my life, or as inspiration to give me strength to continue when things were really bleak. My girls knew my affinity with music and often used it to express how they felt when their own words failed them. The song is about a girl whose boyfriend is never there for her and treats her badly. Grace was crying in the back of the car and I was terribly upset. I had just left my eldest daughter in another country because she could no longer stand the pain of rejection and watching her Mother hurt by the man she professed to love. But if I hoped the words might sink into Olivier's subconscious and convict him of his bad behaviour, I was wrong. He reminded me I had made the choice to leave Taylor, but if I was unhappy with that decision he would be happy to turn the car around and take me back to the airport to fly back to Germany.

His unchanging approach to life: so black and white, I wanted to slap him there and then. As far as I was concerned I had not made a choice between him and Taylor; I had not chosen to abandon my daughter. Rather she had begged me to give her more time to think about what she wanted to do in the long term and I was respecting that. Understandably she was tired of living with all the abuse from Olivier and sick of being blamed for everything. She didn't want to grow up believing all family life was dysfunctional. I recalled promising her in France that if she was really unhappy I would allow her to go back to Germany. I know she felt responsible for her grandparents, constantly worrying something would happen to them if she were not there to care for them. Life is never just simply black or white, one choice or another. In every situation there are a myriad of considerations and I was trying my best to contemplate all the options to ensure my children were happy.

Life back in England had not been transformed to domestic bliss in my absence, and the headaches and sickness continued to plague me as I spent more time in bed than out. The phone was barred again as I was unable contributing to the bills, meaning I could not make calls to Taylor. Desperate to speak with her every day, to assure her of my love, I was forced to use my mobile phone often spending twenty pounds in less than ten minutes. Because Grace still refused to speak to Olivier his anger escalated, and he became more abusive towards us always shouting as he reiterated my family was worthless and ungrateful and not worth pissing on if we were on fire. It was always the same theme, like a record stuck in a deep groove. The physical abuse increased too, and whether I ignored him or dared to answer him back he would spit in my face and aggressively threaten me.

Taylor called one day in tears as my Mother had registered her with the local school. She was experiencing something of the control my Mother usually exerted over my life and did not like it. I asked her to come back to England but she flatly refused, saying she would not live in the same house as Olivier. She needed more time to think before deciding where she wanted to be permanently. I tried to explain to her how my parents really were, but it was useless. For Taylor, anywhere was a preferable alternative to living with Olivier. When it felt like my heart would break with the pain and my head would explode with all the worries, I would take Olivier's car whenever he left it and the keys at home and drive to the nearby beach and sit there for ages listening to music, shutting off from everything in the world. Songs by Anastacia and Christina Aguilera spoke to me powerfully, expressing my innermost thoughts. It was as if these people knew the minutest details of my life and had written songs about them. What I did not know until much later was, many shared similar experiences of domestic abuse and violence and had chosen to use their talents to express their most intimate feelings to the world, and in doing so inspired someone they had never met to carry on when their own strength failed.

"…I considered taking my own life: I contemplated crashing the car – but always the thought of my children with no one to love and take care of them haunted me, and stayed my hand."

Awareness that my two oldest children had lived with such abuse, first with their own Father and then with Olivier, brought tears that would not stop. What could I do? I knew beyond doubt that Olivier, too, was an abuser but how was I supposed to leave, where could I go, how would we survive? Sometimes my mood would sink so low I considered taking my own life: I contemplated crashing the car – but always the thought of my children with no one to love and take care of them haunted me, and stayed my hand. I even thought about crashing the car with them in it, but that terrified me too, incase they survived me in the crash. Depression insidiously enveloped me, sucking the very life from my physical body whilst mentally keeping me the victim of my aggressor. I still believed I was worthless and had no way of surviving by myself. In rare moments of self-assurance, plans formed in my head to leave Olivier. I considered going back to Germany with only our 'black bin-liner rubbish' as he callously referred to our meagre possessions, but the embassy required his signed consent for me to take Summer out of the country to prevent legal battles later. I knew he would never agree, no matter what he might say to the contrary. Although he never shared in Summer's upbringing, I knew he would not allow her to be brought up in Germany or anywhere near my parents.

"Strangely, when confronted with the women there, some with bruised faces and broken bones, I did not associate myself with domestic violence at all."

The time came for the children to return to school. Receiving motivation and strength from somewhere, I called Taylor's school to tell them she would not be back until further notice. The lady I spoke to sensed my distress and when I explained recent developments she suggested I see the school counsellor assigned to Taylor, so I arranged a meeting when I knew Olivier would be out. After a chat she took me to the local drop-in centre for domestic violence. Strangely, when confronted with the women there, some with bruised faces and broken bones, I did not associate myself with domestic violence at all. I assured myself there were far worse cases than mine and my life was maybe not as bad as it seemed and probably even normal. This, of course, is a common reaction to domestic abuse and violence. Victims programme themselves to see their personal situations as unique, possibly better than it really is because if they actually admit how bad things are, they finally grasp their need to escape and that means making a decision to leave.

The staff at the centre were very kind and helpful. They affirmed me in ways I was not used to and suggested I seek a place in a refuge. It seemed ludicrous at the time, as I still refused to admit to myself that we were at any risk from Olivier physically, but the staff, with their professional understanding and experience to draw on, read the signs far better than me. I was asked to make a statement against Olivier and was taken to a solicitor for an appraisal of my survival chances in England and what maintenance I could expect. I was still in denial about the gravity of our situation when I discovered Olivier was seeing someone else. There had been several signs indicating his infidelity, but until now I had been blind to them. When I read glaringly obvious text messages on his mobile and challenged him he chose the aggressive approach accusing me of spying on him, all the time denying anything was going on. Although just under six foot tall, I weighed less than ten stone but Olivier always told me I was fat and ugly and nobody could possibly love me; I believed him but had not made the connection he was having other relationships. Peculiarly, devastated as I was by that knowledge, I felt an even greater need for him to love me. I nurtured ideas of secretly leaving, calling to tell him what I was doing only when about to board a plane at the airport.

"It didn't seem like any church I had heard of and Grace and I smiled at each other convinced we were with a bunch of loonies!"

My friend Erin arrived back from Australia and called to see how I was. I burst into tears on the phone as I updated her about events in her absence. She was very concerned and asked me to join her and some friends the following Sunday. I asked Olivier if I could borrow the car, as the meeting was some distance away and was surprised when he agreed. When I arrived I found myself in a college hall. There were lots of people gathered there and as they started to sing songs together I was told it was a type of church meeting. It didn't seem like any church I had heard of and Grace and I smiled at each other convinced we were with a bunch of loonies! Tea and coffee was served and some talks went on about the recent 9/11 event in America and questions were raised about how a good God could let such tragedies happen. I was keen to listen, as I wanted to know why God couldn't prevent such atrocities. Grace and Summer happily spent the time with many other children of their ages, participating in different activities which was something I was not used to; their care and entertainment was normally my sole responsibility.

When Erin asked me afterwards if I had enjoyed the morning, I lied to her and said yes. Although I really liked the friendly atmosphere and the peace I felt in that place, I felt tricked into the whole church thing. We went out to lunch with Erin and her husband after the service and I learned he was a foreigner like me, from the Netherlands. He, too, was really nice and friendly and asked lots of questions listening intently as I told him something about my life, but when he offered the advice that I should leave Olivier, I was offended that he should tell me what to do. Olivier soon stopped allowing me to use the car on Sundays but Erin and her husband always gave us a lift. I wasn't completely comfortable with that, feeling coerced into doing something I wasn't sure I wanted to do, but I was still drawn to the amazing friendliness of the people who met there, and the wonderful peaceful atmosphere that seemed to engulf me each time I walked in the hall.

Olivier continued to bar the phone from outgoing calls, when he was not home and Taylor would try and call when she knew he was out. One day, however, he was home and talked to me continually while I spoke with Taylor, telling me I should kick her out of my life as she would inevitably treat me the same way his son had treated him. I ignored him, as there was no way I would ever do that to any of my children. His spiteful response was to unplug the phone socket in the middle of our conversation, reminding me it was his house and his phone and he could do what he liked. The next morning, the whole socket had been removed from the wall and he took it to work with him. The satellite receiver also disappeared, and we were no longer able to watch television. Undeterred by his childish behaviour, the girls and I would sit in their bedroom at night, listening to music and chatting. He countered our attempt to carry on as if nothing had happened by disconnecting the electricity, telling me it was his radio too; he paid the bills, we deserved nothing, not even to breathe the same air.

The daily stress was made worse by my Mother requesting permission to care for Taylor on a permanent basis. She insisted it was necessary in order for them to claim allowances to buy the things Taylor needed. I kept refusing all the time, begging Taylor to come back to England, but she would not agree. Why would she? As far as she was concerned, coming back to England meant a life of misery for her under Olivier's regime of hate. Her grandparents had done nothing to harm or concern her then, and she was unaware of the complexity of their personalities that lay simmering beneath the surface. I had little choice, it seemed, than to watch my child head straight towards a huge tornado. I sunk into deeper and deeper depression, knowing I was losing my child to my own Mother.

Where once Taylor would always be with Summer helping me look after her, now Grace shared that role and also provoked Olivier's displeasure. Now it was Grace's turn to be blamed for everything. She still refused to speak to him and he verbally abused her whenever he was around. We continued to go to the church and I desperately wanted to be like all the people I met there. They accepted us for who we were, and so when Erin asked if I would like to join them officially and I accepted, she called their vicar over to speak to me. He talked and prayed for me and his words had an amazing effect, although I did not fully understand what they meant. Erin and her husband Ed gave me a Bible but I had no idea what to do with it – certainly not read it, it was so big, with so many chapters, I found it too daunting.

"…that night the three of us slept like angels. I dreamt I was resting on a soft white cloud that had been placed under me. It was the most amazing and peaceful sleep I'd had for a long, long time."

After that Sunday I prepared to sleep with Grace and Summer in one bedroom, no longer wanting to share Olivier's bed. That action made him more angry and aggressive, because according to him, it was an act of disobedience on my part. He argued we would never be able to resolve our differences if I let the girls come between us, but I knew it was because he wanted sex from me whenever it suited him. I did not deliberately set out to annoy him, I was exhausted from all the conflict, but I refused to return to his bed. In a display of spite and temper he banned us from sleeping in any bed and consigned us to the floor. Oddly, that night the three of us slept like angels. I dreamt I was resting on a soft white cloud that had been placed under me. It was the most amazing and peaceful sleep I'd had for a long, long time.

Another Christmas was just around the corner and I was missing Taylor so much I buried my pride and begged Olivier to loan me enough money to buy a ticket for her to visit. She agreed to visit, but planned to return to Germany in time for the celebrations there. Olivier's condition to her visit was she had to thank him for paying for her ticket. Pathetic as his request seemed, I told Taylor to be prepared and was shocked when she refused to do so, saying she would not get on the plane if that was a requirement of her trip. Desperate to see her I lied once more to my daughter, telling her that would not be necessary. Grace and Summer both needed to see her too, I could not live with their disappointment as well as my own.

Daily distractions passed the time as we waited for Taylor's arrival. There was always something to offend Olivier, and my recent association with a church provided him with another reason to abuse and bully. He did not approve of me going to meetings on Sundays and threatened to turn up and embarrass me. According to him, only weak people believe in God and attend church. The Bible was all lies, made up by drunken fishermen and Jesus' Mother Mary was really a prostitute! I tried to argue with him sometimes, but my scant knowledge of the Bible made me vulnerable to his unkind attacks. All I knew was, Sunday mornings were an oasis of calm in the violent storm that engulfed our everyday lives.

When it was time for Taylor to arrive, Olivier agreed to loan me his car to collect her from the airport. According to him, it was a gesture of his boundless generosity. We had a few hours together, all four of us, before he arrived home from work. Taylor found it hard being back in the house because, unlike our spartan existence, her life in Germany was already filled with many material things as my parents spoiled her. Her English friend and her Mother came to visit, which annoyed Olivier. He did not like the Mother because in his opinion she was overweight. He hated fat people and made no secret of it. When Taylor walked past him without speaking to him, he lost his temper and threw her out of the house. I was devastated, but Taylor was more than happy to knock on our neighbour's door to ask if she could stay the night. Knowing something of our history, they agreed and I was left shocked and in despair.

Instantly Olivier's mood was transformed: he was smiling and cheerful, clearly delighted Taylor had left. He tried to cuddle me, telling me how evil my child was. My child was not evil, and I was speechless with anger yet too frightened to tell him what I really thought, too scared to challenge him. Grace and Summer went to bed, clearly shaken. I stood for ages in the shower with tears streaming down my face until Olivier came to see where I was. I dared not go to bed, as I feared that would antagonise him further so I sat on the sofa pretending to watch television, all the while thinking about Taylor and wanting to be with her. Olivier did not go out that evening as he had every other night, I could not believe it when he sat next to me and cuddled me. I was revolted but worse was to come. He kissed me and pulled me down beside him, then climbed on top to have sex with me. I was so disgusted I wanted to puke but a tiny instinct inside kept me from pushing him away. I knew I should not antagonise him – I needed to survive at all costs. It was imperative for my future and that of my children.

When he left for work the following morning he left his car

keys, indicating my obedience and acceptance that my child was evil allowed me use of his car. I immediately went to see Taylor and apologised for Olivier's behaviour. She agreed to spend the day with us and I was grateful, but she refused to stay in his house. My neighbour agreed Taylor could remain with them until it was time to return to Germany. I did not feel at peace. The next day when I called for Taylor I discovered she had been sick all night and fainted. Overwhelmed with guilt I could not hide my tears. She gave me a letter saying she was not angry and she loved me no matter what happened. It was such a relief to know she loved me regardless of all she endured. Feeling rebellious, I made her come back to our house and rest on the sofa. When Olivier returned, he told me to get Taylor out of his house and kept telling Summer her sister was a horrible person. I knew there would be further consequences for disobeying him, but for now he turned off the television. We sought refuge upstairs in the girls' bedroom, listening to the barrage of foul language and insults directed at me and Taylor. Summer was disturbed by her Father's unfriendly manner. At two she barely understood a lot of what he said, but she picked up on his overall mood and would always keep close to us. We all stayed together again that night, huddled close in one room. Whatever else Olivier deprived us of, he could not destroy the bond of love we all shared.

Taylor's week with us was over far too quickly, and it was time to take her back to the airport but Olivier refused either to drive himself or loan me his car. I called Erin who enlisted the help of a lovely couple from church and they took us in their car apologising for the treatment we received at the hand of one of their countrymen. When I got back to the house I was beside myself with heartbreak at saying goodbye. I told Olivier I was not prepared to play happy families with him over Christmas when my family was torn apart because of him. He promptly booked himself on a trip to leave two days before Christmas. I could not believe his callous stance and phoned my Mother to ask if we could stay with them if I could get us to Germany but she refused, saying she could not afford to feed us all. Inexplicably, like a silly schoolgirl, I harboured the foolish hope that Olivier would change his mind about going and take me in his arms, saying he wanted us to try and work things out, but his heart remained cold towards me. The night before he was due to leave I took Grace to see a special Christmas presentation by the church. We enjoyed the play but when it was time to return home I was overcome with violent shaking and could not drive the car. Grace was worried and wanted to get help but I begged her not too, ashamed people would see me in such a state. I took deep breaths in an attempt to calm myself down. After some time the shaking stopped and I was able to drive us slowly back home.

As it turned out, Grace, Summer and I spent Christmas day with a lovely family from church who lived in a village close by. It was the most wonderfully peaceful Christmas day I had ever experienced, full of love and joy and in no way marred by the spiteful way Olivier provided an abundance of gifts for Summer, whilst giving nothing at all to Grace and me. I was used to that type of rejection but my heart broke anew for the pain it caused Grace. I was surprised when he called to wish us a happy Christmas saying he was not happy where he was at his brother's house in Bulgaria. I could not help but feel a sense of satisfaction as our Christmas, by contrast, had been the best ever. He had left his car for me to collect him from the airport. Like a silly child I imagined he might be pleased to see me, perhaps even missed me. It was only as we approached the airport it dawned on me how stupid I was. Of course he wouldn't be different, he would continue to use and abuse me, punishing me if I stepped out of line.

Erin helped me to see I was not to blame for everything – I wasn't worthless, the problem was with Olivier. With the patience of a saint she insisted I was not a bad mother, a prostitute or any of the other derogatory things he accused me of being. One part of me was so frightened of this strong-willed, often violent man who lashed out spitefully when he couldn't have his own way. Another part of me still loved him, and was so grateful he had rescued me and my children from the horror of life with my alcoholic husband. I felt indebted to him for providing a roof over our heads, but his continual denigration of my character and confidence left me unable to separate the two opposing emotions long enough to get a clear picture of the hell that was our daily life. I had a favourite photograph of Olivier wearing sunglasses and looking relaxed and smiling. I carried it with me everywhere, treasuring it because it represented happy times and I yearned for that man to return. Although physically close, he was so far away; my hero had gone.

I was invited to attend an evening Alpha Course at church and I really wanted to go each week, but Olivier made it extremely difficult for me to attend. Sometimes he would flatly refuse to look after Summer for the couple of hours I would be away, other times he would stand with her at the front door as I left, letting her cry her eyes out. It was so heartbreaking, I would inevitably turn around and walk back indoors. Once, as I walked out the front door, he walked out the back, leaving Summer alone, spitefully forcing me to return. It seemed he didn't want me when I was there, but could not bear to allow me any freedom either. I thought I was in danger of going insane. He was accomplished at the mind games he played. It was only by chance I found proof of his infidelities when I saw the phone bill; one number in particular had been called over eighty times. When challenged he denied anything was going on, and insisted he'd had as much as he could take from me. He called his friend in France – with whom he accused me of having an affair – telling him he planned to visit for the weekend as he and I were finished.

Listening to renewed insults I plummeted down into the depths once more. Even though it was a repetition of everything I had heard before, I was unable to rise above the lies: I was a cheap slut, a parasite, no wonder my husband had a drink problem, it must be the only way a man could live with me. Olivier claimed he was not having an affair but his fixation with his mobile phone – taking it everywhere with him, even to bed, never leaving it unattended, and text messages arriving at all times of the day and night – persuaded me otherwise. I then became obsessed with discovering what he was playing at, and after he booked his ferry crossing to France, I checked on the website to discover the booking was an overnight cabin for two adults. More neurotic detective work revealed the telephone number he called so many times belonged to a married woman who lived locally. My consuming need to have proof of his affair compelled me to arrange for the girls to be looked after for a few hours. I planned to leave the house on some errand and wait at the ferry port until he arrived. As I left, he strangely chose that moment to reassure me of his fidelity and kissed me! I could not believe it. After insisting I was revolting to him, and wanting my disgusting face and presence out of his life, those actions confused me.

My mind in turmoil, I waited almost three hours at the ferry terminal and had almost given up when I saw his car arrive. A woman was sitting next to him in the front seat. I could barely breathe my chest felt so constricted. I wanted to confront him there and then, so that he could no longer deny what I knew to be true, but I was in such a state of shock. The little girl inside me could not bear to be rejected so blatantly. I wanted to be wrong, I desperately wanted Olivier to have a valid explanation that would make everything alright between us. As long as I didn't face up to the glaring truth, I could withdraw back into my safety zone a million miles from reality. In an irrational twist of reasoning I convinced myself this must all be my fault. I became more paranoid and finally put a call through to the ferry operator. I pretended there was a home emergency and urgently needed to contact a passenger. Despite putting out several announcements, Olivier did not take the call. I drove home feeling at my lowest ebb. He had even sworn on his own daughter's life that he was not having an affair with someone else yet what I saw with my own eyes said otherwise.

Shortly after arriving home Olivier returned my call, asking if we were all well and why I tried to contact him on the ferry. I questioned him as to whether anyone was with him on the boat, but he assured me he was alone. I challenged him saying I had actually seen him get on the boat with another woman. He promptly hung up and switched his phone off for the remainder of the weekend. When he finally ordained to come home, he reiterated I had no proof of his affair as I hadn't witnessed him kissing anyone, and anyway I should sort my shitty little life out. The penny dropped heavily and even I had to admit there was no relationship I could salvage. I made plans to go back to Germany and asked him to sign the papers giving me permission to take Summer. He refused. I was left in limbo, only able to leave the country for less than twenty eight days at one time. If I did not comply, he was entitled to approach the authorities and pursue me for kidnapping his child.

"…I nurtured a dream in my heart that one day I would find the strength to break out of the continual cycle of abuse and low self-esteem in which I existed. But the reality was hard to accomplish, and so I chose to remain in my cage, although I alone held the keys to freedom."

I needed to escape, it was imperative for my sanity but thoughts of where to live and how to survive financially on my own kept me shackled to a man I now despised. I immersed myself again in songs by Christina Aguilera, the lyrics to Walk Away and I Am Leaving echoed my desperation and even pointed to an escape route; I nurtured a dream in my heart that one day I would find the strength to break out of the continual cycle of abuse and low self-esteem in which I existed. But the reality was hard to accomplish, and so I chose to remain in my cage, although I alone held the keys to freedom.

Chapter 17
BLEEDING LOVE...

L ife continued like a game of cat and mouse. I felt weak and helpless pitting myself against Olivier's callous treatment and matter-of-fact attitude one day, and bizarre change of character the next. It was like living with two personalities inhabiting the same body. Every day he fixed the phone so I could neither make nor receive calls in his absence. The isolation was stifling – being unable to speak to Taylor, torture. He reiterated if I did not like the way things were I was free to leave – he would even pay for my fare to go back to Germany. Paradoxically he booked a holiday for the four of us to go to Spain together. My heart pleaded a break somewhere different might rekindle something of the love I believed we shared in the beginning, but my head protested it would never work, screaming for me to get out. It is only with hindsight I see the repetitive pattern of Olivier's dual nature. Abuse would often be followed by brief episodes of kindness, giving me false hope, keeping me frozen in place. Returning to Germany a complete failure was one of my biggest fears, but eventually the strain got too much and even the prospect of that seemed to pale in comparison to remaining in England.

Finally I made plans to leave the country once more, but having no finances, I had to degrade myself further and ask for Olivier's help. Childishly, he refused to pay for our tickets in advance, saying he would give me the money as I left the house and I would have to pay at the airport. I reserved our places on the plane and prepared to leave the next day. With no choice, I buried my pride and contacted my Mother who agreed to let us stay with them initially, but she could not resist the opportunity to say 'I told you so' and repeat that she knew all along it was a mistake for me to go with the foreigner. Taylor was far more gracious, saying she would love us all to be together again, but I should only leave Olivier if it was what I wanted to do. I struggled against begging him to stop this vortex of destruction we were all caught up in. He remained cold-hearted and aloof insisting when I returned to my old life I would realise what I had lost with him.

"The day before the planned Spanish holiday, a taxi waited outside to take us on the first leg of our journey back to Germany with our suitcase of meagre belongings."

The day before the planned Spanish holiday, a taxi waited outside to take us on the first leg of our journey back to Germany with our suitcase of meagre belongings. I stood in the house holding my children's hands, overwhelmed by emotions of despair and guilt about our uncertain futures again but needing to make this break if I was ever to retain my sanity. Finally we were on our way to the airport and I kept looking back over my shoulder, willing Olivier to be behind us. Even as we passed through check-in, I naively entertained the notion he might arrive and beg me to come back to revive the fairy tale from the ashes but he did not appear. Grace and Summer were excited by this time at the prospect of being reunited with their sister, they missed her acutely, we all did. I sent Olivier one last message to say goodbye, expressing sorrow at this outcome: it was not what I wanted. I don't know whether I really expected a reply or not, but one came through as we boarded the plane. He actually apologised and asked me to turn around and go back to him. He promised to try and change for the better imploring me to go to Spain with him. His message was marred by one disturbing condition: he did not want to hear anything more about Taylor; as far as he was concerned, she no longer existed. As the girls looked at toys in an airport shop, hope surfaced in my heart to be cast back down. Tears streamed down my face and I knew I couldn't let Taylor down, she would be waiting excitedly for our arrival. The plane took off and once again my world was split in two.

"…my addiction was too complete, even though I could not see it…"

I told Taylor what had happened as soon as we arrived. She did not seem surprised at Olivier's latest strategy, it was as she expected. My Mother gave me no time to draw breath before bombarding me with a long list of things that needed immediate attention: Summer had to go into the local nursery, Grace must be enrolled at infant school and I must visit Social Services to request financial support and find a permanent home. Already she was taking over my life, giving me no time to adjust and reminding me my Father would get mad if I so much as cried or couldn't cope. It should not have been her role, but Taylor was an amazing source of strength to me even though I believe she always knew I did not intend to stay in Germany. What I did not know then was how broken she was, and how my continually changing plans were damaging her trust in me. She begged me to open my eyes and take a long look at how things really were with Olivier. But remaining in Germany looked less and less inviting as other family members expressed concern for Grace living with a mother incapable of caring for her children properly. Their overall dislike and mistrust of English people made them bigots with no experiential backing. I wanted to run away again for all the same reasons I had left in the first place. I hoped to use my time there to convince Taylor to be part of our lives in England once more, but understandably she was not willing to return to a life of persecution with Olivier, and warned me she would soon give up on me as a Mother if I did not see sense. She pleaded with me to see things from her perspective, saying she could no longer bear to watch me destroy my life. But my addiction was too complete, even though I could not see it, and I chose to return to England with Grace and Summer, leaving my darling Taylor behind once more.

I returned to Olivier like a chastised animal with its tail between its legs. He laid down new rules: we must spend more time together as a couple, going out more and mixing with his friends. I was surprised at the latter suggestion, since I was unaware he had any friends; I had never seen them in all the time we had been together. He repeated he did not want to hear anything about Taylor because as far as he was concerned she was evil. My unrealistic hopes of reconciliation between them were finally dashed but I told him I could never forget her or exclude her from my life, she was my child. Our relationship was never going to be an equal partnership, he would always be the authoritarian father figure, and his attempts at making it work lasted less than a week. I am shocked I tolerated another year of constant abuse, allowing myself to become more and more depressed.

Taylor would call me whenever the phone was not disabled, at other times I would shamelessly ask neighbours to use theirs. It was imperative I maintained constant contact with her, but our relationship suffered a huge setback during that time. She saw me as a failure, ably assisted in her opinion by my parents who perpetuated my demise at every opportunity. As far as she was concerned, she was not interested in seeing me until I made a final decision to leave Olivier for good. Throughout her short life she had been my friend and confidante, and now wanted to live life for herself instead of propping me up all the time. She even stipulated I stop calling if all I could talk to her about were my problems with Olivier. In a state of panic I persuaded her to come to England for a short visit. I didn't tell Olivier until two days before her arrival and he promptly booked himself on a holiday to Spain for most of her visit.

Taylor kept her distance from Olivier and was withdrawn from me, spending most of her time with Summer: I could not blame her for the way she felt, after all she was right in that I was wasting my life chasing an illusion. I just could not see it at the time; like any addict, I was still in denial. Olivier tried constantly to upset her, accusing her of trying to take Summer away from him. He would snatch Summer from Taylor's arms, insisting on bathing her, putting her to bed and reading her a story himself. Things he never bothered to do before now suddenly became his main focus, just to punish Taylor. Meanwhile Summer would scream and cry to be with Taylor, and we continued to live our fraught and traumatic lives. Though only two, Summer quickly learned how to control situations; she became very possessive of me, especially disliking any attention I paid to Grace. She would push and kick her sister if ever she approached me for a hug. Siblings often vie for parents' attention within the family structure, but my children had experienced so much change in their young lives, they all needed constant affirmation they were loved to compensate for their insecurities. Olivier made matters worse by condoning Summer's bad behaviour. Taylor could not believe I allowed the situation to continue, and said Summer mimicked Olivier, spitting at Grace and me and hitting us whenever she could not get her own way.

My ability to react to this latest manifestation was paralysed by years of abuse and low self-esteem, and part of me carried overwhelming guilt for what I subjected my children to. I accepted much of the punishment and criticism, believing I deserved it. I accepted all the derisory images Olivier projected onto me believing I was a fat, ugly and worthless slut of a mother who could neither speak or understand English. My punishment for listening to Taylor, and not rejecting her as he demanded was more spitting and insults as he continued to tell me she was evil, influencing his own child against him. Though only thirteen, Taylor was still the only one strong enough to stand up to Olivier and shrewd enough to see through the mind-games he played with me. She would accuse him of being like her own Father in his treatment of me. Olivier of course hated her for her openness – and maybe the truth challenged him on a deeper level. She was also quite aggressive towards me during her stay that time. I can see now it was inevitable as not only was she witnessing me being controlled completely by Olivier, but her prolonged stay with my parents had fed her opinions to line up with theirs. They made every effort to spoil Taylor with material things, something I could not do, at the same time filling her head with prejudices and bigoted view-points.

In preparation for taking Taylor to the airport for her flight back to Germany, I suffered further humiliation by ingratiating myself to Olivier and obeying his every whim in order to use his car for the awkward journey. Taylor made it clear she did not approve of my doormat mentality. She was mature for her age but how could I explain the intricacies of relationships. I was ill-qualified to advise her and she was right: I could not manage my own life, so what right did I have to influence her thinking. All I knew was I loved Taylor with all my heart, as I did all my children. I could not bear the thought of letting her go back to Germany to stay with my parents, I was losing her physically and emotionally and the realisation tore me apart. She was leaving what she saw as an undesirable, stormy existence with me, but I knew she was only heading into an equally unstable situation but all I could do was watch in despair, silently crying for my baby.

After she left I was inconsolable, despite having Grace and Summer with me. To my shame I was not a good mother and neglected them, leaving Grace to get herself to and from school, whilst sitting Summer in front of the television to watch videos all day. Olivier continued to control me, his preferred method of punishment if I did not obey him was to prevent me from speaking to Taylor by disconnecting the phone, or pulling the socket out from the wall. I was living a slow death sentence separated from Taylor, not out of choice, not due to some law or legislation, but through other people's manipulation of my life and my own choice to remain a victim. It was a punishment effected by people who claimed to love me at one time or another, yet who systematically demolished my confidence, rendering me incapable of breaking out of the cage I was in. It felt like someone had stabbed me in the heart over and over again and I was slowly bleeding to death.

I chose to remain shackled to my insecurities that summer. My depression plagued me with more migraines and sickness, I seldom went out and often stayed in bed. Prohibited from having friends visit, Grace would disappear off to their houses, sometimes taking Summer with her to give me a break. I had no idea where they were for much of the time, too engrossed with trying to unbar the phone, or fix the socket back into the wall. Whenever Taylor managed to get through to me she apologised for things she had said, and told me she loved me. I was not angry with her, how could I be? Even in my volatile state of mind I knew her observations were correct. She encouraged me to listen to more music and a particular track by Christina Aguilera called *Fighter* inspired me and made me feel stronger.

Feeling good about myself for possibly the first time in my life, I was motivated to buy the album and discovered another song called *I'm OK* in which Christina sings about her experience of abuse during her childhood.

"I admitted to myself I was living with domestic abuse, that my children had witnessed almost everything I had suffered and that made them victims too."

Although her experiences were different to my own, the song's message had a profound impact on my mental state, causing me to cry until tears streamed uncontrollably down my face. I sat on the sea front near our home, looking out to sea at the distant horizon that reminded me Taylor was so far away. I admitted to myself I was living with domestic abuse, that my children had witnessed almost everything I had suffered and that made them victims too. Although I did not feel strong enough to leave Olivier immediately, I prayed one day I would have the strength to walk away and break the insidious cycle that affected three generations of my family.

As another Christmas loomed on the horizon, I managed to care for Grace and Summer on a superficial level, cooking their meals and washing their clothes but mostly I was distant, in my own little world. Grace spent most of the time away from the house, and it was plain from Summer's crying that she preferred to be anywhere but home too. Fights and arguments occurred on a regular basis, as Olivier expressed his dislike of everything about Grace. It was two years since he had thrown Taylor out, and Grace still refused to speak to him, annoying him intensely, so he made every effort to make her life hell. Although I totally understood why she behaved the way she did, and secretly agreed with her, fear prevented me ever expressing those thoughts to Olivier myself. Grace put on a lot of weight, mostly because she was comfort eating. When she could no longer get into her clothes Olivier was quick to insult her verbally, calling her a big fat lardy. He taunted her, telling her to wear plastic bin liners to save money on clothes.

As his attacks on her increased, I refused all sexual contact with him and slept every night with the girls. In the mornings we would listen as he typed in the code to bar the phone from outgoing calls, praying he would forget, but he never did. I was convinced he was seeing the woman from the ferry, and probably others. Perhaps it explained why I was not subjected to his forceful advances anymore. Out of the blue, he amazed me again by asking if I would join him on a skiing holiday, as we prepared ourselves for another Christmas without Taylor. When I tentatively agreed, he allowed incoming calls on the phone once again but this still did not enable me to speak to Taylor at my instigation. With two weeks to go before Christmas, I was desperate to call her one morning and checked the phone, but it was barred as usual. Unable to repress my frustration any longer I challenged him, saying how much I needed to speak to my child in Germany, and called him a control freak. I knew immediately I had made a serious mistake. He rushed towards me putting one hand around my throat, using his other arm to pin me up against the wall. Caught off-guard I was unable to move and stood there, frozen with fear, while he shouted a tirade of abuse at me.

"The movie was cut as I passed out, and I remember thinking dying was not as bad as I anticipated."

I was completely taken by surprise by his sudden attack, but hoped he would soon tire of shouting and let me go but the look in his eyes scared me; he reminded me of my ex-husband. He pressed even harder against my throat and in that instant I knew I was in serious trouble and terrified that Summer, who had followed me from the bedroom, would witness a terrible scene. By now she was crying and screaming for her Daddy to let me go. I remember hoping Grace would not wake up, then I could not hear anything at all. My hearing had shut off and my eyes felt as if they were getting bigger, threatening to burst from their sockets. In a surreal moment I saw scenes from my life play fast in my mind, like watching a movie. I could feel different parts of my body shutting down and at that moment I accepted I was actually going to die. The movie was cut as I passed out, and I remember thinking dying was not as bad as I anticipated.

When I regained consciousness, Olivier still had his hand on my throat, pinning me against the wall but he suddenly let go as if someone was forcing him to take his arm off me. I clearly remember he looked over his shoulder to see who was responsible, but there was no one there to see. He promptly walked away saying I deserved that because I was too mouthy. Gasping for air and in shock, I collapsed on the floor as Summer rushed to hug me. I quickly got up and ran to the phone to dial the emergency services. Olivier pulled the plug out of the wall again and beat me to the table where my mobile phone lay, throwing it against the wall violently. I hesitated, unsure what to do. If I grabbed Summer and ran from the flat, I would leave Grace still asleep, possibly at the mercy of Olivier. I did nothing, and he finished getting ready for work and left as if nothing untoward had happened. I woke Grace up and prepared her breakfast, trying to remain calm, not wanting to tell her what had happened. As soon as she left, I retrieved my mobile phone which had fallen apart as it hit the wall. It still worked, but I was angry and impulsively sent Olivier a message telling him he was no better than my ex-husband and I was leaving. Within minutes he was actually back in the house telling me I deserved everything I got, and there was more if I wanted it. Sobbing in shock, I asked him if I deserved to die but he callously walked out again, offering no retort.

My throat was very swollen and extremely sore, making it difficult to swallow. I momentarily considered calling the police again, but worried in case I would be taken away; what would become of the children if that happened? I could not take the risk. He returned an hour later, and just sat in a chair watching television until he eventually fell asleep. I sat on the kitchen floor contemplating everything that had occurred, and trying unsuccessfully to make sense of it all. Some time later, Olivier came and sat on the stairwell overlooking the kitchen, apologising, telling me he was sorry and did not mean to do what he did. Promising it would never happen again he made excuses for himself saying it was the only way he could survive in this life. He asked me not to give up on him, reminding me he had booked us a nice holiday. I had no intention of going anywhere with him after what had happened, I wanted to put as much distance as possible between him and us. I could not believe it when he said he wanted to hold me in his arms, but I did not want to be held by him. I asked him what he would have said to the children if he had killed me.

He did not answer that question, but talked and talked for the rest of the day. He insisted his behaviour was a one-off incident, discounting all the other times I suffered physical and verbal abuse at his hands. Foolish as it sounds he wore me down by his continual pleading; suppressed by my own fear I accepted his excuses. All my anger and frustration once more locked away with the disappointments and rejections of all my yesterdays. When I later told Taylor she was worried and alarmed enough to phone Erin who phoned to see how we were. I explained Olivier had apologised, everything was okay, and the four of us were going on holiday together. Who was I fooling? Looking back I can see how ridiculous my reasoning appeared. Yet again hindsight brings perfect vision. I still believed I could only survive with Olivier, not without him and I was convincing myself as much as anyone else.

As soon as we arrived on holiday, Olivier adopted his familiar pattern of being nice to me for one day, and ignoring me the rest of the week, leaving me alone with the girls in our hotel room. I was surprised to discover his sister and brother-in-law were at the same resort. Summer had no interest in skiing – it was too cold for her and she did not adjust well, sleeping a lot of the time. Olivier did not tolerate her apathy well, and spurred on by Grace's silences, concentrated his bullying on her, calling her appalling names, intent on hurting her feelings. She spent most of the holiday crying and I contemplated whether I should just leave and head back to Germany. However I was dependent on Olivier for all our finances and decisions like that are more easily made when not involved. One saving grace was we were joined there by his sister and brother-in-law. They are lovely people, very down to earth and normal. They were fun to be with and made it possible to stay, his sister even offering to look after the girls so I could spend time with Olivier and her husband on the slopes. She was unaware of our history or indeed of Olivier's treatment of me, Grace and Taylor in general. He cleverly kept up a pretence of us being a happy family unit. My anger towards him grew along with my fear of the unknown as we took the ski lift up to what was supposed to be a beginner's slope.

"Suddenly my paranoia took over, as I envisaged Olivier had a plan to kill me up there on that mountain and I screamed at him I would not ski down."

After a seemingly interminable journey up the mountain, we reached the top, and I stared in disbelief at the steep runs back down the valley. Suddenly my paranoia took over, as I envisaged Olivier had a plan to kill me up there on that mountain and I screamed at him I would not ski down. It was too late to take the lift back down as the last one of the day had departed. His brother-in-law assumed I was joking and laughed, but such was my irrational fear, I imagined he and his wife were involved in the plan, and that was why she offered to look after the girls. Olivier told me to stop making a scene and stood by me at the top of the run. His brother-in-law stood close by. Overtaken by anxiety, I took off my skis and threw them in the snow, refusing to go anywhere with him and declaring I would rather die on the mountain than trust him to get me down on skis. I could only think of Taylor in another country with her grandparents, knowing everything she had accused Olivier of was true. Perhaps feeling guilty because of what had occurred between us two weeks before, and worrying that his family might think I was an hysterical lunatic, Olivier followed me down the mountainside on foot, carrying my skis and sticks.

What should have taken twenty minutes on skis took us over two hours on foot. It was intensely hard work and I was in agony, as the heavy boots rubbed blisters on my feet that chaffed with every step. I was acutely hot in my ski suit and wanted to give up many times during the descent. A raging thirst made it necessary to repeatedly melt snow in my mouth before continuing. Olivier's mobile announced several text messages, and I was concerned in case it was his sister and the girls, but he refused to acknowledge them. I learned later they were, in fact, from his mistress. When we finally reached the resort he removed my boots, still trying to atone for his behaviour. My feet were bruised and covered in weeping blisters. Unaware of our history, his sister merely saw the incident as amusing, but the rest of our stay was marred by my continued mistrust of Olivier. Somedays he chose to remain in bed, rather than spend any quality time with his daughter. He refused to play in the snow with Summer, take a sleigh out with her, or ski with her on the children's slopes. All his promises of being together and enjoying a great holiday proved nothing more than the usual empty words. I could not wait to get back to England to make plans to leave him for good.

"…I still didn't look upon the arrangement as permanent and was in no way prepared to sign my daughter away with the stroke of a pen."

Home in England, Olivier refused to acknowledge I intended to leave him at all, adding to my confusion and insecurities. In an unheard of flourish of social activity, he took us to his Mother's birthday party and we spent leisure time with his sister and brother-in-law. Although I can see now he was doing no less than controlling my life, I began to feel alive for the first time in ages and hung around him putting off the inevitable, soaking up what I assumed was genuine affection. Amidst all this change of lifestyle, I suddenly had to fly out to Germany. My Mother called to say the benefit and maintenance she received for looking after Taylor wasn't enough, and in order to receive more I must sign a form giving her sole custody of my oldest daughter. I was seriously alarmed; just how much money was required to feed and clothe a fifteen year old? As far as I was concerned my Mother was already receiving enough money to support a small orphanage. Whilst grateful my parents had offered her a home at a difficult time, and Taylor believed it was where she preferred to be, I still didn't look upon the arrangement as permanent and was in no way prepared to sign my daughter away with the stroke of a pen.

Taking advice from a lawyer in Germany, I learned custody would never be given to my Mother without my consent, and no court would award it to anyone other than me unless there was proof of neglect or mistreatment. Armed with this information, I was shocked to arrive in Germany to discover my Mother had set up a meeting at their house between me and welfare officers. Perhaps I should have suspected she would stop at nothing to get what she wanted. At first I imagined Taylor's involvement, but she was as upset as me. She did not want me to give up custody of her and felt as betrayed as I did. I was accused of being an unfit mother and advised it was in Taylor's best interests to sign the document. Outraged, I left the table refusing to sign anything. Taylor was angry as she did not want me to go, but what she didn't understand until much later is her Grandmother is a very manipulative person. She does not handle money well and will go to any lengths and say anything to obtain more, without concern for those around her. The atmosphere in my parents' house was horrible. My Father shouted at me to leave without further discussion and my Mother repeated over and over it wasn't her fault, but she needed extra money otherwise she could no longer look after Taylor.

Left with no choice, I reluctantly signed a partial fostering agreement giving my Mother the extra money and permission to sign for urgent operations, doctors, dentists and school matters. My Father's anger frightened me. I feared he might hit me as he had always done but instead he resorted only to verbal abuse. Devastated and heartbroken, I flew back to England without Taylor, who failed to see she was being used to get back at me. I could not blame her. To her young mind it was preferable living with her grandparents, remaining with her friends and boyfriend, and completing her studies in Germany, than returning with me to Olivier's house and his cruel treatment. My parents literally spoiled Taylor, giving her every imaginable material thing she desired. I could not even begin to compete. As my plane landed in

England, Olivier's was taking off bound for Spain. Thinking I would be away for a few more days he had arranged to fly out to view some land with plans to build a house there for us. He left a massive bouquet of flowers for me on the table and had slept with my nightdress under his pillow. I was impressed by his efforts but it was not enough to deaden the pain of leaving my baby in Germany. I was grieving for her big time.

I continued to spend more time with his sister until it annoyed Olivier to see me independent of him, and he told me to cool the friendship accusing her of being nasty and talking too much. He implied she would hurt me just as she had hurt him, taking him to court over some trivial matter. I was shocked, I accepted his sister's friendship as genuine but, characteristically, Olivier objected to anyone I became close to. Influenced by him I withdrew from his sister, only later to discover that it was Olivier who took her to court, not the other way around. When I acted cool towards him he retaliated by verbally bullying me. He told Summer I was a horrible, fat bird nobody would want, and a slut and prostitute. Even though Summer didn't fully understand or know what to make of his outbursts, his assassination of my character to her was cruel. Visibly afraid of him she would crawl into my arms and hide, aware that Daddy was not playing games. Then he would turn on Grace, calling her despicable names, but she stood her ground, still refusing to speak to him at all. For three years she had kept it up, and although I did not appreciate it at the time, she was an incredible example to me of how to stand up to a bullying tyrant. But Olivier always knew how to reduce me to a piece of worthless humanity, down on the floor begging for his attention. By taking the phone away, or tearing the socket out of the wall to prevent me calling Taylor, he could control me like a spineless puppet.

To survive at all I learned what to say, how to say it and when. Sometimes I passed the test, but mostly I read him wrong or made no allowance for his volatile mood swings. Then he left me in the house like Cinderella, feeling guilty because I had not done what he wanted. On the rare occasions I felt brave enough to challenge him, telling him we were not a couple and I need not do anything for him, he would respond spitefully, with his familiar barrage of insults. If I dared him to kick us out he would decline, refusing, he said, to make his child homeless. All the more surprising when, one month later, he decided it was time for me to go – back to Germany. As far as he was concerned I was a f…… user, an asylum seeker, living off his government's money and if Hitler was alive he would kill vermin like me.

I was more than happy to leave by then; I had nothing to gain by staying. If I returned to Germany, at least I would be with Taylor with a possibility of gaining acceptance from my family at last. He telephoned and booked us flights for the following day. Again, I prepared to go with just our two suitcases, once more happy to leave everything behind and escape with my children and my life. Olivier's tone took a sinister turn, though, as he warned me to watch my back as accidents can happen. He warned me especially to look after Taylor who may be the first one to experience a fatal accident. He insisted it was her fault we had problems in the first place. I could not believe he was still blaming Taylor for everything. She had not lived with us for two years, yet in his mind she was the cause of all his troubles; and if not her, then Grace and if not them, then it was my turn to be the scapegoat. We were all scum and parasites. I wondered at the level of his delusion. But first and foremost I was scared of what he was capable of doing, especially to Taylor.

"For once I left without a backward glance, even though it contradicted my desire to live happily ever after…"

For once I left without a backward glance, even though it contradicted my desire to live happily ever after, but I realised no one in my life was able to fulfill that pipe dream. I knew I could not exhibit sad emotions to my parents meeting the flight, and crying was not tolerated by my Father, it made him mad. Taylor was understandably cautious of trusting me again, although she did hug and kiss me. At least we could still do that, something I had never been able to share with my Mother. On the extremely rare occasions she would kiss me, I inevitably wiped off traces of her touch with my hand. Though I was grateful they took us in again, I did not feel comfortable and began looking immediately for a home for us all. Selma's former house was available, and we were all excited to move there as it held so many happy memories, as well as being the place I had met Olivier. If I could not live with him, at least I could remember there had been some good times.

We settled in well and felt a peace for the first time in ages, apart from Summer who was not happy away from England. In order to survive I needed some initial financial help from the government, but unlike England, Germany does not offer much in the way of assistance to single parents. I had no national health medical cover for me and Grace, despite being German nationals, and no private insurance would cover Summer. It was expected I get a job immediately, with no time to adjust for the children or myself, which, considering what we had all been through, was a daunting prospect.

Summer missed her Daddy very much, and I let her speak to him by phone. He assured her he would visit her once in a while, but if I tried to discuss her maintenance he accused me of using her to get to him and hung up. For some unknown reason, Summer did not like the attention showered on her by my Mother, and she cried every morning and evening around the times she would normally see her Father. She would finally fall asleep exhausted from crying, hoping her Daddy would be there when she woke up. Whenever she spoke to him she asked when he was coming to take her back home. It broke my heart,and I think it finally penetrated his hardened spirit. Still able to access his email account, I shadowed his social activities like some covert detective. He moved on quickly from our relationship, and I discovered he was dating women he met online. It was deceitful and stupid of me to chart his movements but I could not stop, it was like drinking a poisonous liquid, I knew it would kill me, slowly and painfully, but I drank it anyway. I learned he booked himself a holiday flight. Feeling cheap I opened the email with trepidation, and was staggered to see the flight was to Germany. The discovery threw my mind into more confusion. I was sick and tired of always being sick and tired. I wanted a peaceful life and was trying to settle back in my village in Germany. The knowledge that he was coming exerted the old power he had over my life. I was not free of my addiction and fraternising with the enemy would not be wise.

He called a couple of days before his booked flight but I did not let on I had advance knowledge of his visit. I questioned his motives for coming, and he said he just wanted to talk. It scared me. On the way he sent a text asking what I would like him to bring from the airport. I could not believe it after all the times he had accused me of being a gold-digger, and all the times I could not rely on his support for us, he now asked me what present I would like. Sarcastically I replied saying I would like a fat gold necklace just like he wore, hoping he knew me well enough to know it was the last thing I would ask for. He arrived at the house the shy Olivier I met once in that very place, and he handed me a nicely wrapped big fat gold necklace; after six years of living together, he did not know me at all!

Pleasantries over, his manner quickly changed, and offering no explanations or apologies he made it clear he did not want Summer staying in Germany any longer than absolutely necessary. He also added that he was happy to have Grace and me back with him in England, but not Taylor – she no longer existed as far as he was concerned. The choice was mine and I had two weeks to decide, after which time he would hire someone to get Summer back, he would not allow her to grow up in Germany. I laughed when he dictated his terms but inside I was anxious in case he was really able to take Summer away from me. I now knew he was capable of many things and I was worried when he told me he knew people who could arrange a fake passport. From my experiences of both countries, England seemed more proactive when it came to helping victims of domestic abuse. I wondered if it would be better for us if we did, in fact, return to the United Kingdom. I could not bear to think of Olivier having full custody of Summer, he had done nothing to help raise her so far, and I was not about to give up another of my children.

Taylor planned to be baptised in the village church – the one close to Aunt Becher's house whose bells I heard every Sunday whilst growing up. Aunt Becher, who told me about God all those years before – the God I had not prayed or spoken to in a long time. I really wanted to attend the service for Taylor's sake and my own. I hinted to Olivier that I might consider returning to England, but I wanted to stay in Germany at least for Taylor's big day. He was insulting as usual and dismissed the event as if it were nothing, which of course to him it was. He swore and told me to think about us, which was laughable considering his abuse of our relationship.

As suddenly as he had arrived he returned to England, leaving his ultimatum like a bad smell: I had fourteen days to join him or he would pay someone to get Summer. Although I was relieved when he left, my mind was in turmoil about the decision I was being forced to make. In my heart I wanted to be with all my children, and although I had spent almost six years in England, I was still a foreigner. But the alternative was no more attractive. If I remained in Germany, I would always be under the control of my parents, living in a small village with its small-village mentality and prejudices. I had no financial help in Germany as my ex-husband managed to avoid paying maintenance. Thanks to Olivier's relentless belittling of my character, I lacked the confidence to get a job. Although Summer was a German national, she had lived all her life in England, did not speak German and would be desperately unhappy in German speaking institutions. Grace was content to remain and attend school with her older sister and Taylor would not change her mind about leaving Germany and her grandparents.

"How had I allowed the men in my life to blind my judgement so that I placed their demands before those of my children?"

With the deadline fast approaching and receiving harassing calls from Olivier, my dilemma caused me to fly back to England with Summer, reluctantly leaving Grace and Taylor at my parents' house. I was surprised I cried as the plane took off as I intended to stay in England no longer than a week; long enough to arrange maintenance for Summer and Olivier's signed permission for her to live with me indefinitely, though I doubted he would consent if that meant Germany. It was imperative I returned in time to witness Taylor being baptised, that much I owed her. Despite all the traumas I had put her through, Taylor still loved me and believed in me. My self-appraisal was much more scathing: how could I be a fit mother when I exposed my daughters to such upheaval and heartbreak in their short lives? How had I allowed the men in my life to blind my judgement so that I placed their demands before those of my children?

I told Olivier of my intention to return for the baptism and he went berserk, shouting I needed his consent to leave the country again with Summer and he would not give it. He barred the phone, removed the wires from the computer, put her in his car and prepared to drive off. I followed to get Summer out of the car and he told me if I ever left England he would hire someone to shoot me. At this point Summer was crying, begging me to run away as she didn't want me to be shot, saying she would be fine. It was heartbreaking to hear my little three year old, fearing for her Mummy's life and trying to be strong so that I would not be hurt. With the strength of a lioness protecting her cubs, I pulled Summer from the car, making a decision never to let her out of my sight. I laughed as I told him he would not dare to harm me because too many people knew what he was capable of – Taylor would hunt him down and he would lose Summer forever. I could see his eyes, filled with so much anger towards me and he told me again I had better watch my back as he could arrange to have me killed in no time.

"Then, like a cunning snake, he changed his tactics… Once again, mesmerised by his guile, I found myself thinking his suggestion sounded plausible."

Then, like a cunning snake, he changed his tactics, suggesting we go to Germany together and try and work this out. Once again, mesmerised by his guile, I found myself thinking his suggestion sounded plausible. We would travel by car and ferry and leave in time to attend Taylor's big day. I was ensnared but not so Taylor. When I rang to explain the change of travel plans, she doubted his intentions – both to get us back on time and to change his treatment of me. To reassure myself it would happen according to plan, I made all the bookings and packed everything into the car in plenty of time to leave, little believing Taylor's instinct would again be correct. Just as we were about to leave, Olivier put on his new sunglasses to find a scratch on them. He blamed me saying it was my responsibility to take care of things. I was an unfit mother and wrong to allow Summer to climb over everything. Thinking he should take care of his own sunglasses, I nonetheless apologised immediately, focusing only on getting back to Germany in time. I sat playing with Summer as he drove off but he would not stop berating me about his sunglasses, going on and on and on. After a short while it became unbearable and I instructed him to turn the car around and go back to the house. He happily complied, his mission accomplished.

Determined not to let Taylor down I booked a flight for Summer and me for the following morning, still giving us enough time to make the church service, which was all that mattered to me. It cost me all the remaining money I had, leaving me with nothing to get to the airport in England or from the airport in Germany to the church. I knew I could not ask my Father for help at the other end as I knew he would refuse. He banned me from his house when I left for England with Summer the week before. All the while Olivier watched television, obviously enjoying the problem I was having, until suddenly in a perverted twist of mood, he offered to drive all the way to Germany, catching the next available ferry. I was completely bemused at his change of heart, as it meant he would have to drive through the night to get us there on time. Looking back I am amazed at how many times he could manipulate my thinking, that I could entertain the idea he was sane and cared about me. But such is the total destruction of a victim's personality. All I cared about then was getting there for Taylor, and so I agreed. We shared the driving, and actually arrived in time for me to have a couple of hours sleep before the service. I went alone to the church, leaving Summer with Olivier at the hotel. Apart from supporting my daughter and being there for her, the day was not easy for me. It was obvious my entire family judged me badly for my involvement with the foreigner, and considered me an unfit mother and daughter. They mostly ignored me but I stayed close to Taylor, her joy at my presence there was all I needed to know my efforts were worthwhile.

Finally conceding to Olivier's threats concerning where Summer lived, I resigned myself to the prospect of returning to England once more, and made plans to leave the next day with her and Grace. I was scared by the things he had said concerning my safety, and until I had time to investigate where I stood legally, I decided it was better to do as he demanded. Yet again it was my children who suffered most. Grace had just begun attending school in Germany and she was uprooted once more. Olivier didn't care, as far as he was concerned it was neither his responsibility or problem; I would have to deal with the upheaval and heartbreak alone as usual and Grace would receive more messages that she was not a priority and her life was unimportant.

Chapter 18
LEFT OUTSIDE ALONE…

It came as no shock when Olivier resumed his self-centred life back in England. He arranged a holiday to Canada with an older lady and her daughter and expected me to drive him to the airport; I refused. I was furious and expressed my dissatisfaction at his treatment of us, but my protests only unleashed the usual verbal abuse and he removed the phone and computer leads before leaving. By this time I was becoming quite an expert at surviving his ploys and quickly replaced the necessary equipment enabling me to communicate with Taylor everyday. Once I overcame the initial panic of fending for myself, we enjoyed the peace that reigned in his absence. He'd adamantly refused to sign papers allowing me to take Summer to Germany to live but in his new life as a single man, I hoped he would choose to move out of the house, leaving us there to get on with our lives. I held tight to my dream that if that happened, Taylor would return to live with us, too.

Olivier called several times from Canada to speak to Summer, but she was not interested, preferring the neighbour's children than her own Father who had abandoned her again. Of course, he blamed me for her attitude and when he called again a few days later to say he was bored and ready to come home I could not resist telling him it was his own fault and we were having a much better time without him there causing arguments and fights. He demanded I call him back in Canada, but the phone was fixed to receive calls only and anyway, I had not taken down his number. Later that night he sent a text message to my mobile asking if I still loved him and wanted to marry him. I could not believe the audacity of the man – he was obviously out of touch with reality, unaware of the mind games he played. He asked me to meet him at the airport on his return, but I reminded him he had not left his car for me to use. He arranged for it to be delivered immediately, but for once I refused to be his servant, knowing there would be dire consequences for my rebelliousness.

"His menacing threats included me being shot and buried alive and he continually spat in my face…"

Indeed there were consequences. As soon as Olivier returned from his holiday he ordered me to leave his house with my pathetic kids and belongings, and he would begin legal proceedings this time to ensure I did as I was told. At first I thought his words were just threats, as they had been so many times in the past, but as the intensity and severity of abuse grew I knew it was not safe to remain anywhere near him. His menacing threats included me being shot and buried alive and he continually spat in my face whenever he spoke to me, and his verbal attacks on Grace were relentless. Summer was terrified of this person who looked but didn't act like her cuddly Daddy, and she would always try to stay close by my side. A letter from his solicitor giving me permission to take Summer out of the country came as a complete surprise as did an injunction to evict me from the house within fourteen days. All I would be allowed to take was my children.

I had no choice but to contact the housing services and ask for their immediate help. I needed somewhere to live. We had no furniture or money, as Olivier flatly refused to give me anything at all, stating everything, including the house was his and I had no rights. Meanwhile, he forced us to move into the smallest bedroom with our personal belongings wanting all reminders of us out of his sight. I pleaded with him to at least consider his own daughter but he ignored my appeals saying it would be worth making his own child homeless to get rid of me. I could not believe what I was hearing. When I failed to meet his irrational demands and move six years of our lives into one tiny room, he put a lock on the door of his bedroom, denying me access to important paperwork including birth certificates and family memorabilia. I attempted to get in the room, but he pushed the door against me, trapping my back and leg. Feeling frightened and reminded of a similar incident with my ex-husband, I alerted Grace who called the police. When the unit arrived, my leg was badly bruised and my back cut and bleeding. The officers advised me to leave immediately. All the while, Olivier insisted I was his cleaner, and that we had no relationship. I listened in disbelief as he not only maligned me and Grace, but disowned his biological child too. At first I refused to go but the police advised me to leave as I did not have the owner's permission to be there. I felt like a low-life someone was trying to exterminate.

In contrast, at Social Services the next day, I was relieved when someone took me seriously. My contact there, appalled by the evidence of abuse was keen to get me rehoused as soon as possible for my safety as well as sanity. They gave me a form to complete for emergency funding for a house, but Olivier laughed in my face and tore it into little pieces in front of me, saying he would rather see me on the streets. He would deny all charges leveled against him, insisting we had no relationship; I was only his cleaner with whom he'd had a one night stand, and who was using menacing behaviour towards him. My body revealed much physical bruising and so Social Services informed the police to put us on alert. I was advised to call the emergency services immediately I felt physically threatened or was beaten. In the meantime, I had no choice but to wait for the slow wheels of administration to turn. Fourteen days passed and D-day arrived. Olivier got up at six in the morning, threw all our clothes into one suitcase and dismantled one bed he was generously donating, in preparation for us to get out. The abuse worsened considerably and I called the police to discover they had already been alerted by our neighbour who witnessed his horrendous ranting at Grace from her garden. I knew my call, being the second in twenty four hours, would culminate in us all being made to leave the house immediately and for good. The accommodation we applied for was not available, and it could take another three months for us to be re-housed, but I had no choice.

Four police units were promptly swarming all over the house, guarding back and front exits. Officers went upstairs to question Olivier and I had to give a statement about every incident that had occurred over the years which took two hours. Afterwards they had enough evidence to arrest Olivier for grievous bodily harm. I was asked to leave the house and not allowed to return. I stood in my next door neighbour's house, in shock and outraged, as Olivier took advantage of the situation to change the locks on the doors. Finally I was out and he was in! I had not wanted to leave, how on earth would I survive? We had no belongings, where would we go? I could not see how they would arrest Olivier, although the officer taking my statement said it was an extreme case of domestic abuse. I regretted calling them as it seemed I suffered further, while the perpetrator remained free, but by three that afternoon I received a call confirming Olivier had been arrested pending further enquiries.

I did not feel victorious, I had seen the look of absolute hate and anger in Olivier's face. I crumpled onto the floor of my neighbour's kitchen while she danced around celebrating. She witnessed many events of my turbulent life with Olivier since we lived next door and was herself going through a bitter divorce. We had become linked in friendship through adversity. Her husband subsequently blamed me for the breakdown of their marriage, believing my association with his wife influenced her decision to leave him. I don't believe that was true. Apart from sharing our common problems, our lives were very different and the choices we made were unique to each of us but her husband did not see it that way. Furious I was sheltering in his house, he shouted at me to leave.

My initial concern was to find somewhere to stay, as it was ten at night and the nearest homeless shelter was full. My friend offered to let us stay with her but I was reluctant to upset her husband any further. Eventually she called another friend who took us to stay in her Mother's house in a different part of town. At midnight a call came through from the police station. It confirmed Olivier was to be charged with harassment, and if I needed to collect anything from the house, now would be a good time, as he would afterwards be released on bail, awaiting trial. By then it was too late. Grace and Summer had finally fallen asleep exhausted, we were in an unfamiliar part of town with no means of transport, and I had no money. So I had little choice but to remain where we were. Olivier was subsequently released on bail with the condition he did not attempt to see me. Finally, in the early hours of the morning, I tried to join my children in sleep, but I was too numb from the day's trauma and could only dwell on our homelessness.

Early the next morning I went to the council's housing department to seek emergency housing. With Olivier released on bail, I was not allowed back in the house so we had only the clothes we wore and had slept in. Social Services said they would get back to me later. Things had turned out exactly as Olivier planned: I had no money in my pocket, no bank account and it was a cold and rainy November day. I clasped my children's hands and walked along the streets of a town I had come to despise, unable to think of any solution to our dilemma. Miraculously, at that moment, my neighbour and the daughter of the lady in whose house we stayed overnight, walked towards us in the rain, they looked like two guardian angels to me. They had come looking for us and the lady I did not know offered help, inviting me and my daughters to her house for the day. Overwhelmed at her kindness, I accepted and wept.

The lady's name was Lucy, and we remained at her house for much of the day. Another visit to Social Services proved fruitless, as they had nowhere yet for us to go other than a refuge. Lucy was reluctant to see us go to such a place and offered accommodation in her house if her husband agreed. I was overwhelmed and with four children of their own, loathe to put them to any more trouble, but we were desperate. At my neighbour's house I learned Olivier had been escorted home in a police car in the early hours of the morning. Having reported him to the police I knew, with a certainty, there could be no further reconciliation between us: Olivier would never forgive me. His threats echoed in my brain: if ever a woman crossed his path, she would never be happy again; nobody ever reported him and got away with it. I had lived with his menacing ways for six years, but I felt more vulnerable being outside the house and relationship, no longer able to monitor his behaviour and reactions. I was exactly where he threatened I would be: alone on the streets with my children.

I called into the drop-in centre for domestic violence for guidance as to what I could do next. I was advised to contact the officer in charge of the case, in order to gain safe access to the house to collect some belongings as we all needed clean clothes. As soon as we were allocated somewhere to live an alarm would be fitted for our protection. Meanwhile, my life took on a dreamlike quality, as if this were happening to someone else and I was merely an observer. The officer advised me to wait at my neighbour's house while he ascertained if it was safe for me to enter. Olivier would not let me in the house, insisting it conflicted with his bail conditions, but eventually the officer persuaded him to give us some clothes. I should have guessed Olivier would somehow manage to humiliate me further. He stuffed our clothes into black bin liners, dirty and clean thrown haphazardly in together. I knelt on the floor in my neighbour's lounge surrounded by rubbish bags, drowning in the tragic reality that they represented the mess of my life. I had nowhere to live, nowhere to store anything, and Olivier had spitefully withheld the children's toys along with my personal documents. My neighbour kindly offered to wash our clothes and keep them for us until we were rehoused. The police officer expressed sympathy at our situation, intimating it should be Olivier on the streets not us.

"…relieved at being away from the constant abuse…I actually missed Olivier's presence. Even though he treated us appallingly for so long, it was a familiar situation; removed from that I felt uncomfortable and exposed."

I experienced a weird paradox of feelings: part of me was numb and in shock from the trauma of the past few days, though relieved at being away from the constant abuse. I was hurting and scared, but strange as it may sound I actually missed Olivier's presence. Even though he treated us appallingly for so long, it was a familiar situation; removed from that I felt uncomfortable and exposed. I had been released from a prison, but did not know where to go or what to do with that freedom. My relationship with Olivier was an addiction and without my next fix, unable to speak to him or look to him for our provision, I did not know how to survive. Inside I screamed silently for him to come and rescue me. I thought I needed him, I was lost without him. The girls were living their own nightmares too. Summer could not understand what was happening. Even though he did not spend much time with her when we lived under the same roof, she missed her Father and found it hard visiting the house next door, yet unable to see him. Grace too was in shock, she couldn't think straight. In her eleven short years of life she had experienced excessive unhappiness and persecution and though incredibly resilient, her self confidence was at rock bottom. The human body and mind is capable of withstanding extreme assaults, but the long term effects can cause damage that is not repaired easily, if at all. I worried about the repercussions of this on my daughters, and have since discovered many issues can lie buried for years.

Lucy was a source of love and practical help to me and the girls. She and her husband invited us to stay until we were suitably accommodated. The time we spent at their house made us feel safe, and amidst all the heartache we managed to experience some laughter, and hope for a future not overshadowed by abuse. She had a strong Christian faith, and the church she attended answered her urgent request to help us. Their response was overwhelming, and many essential items were donated to us for our new home. I was suddenly reminded that I, too, was a Christian, though my faith could barely be described as active, let alone strong. It was Lucy who recommended I ask a health visitor to see the children to help them deal with their emotions. When I did I was also advised to speak to the NSPCC (National Society for the Prevention of Cruelty to Children). I had heard of the organisation but I wasn't convinced our case merited their involvement, as I assumed they were concerned with only helping children who were neglected, beaten and abused. To my surprise they agreed we were living with domestic abuse, including violence, and it slowly began to dawn on me the gravity of our situation and the length of time it had continued. Life had been that way for so long, I considered it normal. I needed to be re-educated concerning balanced and healthy family life.

With no house or suitable accommodation forthcoming, Olivier, desperate to be rid of us for good, took matters into his own hands and paid the deposit on a rental house in the town. It suited him to ensure there was no way we would be allowed back into his home or life. Lucy and her husband encouraged us to move into that house after only a week with them. The house was not in a good condition and so I was surprised at their advice, but moved to avoid burdening them further. It was not until a few months passed I learned the real reason behind their advice. They were influenced by unkind and untrue gossip, which branded me as a needy person who would require high maintenance, advising them to withdraw from close involvement. So it was one cold mid-November day I took Grace and Summer to a dirty, uninviting house, furnished with an old grease-smeared sofa and bunk beds with no mattresses. Drained of energy, hope and will, I could not even assemble another bed donated to us. Outside it was freezing; inside I lay awake shivering on the floor trying to hug my innocent babies as if to protect them from the ravages of a life they did not choose. Being pushed around from one place to another for years finally caught up with me, as the old abandoned smell permeating the house reflected my life. I felt like unwanted junk, discarded as useless and of no worth.

It would be easy with hindsight to gloss over the weeks that followed, because I am looking at my past through the eyes of victory. But in deference to what I and my daughters survived, I want to document the misery that was our daily lives then to remind us what we survived, and inspire others that it is possible to overcome the most adverse situations. Olivier refused to hand over the girls' belongings, denying them comfort and pleasure from familiar things. Financially my life was in a mess. Although eligible for benefits they were never enough. Every day I struggled to make ends meet, to feed us and pay the bills. I also owed three thousand pounds to the German government, because I listened to Olivier and claimed child allowance whilst living in France without completing all the relevant paperwork at the time. Now it was being deducted from my English bank account, making me permanently overdrawn. I continued to lose more weight and despite the health risks and additional drain on finances I was smoking heavily and unable to give up that addiction.

Conversely as I saw no end to the practical difficulties, it was at that time my spiritual condition began to improve. I had always felt controlled by others, now I was responsible for the choices and decisions I made. I had to learn how to be free in every aspect, including being myself. It was extremely difficult to adjust but one thing became apparent: no one could come into the house anymore and punish me, shout at me or verbally abuse me. I was seeing an unfamiliar side of life that attracted me and gave me determination to cope alone. From early childhood I chased the illusory man of my dreams to fulfill an unrealistic fairy tale life believing I needed someone else to validate my worth, unaware I could cope alone as a valuable human being.

I had an opportunity to talk to Lucy and discovered why she and her husband had drawn back from our friendship. My ex-neighbour had unaccountably chosen to gossip to her, implying all kinds of negative things about me, and advising them to steer well clear. Fortunately Lucy kept an open mind and we renewed our friendship. She invited me to visit her church again and I agreed, keen to meet these amazing people who had given so much to a complete stranger. I spoke to my friend Erin, who had originally introduced me to Christianity and I told her I wanted to get more involved with a church. She agreed it was a good idea. Soon afterwards I was baptised in the sea near where we lived, and although I did not fully appreciate it then, a life-changing journey began for me that is still continuing to this day. I have since moved to another church which suits me and my family well, and my faith continues to grow daily. I know there is a God who loves me unconditionally and knows everything about me, just as Aunt Becher told me all those years ago.

Life without Olivier was still proving a challenge. I found the night times tough, and I hated the dull orange street lamps in the town that reminded me of the countless nights I waited for him to come home. Summer was constantly ill, suffering from high temperatures and coughs. She, like Grace, was eventually diagnosed with asthma. The house was always cold and that did not help. The night storage radiators seldom gave off sufficient heat and we all slept in track suits, woolly jumpers and thick socks. I invested in some fan heaters, but the cost caused the electric meter to continually run out and I could not afford to keep them running when we so desperately needed them. My relationship with Grace hit an all-time low. On one hand she was relieved to be away from Olivier and his constant menacing, but she was suffering deeply from the effects of our fractured existence and being bullied at school and chose to reject my attempts to get close to her or even hold her close. Her comfort eating caused an increase in her weight that compounded her unhappiness. Our discussions often led to arguments and she began to hit and punch me, the way Olivier used to. I constantly bore the bruises of her attacks, and she even resorted to hurting Summer at times. We were all struggling with our own frustrations and crying out individually against a past that refused to free us from its tentacles. Although we had that freedom physically, the aftermath of the emotional battle had just begun. Earnestly putting my new faith through its paces, I prayed for the children and myself but I was constantly distracted by thoughts of Olivier. He was still very much on my mind, the addiction still evident, although we were forbidden contact with each other to comply with the bail conditions.

I communicated with Taylor frequently, but it was difficult for her to appreciate the situation at the end of a telephone line. She was unsure if my relationship with Olivier was truly over, after all, she had witnessed me like a bouncing ball returning to live with him time after time, no matter what cruelty he dispensed. Summer's bouts of ill-health, manifestations of her mental state, were a constant challenge. She was fearful of everything and would not go anywhere on her own, even indoors. I would have to accompany her to the toilet and she would not sleep anywhere other than curled up next to me in my bed. I knew she needed to see her Father and once, at my request, he did see her, using promise of any future visits as leverage to persuade me to withdraw my evidence. The decision to take Olivier to court was not in my hands as the Crown Prosecution Service were taking him to trial and I would be required as the victim and witness only. Whilst the case was pending we were not allowed to leave the country, a ruling I struggled with, as I desperately needed to see Taylor. There were countless times I wanted the case dismissed and I'm ashamed to say, some of those times were due to my volatile moods and fear of being alone. Constantly battling with my emotions when it came to Olivier, I could not quite decide whether he was the person I most hated or loved and I nursed a delusion he might change his attitude towards me and my fairy tale could be redeemed.

It was a relief when the NSPCC finally arranged counselling. In the beginning it was group sessions for Grace and me only as Summer was considered too young. Grace gained nothing from those early attempts at therapy, and withdrew even further into her own dysfunctional world. Initially it helped me to open up and share with other women suffering in similar ways. I was loathe to burden the few friends I had with my experiences and feelings in case I bored them or worse, they judged me. Strange as it may sound, it was a comfort to discover my situation was far from unique: there are countless men and women suffering in similar ways but I had no idea of the vastness or frequency. It was a revelation to learn it wasn't my fault. I always blamed myself, and found that particular fact the most difficult to accept. Erin strongly advised me to write down my experiences – in the hope that it would help me in a healing process, but also because she felt by openly speaking about domestic abuse and all its sinister manifestations, others may be inspired to break out of their own personal prisons. In those early days my life still seemed worthless, I had been told too many times I was not worthy to breathe the same air as my abuser. The prison door was open and I had made the first tentative steps, but the journey to living in that freedom had only just begun. I was not in the right state of mind to fully understand what we had survived, let alone express those thoughts on paper. Life still yawned like a big black hole with many gaps in my understanding, acceptance and confidence in myself. Events of the immediate past and Olivier were uppermost in my consciousness – I recalled little of my childhood or marriage.

I continued to crave Olivier's attention like an addict suffering withdrawal. In order to allow him to see Summer in her own dire need, I was forced to bury the irrational feelings I felt towards him. I mistook them for love then, only understanding later they were classic signs of dependency. Even if I had chosen to confide in him he would not have understood, believing himself to be the victim. As far as he was concerned I had betrayed him: there was no forgiveness, no going back. In his inimitable fashion he used his visits with Summer as bargaining power. I was frequently without money for basic food. Knowing that, he would offer financial assistance only on the understanding I would drop all the charges against him. On one occasion Summer arrived home upset, informing me her Dad had a new girlfriend. Olivier pretended she was simply the cleaner, but Summer observed them kissing and having dinner together and drew her own conclusions.

Once she arrived home stiff, not wanting to move or speak. She was clearly traumatised and the effect lasted for the remainder of that day, throughout the night and even into the next morning. Clearly it was painful, and not just for her but for me too. I called her Father to ask what had happened, but he offered no explanation. By the time I took her to school I was concerned and spoke to her teacher. My anxiety levels hit the roof when Summer finally broke her silence to tell me her Dad had a gun. Once she dropped her revelatory bombshell, she refused to say anything further, causing my mind to go into an overdrive of fear, as I recalled she, too, heard Olivier threaten to shoot me. She was obviously in shock, having seen a gun at her Father's house and believed he was actually going to shoot her Mother. According to his subsequent explanation, he used the gun to shoot rabbits and showed no remorse for having subjected his daughter to a disturbing episode.

Almost a year had passed when I received a call informing me the case against Olivier was to be heard the next day. Distressed at the prospect of Summer's father facing a prison sentence, and frightened of what the procedure entailed for me, I called him to talk. Violating his bail conditions, he came to the house immediately. He was visibly upset, but spoke persuasively, making me think our enforced separation had helped put our differences behind us. I could not bear the thought of Summer unable to see her Daddy if he went to prison. I still felt responsible for separating Taylor and Grace from their Father, so I told Olivier I would attend court but refuse to stand as a witness. Lucy called that night, but I did not pick up the receiver, thinking she would try to convince me to testify. She merely left a lovely message offering her support, no matter what I decided to do. When I called her back she agreed to accompany me to the court, and I was relieved I would not have to face it alone; I was also overwhelmed at her unconditional love and friendship.

When I awoke early the following morning, my heart was racing with fear and I felt physically sick. With tears streaming down my face I prayed earnestly for God's mercy and forgiveness, feeling for the first time my heart was truly open. I asked God over and over again to show mercy, whatever the outcome at court; to allow Olivier to go free and not be punished with a prison sentence, but help him see the pain his daughter was suffering, and make amends to her. With Lucy's help I had finally stopped smoking four weeks earlier. I was glad with my decision, but thoughts of impending stress that day exacerbated the withdrawal symptoms I suffered. I arrived at court with my nerves all over the place. A representative of Victim Support was there. They offered support throughout the proceedings and made sure I had something to eat. I knew it was make or break day: if I gave evidence I knew I would lose Olivier for good, yet if I refused there was a remote possibility he might come back to me. I couldn't let go of a last thread of hope. Knowing involvement with him was dangerous for my health, I still craved his presence in my life; like giving up smoking cigarettes, it was hard to give up Olivier.

When I revealed my decision to the police officers, they explained I could be held in contempt of court if I refused to give evidence. In fear and defeat I stood outside the courts and smoked a cigarette; I could see Olivier – a breath away from me – and I saw fear in his eyes. At his request I allowed him to walk Summer to school that morning, in case it was the last time. But was it, or was this all part of his game? Lucy stayed with me throughout gently offering comfort and strength. Even when I fell silent she encouraged me to share my thoughts instead of hiding them inside but I dared not tell her I still clung to the fantasy of reconciliation with Olivier, I couldn't bear to lose him for good. Further discussion with the police and Lucy made me see I had lost Olivier a long time ago, if in fact he had ever been committed to our relationship, and it was right he should be punished for the way he treated me and all the girls. I did not take the stand until late in the afternoon, as my ex-neighbour in a last minute twist had decided not to give evidence which had delayed the proceedings.

The case for the prosecution was fairly straightforward, as I was the only witness. They ran through their questions quickly and I was expected to answer with a simple 'yes' or 'no'. The defence was another matter entirely. It was like listening to Olivier's abuse all over again. I was presented in a bad light, as an extremely untrustworthy and unsavoury character, who was nothing more than Olivier's cleaner. I appeared as an eastern European immigrant and a gold digger after big money. Again I was not allowed to say anything, except 'yes' or 'no' to the questions. In disbelief, with tears streaming down my face, I glanced at Olivier and saw a look of pure hatred in his eyes that said, 'I told you so: don't mess with me!' It broke my heart to hear the lawyer imply our daughter Summer, the child Olivier persuaded me he wanted, was nothing more than the result of a meaningless one night stand, now being used to extract money. The same child I allowed him access to over the past year, and who he walked to school that very morning. The trial was adjourned until the next day, as I was crying too much to speak coherently. Lucy continued to prop me up for the remainder of the day, reminding me Olivier would use every angle to avoid prosecution and punishment. Another friend, Nancy, looked after the girls that day and offered to do so the next day too. Lucy invited us all to stay at her house that night and I am so grateful we did, it was an oasis of love and calm in the maelstrom of stress and anxieties in head.

"I was devastated and ran out of court convinced people saw me as a liar and a nobody..."

When we arrived at court the next morning, Olivier was already in the courtroom. The other witness, my ex-neighbour, had already been escorted there by the police, and was outraged when she saw us, shouting abuse at Lucy for supporting me. I felt bad about Lucy and saddened that my friendship with my neighbour had been ruined by Olivier's interference. She refused to give evidence against him and I later learned she felt intimidated by his presence next door. Once again Olivier was getting his own way, whilst to me it wasn't about winning or losing but justice for my children. For what Grace, Summer and Taylor had to live through. After waiting hours, the case was dismissed. I was devastated and ran out of court convinced people saw me as a liar and a nobody, a silly foreign woman who made a mess of her life. The jury had been informed I was terrified of Olivier, but also advised I had broken bail conditions and had contact with him during the past year, even though it was for him to see Summer.

"I would like more understanding of the victim's mental state to be disclosed..."

With hindsight I can see how my behaviour might be interpreted as contradictory. On the one hand, I called the police to intervene in Olivier's abusive treatment of me and the children, whilst on the other hand I continued associating with him, contravening the conditions of his bail. I didn't acknowledge the degree of my dependance on Olivier, I don't believe any victim does whilst they are still involved. I was physically and mentally scared of Olivier, but I also needed him. I wanted his attention, even if that meant bad attention and when he was no longer around me every day, I still refused to live without him. My whole worth and personality was by then so completely bound up in

Olivier, I had no existence apart from him. I was what he accused me of – a worthless nobody. Without the familiar bullying and abuse, that had come to be my whole world, I was lost and aimless. I would like more understanding of the victim's mental state to be disclosed when the perpetrator is brought to court, in order that individual and fair judgements can be made. It is extremely difficult to convey full accounts of events or feelings when only able to give simple answers such as 'yes' and 'no' to questions, real life is too complex for that but such is the legal system. Being removed from direct threat of abuse does not signify the abused is automatically and suddenly fine; it is a long process to complete healing because the brain has to be reprogrammed with professional help. Despite a few faithful friends and my faith, which did help me, I was stuck for some considerable time as a battered woman, and it required a breakthrough of significant proportions for me to live a new and free life.

The dismissal of the court case dragged me down towards depression again, but Lucy and Nancy kept watchful eyes on me. Through them another lady befriended me called Lara. I had met her briefly whilst I was still living with Olivier, but now the friendship blossomed. She was quite a private person and a busy family lady, but her straight speaking and empathy helped me emotionally and spiritually at that time. It was she who made me realise I had actually wanted and prayed for Olivier to walk free from the courts unpunished and be able to see his daughter grow up. My prayers had indeed been answered and now I had to summon the strength to live with that, and find it in my heart to forgive him for all the hurt he had caused us. It was the only way I would ever be free from the abuse and move forward with my life and help my girls do the same. I began to write my experiences down in the hope it may help to give them a voice, but the time was not right and progress was slow. It was obvious I would not be able to release myself from my chains; I would need additional help.

Extraordinarily at that time I met another Christian lady who had just finished a book about her quest to find her Father. She was giving a talk and Lucy and Nancy invited me along. Kyla's story was inspiring and illustrated how any one of us can overcome enormous obstacles in our lives, know that we are valuable human beings and live a life free from the shackles our circumstances place on us. I took an advance copy home and became interested in knowing more about this God I seemed to be encountering in other people's lives. I used the internet to feed my curiosity and began attending the local church where Kyla went. They did not have a church building but rather met in a school hall each Sunday and were very active in the local community. I was not comfortable at first; I felt threatened by the sheer number of people there. I preferred to be alone, unwilling to trust and be let down again. I hated the town in which we lived and could not understand why I remained there or why I was still reluctant to return to Germany. It was frustrating and I see-sawed between hopelessness and frustration. What was I supposed to do with the rest of my life? In the coming months I would learn that letting go was the answer and it frightened me. I had known pain and tears all my life; letting go implied I would be empty of everything, with no guarantee Malaika would be there afterwards.

Chapter 19
THE POWER
OF GOODBYE...

I vowed never to let Olivier see Summer again after the trial, but my conscience stirred and I relented because I did not want her growing up without knowing her Father. I read Kyla's book every spare minute I had, and it confirmed to me the hurt being fatherless can cause. Grace and I attended church on a fairly regular basis on Sundays when Summer was with her Father and although Grace seemed comfortable there, I was not: I just did not get it! On one occasion Kyla and another lady prayed with me and afterwards she gave me a hug that made me immediately suspicious. Nobody had given me a hug in years and I was squirming inside, completely out of my comfort zone. Then Kyla told me I was a beautiful woman and I wanted to run out of the building. Call me anything you like: fat, ugly, a gold-digger, prostitute, no-good mother but don't call me beautiful – I can't deal with that! She told me writing a book would bring healing, not just to me but other men, women and children who were living the same hell. Kyla told me she had recently qualified as a counsellor and would be happy to counsel me. At first I could not understand her, unwilling to admit I needed counselling. She smiled, knowingly adding I would be helping her at the same time. She waived charges for me as her first client. I relaxed, that sounded better, I would be helping her, I was happy to do that.

At home we continued to experience problems. I became obsessed with writing my book. If there had been prizes given for the number of pages written in the shortest time, I would have won hands down! Grace was opting out of school more frequently, claiming she felt left out and missed her sister and family back in Germany. She resented Taylor living with my parents and wanted to do the same. As for Summer, she suffered from constant colds and high temperatures. I presumed it was all connected with missing her Father who only saw her when it suited him. He spent much of his time meeting women, either online or out and about. It did not fit in with his plans to have a young daughter constantly demanding his attention. Often, when he was supposed to be spending time with Summer on her sleep-overs she would call me, explaining Daddy was always in front of the computer. He inevitably blamed me for her dissatisfaction, saying I had not raised the children correctly and had influenced Summer against him. All the time he could not see she desperately needed to know her Daddy loved her and considered her important enough to spend quality time with her. Olivier had not participated in raising Summer when we lived together so he did not know how to entertain a young child. Our money was always tight, with never enough to go around, and I selfishly continued smoking after the court case. This placed an additional burden on the finances, but even though I knew I should stop, I could not find the will-power to do so. I felt such a failure in every area.

"I could not believe someone would actually listen to me for that length of time without any interruptions."

Meanwhile, Kyla and I arranged to meet at the local community centre on a weekly basis. I felt extremely nervous at the first session, not knowing what I should talk about, my thoughts still being preoccupied with Olivier and my feelings for him. Kyla prayed before we began, asking for God to be the counsellor, to use her as his helper. Then she sat patiently back in her chair and listened to me talk. I spoke a great deal about Olivier and how much I missed him, despite being hurt by him. I could not believe someone would actually listen to me for that length of time without any interruptions. She asked me to think back to different stages in my life. I was shocked: what stages? What life? There was only Olivier! As far as I was concerned my past life in Germany was gone: never wake a sleeping dog, but Kyla asked me to explain how I felt about those stages. Suddenly the hour was over and our session finished. I was surprised at how quickly the time passed. She advised me to concentrate on 'me time' and then time with my children when I went home. Me time? What on earth was that? All my life I had done what others wanted and behaved as they demanded, now I was being told to do things I wanted to do. I was bemused: I had no idea who I was or what I wanted to do. I felt ashamed to tell her I did not understand, I did not want her to think of me as stupid.

Another week on and Kyla was again the most amazing listener. After the next session she told me to go home and pray, asking God how he saw me. I wasn't too sure what she meant by this exercise but I complied. To be honest I was not expecting anything in particular to happen, whilst secretly hoping something would. The following day after praying the prayer Kyla recommended, I was working on my manuscript, typing furiously when I received a text message from Taylor. Instead of her usual greeting of 'hi mom' it read: 'I love you and believe in you; don't give up keep doing what you are doing, just don't give up because you have us.' I sat reading the message over and over and showed it to Grace; we were both amazed and sure it was an answer to my prayer. Taylor had looked up into the night sky in Germany and thought of me as she listened to one of my favourite songs by Peter Gabriel called *Don't Give Up*. She felt strongly compelled to send me those words, knowing how much music and lyrics always meant to me. I could not believe it but kept turning the thought over and over in my mind that there may be a God out there who actually loved me. I thought of calling my book Highway to Hell but realised God wasn't about hell, there was something much better He planned for me. The right title would come, I just knew I mustn't give up.

"It was a learning process that would not only set me free but help others break the chains shackling them to their abusers."

Life in the daily grind continued. Olivier came and went in our new house as it pleased him, as if he owned it and us. Often he would turn up in the morning to see Summer for ten minutes before school and expect a coffee. It was not an ideal situation, but I irrationally harboured dreams of being reunited with him, and thought perhaps it was what God had in mind. I was to learn through the counselling that this was not what God wanted for my life: to be used and abused by Olivier, rather he had a wonderful life of freedom planned for me, but the transition was not to be an overnight thing. It was a learning process that would not only set me free but help others break the chains shackling them to their abusers.

In my quest to discover whether God was really concerned about all the small details of my life, I signed up for another Alpha Course run by the church. It provided a chance to explore Christianity in a non-threatening way and ask lots of questions. I thoroughly enjoyed the weekly talks, and everything I learned made a lot of sense. Human beings are always in search of something bigger and better in their lives but when they find it, they frequently become bored, just like children with their toys. Through the Alpha Course I learned God was the only thing that could satisfy me completely – the real thing – I should accept no substitutes. It was a profound revelation for me and my newly discovered faith helped me tackle everyday situations and gain a confidence I had not known before. I was amazed to discover God cared passionately about me, and knew me well enough to speak to me in ways I could understand. Hardly a day went by without me hearing confirmation of his love for me in song lyrics. Listening to Celine Dion's song entitled *Prayer* I was reminded again of Aunt Becher's assurance that God knows everything about me. Once, I was a child robbed of childhood in order to please my Father and Mother. Now I was alone, a single parent, wanting to do things differently with my own children because they are worth the utmost I can give – I suddenly knew God would help me achieve that.

"My confidence grew through the continued counselling and I stopped blaming myself."

I called Taylor as soon as I could, apologising for the wrong decisions I made that affected her life; for all the times I had gone back to Olivier and left her broken-hearted in Germany. I asked her forgiveness for not believing her the countless times she had tried to warn me about Olivier. I explained I never meant to abandon or neglect her, or cause her unhappiness. She was somewhat surprised by my call, but assured me she loved me and always would. That phone call released a torrent of healing inside me from the hurts of my past. My confidence grew through the continued counselling and I stopped blaming myself. I appreciated my most important role was to be a good mother to my children, to show them it was normal to play and laugh and enjoy their lives without living in fear of being bullied or abused. Within three months of the first session I was able to let go of my feelings for Olivier. He did not deserve my love, his heart was in a place I no longer wanted to be. The way forward was to forgive him completely for the way he treated me and enjoy the freedom that decision brought. Music played such a big part in my journey, and God knowing me intimately – knew he could speak to me through music, and I would hear and believe. I cried tears of joy because

God was the Father I never had, and tears of bereavement for the wasted years when I lived with abuse. Using pebbles on the beach, Kyla got me to write the damaging words people had spoken over me during my life and then throw them one by one into the ocean. It was an amazing thing to do. I felt cleansed, energised, released!.

I listened to Christina Aguilera's song called The Voice Within and sensed God was telling me to trust exactly that. My past was filled with neglect and abuse and controlled by other people, The future could be very different to that, the choice was mine to make. I had come to hate the town where we lived, but recalling what I'd read in my favourite book all those years ago, I knew running away was not the answer; I would only take all the problems with me. I was afraid of the changes I must make and of being alone, but good people had come into my life at strategic times and given me the hand-up I needed. I had to hold on, be strong. My inner voice told me I could make it. What a powerful statement that is: I can make it! No one can stop me, or tell me what to do.

Music continued to inspire and motivate me. Songs by Anastacia and Christina Aguilera filled my days with hope. Their lyrics seemed to have been written just for me, they echoed the cries of my heart. Although Kyla assured me it was alright to break down and cry during our sessions I never did, preferring to do that alone at home. I felt safe with her during those times, but privacy is something I am more comfortable with. The difference in how I felt was tangible. Three months before I struggled in Olivier's company. Whenever he visited Summer it affected me deeply; I was plagued by the fact that he lived in the same town and yet we were not together. Previously a television programme or place would remind me of him and govern my mood for the day but now I was changed. Before I sought his approval and his acceptance, now it no longer mattered. As I lay down my broken dream of the fairy tale ending I chased for so long. I gained an inner peace Olivier could not take away. He had robbed me of so much during our relationship, material things, my self respect, confidence and most importantly being with Taylor but his hold over me was broken and though there was an ocean between Taylor and me, in our hearts we would always be one.

Summer occasionally spoke of the hurt she experienced living apart from her Father. She asked why he tried to strangle me or swore and spat at me. Olivier denied those things happened whenever she questioned him about it, and he forbade Summer to speak of us, especially Taylor, in his presence. To him we simply did not exist. She was confused as she witnessed much of the abuse firsthand. It was painful to hear my baby girl express complex, adult emotions, I felt responsible for having exposed her to such a cruel world. As I hugged and comforted her during the many nights she missed her Dad, could not sleep or was afraid to be left alone, it it occurred to me Olivier had never offered love or compassion to me when I needed it most. In his eyes I clearly was someone who cleaned for him and provided free sex whenever he demanded it. I figured it unlikely he would be there for Summer when she needed him: children were not his priority, money and the good life were his goals. Nonetheless, I allowed Summer to speak what was on her mind, praying it would help in her healing process. Gradually we both accepted we could not change her Father, he had to want to change, we could only pray he'd wake up before it was too late.

"...I finally felt good about myself. I was free from the chains of abuse."

As memories of Olivier's intimidating conduct were relegated further into the past, Grace opened up more to me. One night she asked to sleep in my bed – Summer already slept there every night – and we talked for hours as she shared her inmost thoughts. The freedom to do that with my daughter without being criticised or ridiculed by Olivier was such an exhilarating experience for us both. We prayed together to be able to let go of the past and live a full and happy future. I remember asking this God I was getting to know if he would stay especially close to Grace, so that she could somehow feel his presence. I was completely taken aback when she said she felt my hand on her shoulder while I prayed because I had not reached out to touch her at all. I was so thankful I was at last able to be the mother I dreamed of, when I was a little girl, without the mother I craved. Especially liberating was the knowledge that no one could stamp out our new-found joy in the simple things we did together. I genuinely felt sorry for Olivier with his hardened heart, he was consumed with how much money he could make, wasting his time with hate and regret and only seeing things his way. My final goodbye to him was in learning freedom only comes when you can let go and have no regrets. I will never regret loving him because it was sincere, but the time had come: I had nothing left to lose and finally felt good about myself. I was free from the chains of abuse.

With ongoing counselling I made changes in many areas of my life. Not everything slotted perfectly into place – life is not like that. Finances were frequently in short supply, I struggled to pay my bills and there was never enough left over for treats or luxuries. Our phone had been cut off and my only contact with Taylor in Germany was by mobile phone which sapped what extra money I did have. She needed to hear my voice everyday and always called me to discuss any problems she faced, before informing her grandparents. Hard as it was, I felt privileged that Taylor loved me and still respected my opinion. I had put my eldest children through two failed relationships crammed with violence and disruption, I could have lost them. Not just through the intervention of Social Services but they could have chosen to turn their backs on me completely.

While Taylor still lived with my parents in Germany she was living a replica of my childhood. She wasn't allowed to show her feelings, no crying was allowed in case it upset my Father and my Mother never ministered words of comfort or love to her, merely reminded her things were never as bad as they seemed. Her school work suffered badly at first, but she somehow managed to improve from being the worst student to one of the best. I was extremely proud of her. A trivial dispute at school brought my Father's wrath down on her, and all the anger he felt towards me, he directed at Taylor until it concluded in him refusing to speak to her. This lamentable impasse continued for a year. In disbelief I witnessed my parents repeating their familiar pattern of abuse with Taylor. When I challenged my Mother, she merely said it was up to Taylor to make the first move towards reconciliation.

"Putting my inmost thoughts and memories down on paper, together with the counselling I received, helped enormously in my understanding of who I was and why I behaved the way I did."

Putting my inmost thoughts and memories down on paper, together with the counselling I received, helped enormously in my understanding of who I was and why I behaved the way I did. At the same time it was extremely exhausting mentally and physically. Often I would feel emotionally drained and suffer physical symptoms the day after counselling, though something inside me was forever changed, and I was always eager for the next session to discover more truths that would set me free. To be listened to, without feeling I was being judged, was a tremendous step towards my freedom. There was once a wall so huge around my heart, like the Berlin Wall as I grew up, I could not see over it, around it or ever hope to scale it. Now, brick by brick that wall was being dismantled by people who cared and I dared to believe there was a better way to live. Were it not for the tiny seeds sown by old Mrs Becher all those years before, perhaps I would not have been open-minded about God. After all I had grown up in a post Christian regime that denied a personal faith; the Communist State did not remove God, it simply replaced him.

When I began exploring the possibility of God's existence I was overwhelmed by the countless and varied ways I believe God chose to assure me of his presence in my life. I recall one particular dream: I was standing in a room with all the people I loved and who loved me during my life, including my children. A bird appeared and flew around the room, hovering over each one of us in turn. A voice explained this was a lovebird giving love and healing. The next morning as I drew the curtains and looked at the back garden I gasped in amazement. There, in the middle of the small lawn was the exact same bird of my dream. It made me feel secure, assured me God was real and loved me. Everywhere I went that day the bird, or one incredibly like it, followed me around. Even as I walked the girls home from school, one deliberately rested on a fence in front of a startled Grace. It remained staring at me, unafraid, as I looked into its eyes. I sensed it was God's way of assuring me He was always with me. I smiled as I remembered the scene from the movie *Bruce Almighty*. Jim Carey wakes up in hospital holding in his hand a bead bracelet he'd previously discarded. He accuses God of showing off because he uniquely produces it again just for Bruce.

"...I am still standing and I declare there is life after abuse. It is not easy to break away and make a fresh start, but it is worth every ounce of effort."

Inevitably, the tears came at the counselling sessions as people told me they would. I cried as I spoke for the first time about the abortions and the children I felt forced to give up before they were even born. I had not before been able to grieve for fear it would anger my Father, but now my emotions finally found space to express themselves and that particular part of the healing began. I cried long past the session, even waking in the night, crying and crying, letting go of the pain. The sessions explained how I had been robbed of so many things in my life, not just through the abortions but also in connection with Taylor now living apart from me. Through the actions of Olivier and my parents, I had been robbed of my oldest child's presence during some of her most formative years. But I am still standing and I declare there is life after abuse. It is not easy to break away and make a fresh start, but it is worth every ounce of effort. If you are reading this book and you are in an abusive relationship, I urge you not to waste any more of your life. Tell someone about your pain, tell them what your life is like and ask for help to get out of the abusive situation. It does not happen overnight – lives don't get messed up in a day and it takes time, perseverance and patience to rebuild them but it can be done. You can walk free from your prison. It is up to you. Our greatest victories are born from our hardest trials.

SURVIVORS...
DON'T GIVE UP
Summer 2007

As each day dawns I have come to appreciate my freedom. Breaking out of an abusive situation, making the decision to walk away – and in many cases escape with your life – is only the beginning of a journey that lasts a lifetime but it is worth every second of effort. When we remain in abusive relationships we give power to the abuser and line up with what they project on us: we are worthless victims living in fear of the next emotional or physical beating. Choosing to leave is not an easy option; there are few enough places we can turn to get the help we so desperately need. But awareness of this terrible offence is growing. Little by little people are prepared to break the silence, dismissing the stigma this silent crime carries: to speak out. However, the crucial difference between someone who chooses to remain in any form of domestic abuse and someone who chooses to get out, no matter what effort it takes is this: if you remain, you remain a VICTIM if you leave you become a SURVIVOR.

Since I started to write our story I have made many acquaintances, through the internet and face to face, with adults and children who have experienced situations similar to mine, some less violent, many far more terrifying. They often refer to themselves as victims but I always correct them if they are no longer trapped in abuse and say they are now survivors. I believe what you speak out about yourself is vitally important. If we continue to refer to ourselves as victims – we will continue to be so. Interestingly an alternative word offered in my thesaurus for victim is the word loser. The dictionary definition of survivor says: 'continue to live in spite of danger or hardship'.

In November 2003 we managed to stay in that dirty unwelcoming house for a few weeks, but eventually the cold wore us all down. We spent much time in bed with all our clothes on trying to keep warm and we were constantly ill. The night storage radiators did little to protect us against the extremely severe winter temperatures and I could not afford other heating. Concerned about Summer's health, I accepted Olivier's offer to move back into his house when he vacated it. Advice from friends and my head told me it was not a good idea but my heart said otherwise. I was, first and foremost, a mother fiercely wanting to protect her children and they needed a better home. It was not easy to do and I did not take the decision lightly and then only after consulting the girls. The inside of the house had barely changed, and when we first walked across the threshold again I could hardly breathe. It was months before I could go to sleep without being haunted by frightening images. Grace and Summer were not so noticeably affected but nonetheless had to face many painful memories in their own way. They survived; we all did.

"…we are no longer under his control by being tenants in his house. Counselling enabled me to make the first steps to live my own life, but how I chose to walk each day had to be my own decision."

It is now 2007, and we have recently moved into another rented house in the same town, independent of Olivier. That, too, proved another liberating decision: we are no longer under his control by being tenants in his house. Counselling enabled me to make the first steps to live my own life, but how I chose to walk each day had to be my own decision. For me it was a gradual letting go of my feelings for Olivier and my dependancy on him. Where once I hated the town where we live, and knew few of the people, I now walk along the streets feeling free and at peace. I am still a single mum and proud of that. I am still in touch with Olivier, who as the Father of my youngest child has a moral right to see his daughter; he has never threatened or harmed her physically. Grace is now fifteen and Summer is eight. I work part time at a local school. Taylor, nineteen, still lives in Germany with her boyfriend, they are setting up home together but it is her dream to move to England to be close to me and her sisters.

"Each day Taylor reinforces her decision to be a survivor."

The years since the court case have not been easy for any of us. Taylor finally realised for herself the problems associated with my parents, decided she could no longer live in that repetitively abusive situation and chose to walk away. We speak to each other everyday either by text, e-mail or phone, and I am so thankful for technology which enables inexpensive communication. We are slowly rebuilding our relationship and I have been freed from feelings of guilt about my past decisions. I miss her so much it causes physical pain, and I should like nothing more than for her to live nearby so I could see her everyday, tell her I love her and support her through life's challenges but it is not for me to dictate to Taylor. I keep faith that circumstances will change. She has her own life; she can choose to learn from my mistakes, though generally we learn better from our own. Taylor's childhood was dominated by an alcoholic Father, appalling abuse from her Mother's second partner, feelings of rejection by her Mother and manipulated by controlling grandparents. The fact that she is choosing to be a survivor at all is amazing, and I intend to support her in whatever way I can. Each day Taylor reinforces her decision to be a survivor. I love her and respect her for that. She is beautiful and precious to me.

Grace is at school preparing to sit her exams. She has been a tower of strength through the bleakest of times, and I could not have coped without her. When I felt like giving up she was always there to encourage me to carry on. Whilst writing this book she has intuitively known when to stand behind me rubbing my back as I fought to put the words on paper. From being overweight through comfort eating she has shown tremendous will power to transform herself into a beautiful young lady. She faces her own demons every day as a result of the abuse she too has suffered, but chooses to include me in every aspect of her life. She is an inspiration and constant source of love that never fails to brighten my day. She has taught me much about overcoming hardships – she is a survivor.

"Children have little or no say in the daily choices we make as adults and parents; their voices and fears are seldom heard."

Summer has witnessed far too many unsettling things in her short life, particularly anger and violence no child should be subjected to. Over-exposure to the adult world has robbed her of innocence too soon. As a result of her experiences she is clingy towards me and possessive of my attention; even now she seldom sleeps in her own bed all night. She has regular contact with her Father but he has not yet proved to her to be reliable or trustworthy and understandably that affects her judgement of him. To her credit, she loves him in spite of his shortcomings. She sometimes experiences problems in her relationships with other children. I hope, in time, she will benefit from counselling, as she requires help to deal with her feelings and walk free as a survivor. She never fails to make me laugh and is uniquely precious to me. Children have little or no say in the daily choices we make as adults and parents; their voices and fears are seldom heard. We need to break the cycle of abuse for the next generations. The effects of domestic abuse on children are deep and long lasting, as seen with my own children. Even if they themselves are not physically or emotionally abused, just witnessing abuse in the home is abuse! They need help to deal with their confusion and pain.

Olivier continues to live a bachelor life with scant knowledge of what quality time with children really involves but he has access to Summer and it is my hope their relationship will grow and bring healing in other areas of their lives. Breaking the bonds that held me to him have not been easy, but unconditional forgiveness has been the key to release and my fear and hate have been replaced by peace and a genuine desire for his well-being. Even abusers are prisoners of their own behaviour.

My parents still choose not speak to me, despite efforts at reconciliation on my part. Whenever I return to Germany I pray they have had a change of heart. For now they still choose to snub me and their grandchildren, but I love them and will never give up hope that we may be reconciled.

I have little contact with my ex-husband, sadly he chooses not to be involved in his daughters' lives. He now has a new partner and many of the trappings that go with a comfortable existence. As far as I am aware he did not seek further help for his alcoholism. My personal counselling helped me forgive him for all the pain and distress we suffered, and I know that decision helps me live free of bitterness and guilt.

"God…gave me the strength to break free and I believe sent people and angels to help me at precisely the moment I needed them."

Rejecting Olivier's slurs on my German heritage I have learned to be proud of my roots. I am thankful to God for rescuing me from the prison of abuse. I could not have survived without him.

He was always there even when I thought I was alone. He gave me the strength to break free and I believe sent people and angels to help me at precisely the moment I needed them. I trust Him to uphold me in that freedom.

If I have one dream, one vision for writing this book, it is to encourage better understanding and help for perpetrators and their reasons for abuse and for the many, many victims held captive by this appalling crime in all its forms, to be liberated from lives of fear and repression, to shine and be all they can be.

As the character Timo Cruz quotes* in the film *Coach Carter*:

"Our deepest fear is not that we are inadequate. Our deepest fear is that we are powerful beyond measure. It is our light, not our darkness, that most frightens us. Your playing small does not serve the world. There is nothing enlightened about shrinking so that other people won't feel insecure around you. We are all meant to shine as children do. It's not just in some of us; it is in everyone. And as we let our own lights shine, we unconsciously give other people permission to do the same. As we are liberated from our own fear, our presence automatically liberates others."

*An excerpt quoted from Marianne Williamson 'A Return to Love: Reflections on the Principals of a Course in Miracles.'

Lifelines for Help
with Domestic Abuse

Whilst it is the author's wish to be able to provide vital telephone numbers and links to organisations offering help to individuals, it is not possible to provide an extensive list due to space. However, the following may be of use in the United Kingdom. Please appreciate that details can and do change and we would suggest you use the following as a brief guide only, whilst researching the internet, libraries and telephone books for up-to-date data.

The following helplines can offer you practical help and advice including:
- emergency refuge accommodation
- safety planning and advice
- translation facilities if you have difficulty communicating in English

National Domestic Violence Helpline
0808 2000 247
A 24-hour freephone number which provides access to emergency

refuge accommodation, as well as an information service. It joins together the Women's Aid Federation helpline and the Refuge National Crisis Line in a single service.

Women's Aid
Helpline: 0808 2000 247
www.womensaid.org.uk
Advocates on behalf of abused women and children and provides services and support including refuge accommodation.

Refuge
Helpline: 0808 2000 247
www.refuge.org.uk
Refuge is the UK's largest single provider of safe accommodation and support to women and children escaping domestic violence.

NSPCC
National Society for the Prevention of Cruelty to Children
Help and Advice – adults – FREEFONE 0808 800 5000
www.nspcc.org.uk

Child Line
Part of the NSPCC
Children – FREEFONE 0800 1111
www.childline.org.uk

Victim Support
National 0845 30 30 900
www.victimsupport.org

M.A.L.E (Men's Advice Line Enquiries)
Helpline: 0808 801 0327
A helpline service for men experiencing domestic violence.

Men's Aid is a registered charity which has been set up in Milton

Keynes to provide free practical advice and support to men who have been abused.

0871 223 9986

www.mensaid.com

Get Connected provides a free, confidential helpline that gives young people in difficult situations the support and information they need to decide what they want to happen next. It could be anything from a listening ear to somewhere safe to stay for the night.

www.getconnected.org.uk

Respect is the UK membership association for domestic violence perpetrator programmes and associated support services. Our key focus is on increasing the safety of those experiencing domestic violence through promoting effective interventions with perpetrators.

0845 122 8609

www.respect.uk.net

If you call any helpline or even 999 they provide you with emergency refuge accommodation as do the Samaritans.

Based in Canada:

www.fathersforlife.org has some info for abused men.

Some American National Helplines:

National Coalition Against Domestic Violence
(800) 799-SAVE (7233)
Spanish-speaking operators available
http://www.ncadv.org

National Resource Center on Domestic Violence
888-Rx-ABUSE
800-595-4889 (TDD)
http://endabuse.org